OUTRAGEOUS, CONTAGIOUS

Five Big Questions to Help You
Discover One Great Life

ED YOUNG

BERKLEY PRAISE, NEW YORK

THE BERKLEY PUBLISHING GROUP
Published by the Penguin Group
Penguin Group (USA) Inc.
375 Hudson Street, New York, New York 10014, USA
Penguin Group (Canada), 90 Eglinton Avenue East, Suite 700, Toronto, Ontario M4P 2Y3, Canada
(a division of Pearson Penguin Canada Inc.)
Penguin Books Ltd., 80 Strand, London WC2R 0RL, England
Penguin Group Ireland, 25 St. Stephen's Green, Dublin 2, Ireland (a division of Penguin Books Ltd.)
Penguin Group (Australia), 250 Camberwell Road, Camberwell, Victoria 3124, Australia
(a division of Pearson Australia Group Pty. Ltd.)
Penguin Books India Pvt. Ltd., 11 Community Centre, Panchsheel Park, New Delhi—110 017, India
Penguin Group (NZ), 67 Apollo Drive, Rosedale, North Shore 0632, New Zealand
(a division of Pearson New Zealand Ltd.)
Penguin Books (South Africa) (Pty.) Ltd., 24 Sturdee Avenue, Rosebank, Johannesburg 2196,
South Africa

Penguin Books Ltd., Registered Offices: 80 Strand, London WC2R 0RL, England

A complete listing of Scripture references is provided on page 373.

PRINTING HISTORY
Berkley Praise hardcover edition / January 2007
Berkley Praise trade paperback edition / January 2008

Berkley Praise trade paperback ISBN: 978-0-425-21908-9

The Library of Congress has cataloged the Berkley Praise hardcover as follows:

Young, Ed, 1961–
    Outrageous, contagious joy: five big questions to help you discover one great life / Ed Young.—1st ed.
        p.   cm.
    ISBN-13: 978-0-425-21185-4
    1. Joy—Religious aspects—Christianity.   2. Christian life.   I. Title.

    BV4647.J68Y68 2007
    248.4—dc22   2006030350

PRINTED IN THE UNITED STATES OF AMERICA

10   9   8   7   6   5   4   3   2   1

Most Berkley Praise books are available at special quantity discounts for bulk purchases for sales promotions, premiums, fund-raising, or educational use. Special books, or book excerpts, can also be created to fit specific needs.

For details, write: Special Markets, The Berkley Publishing Group, 375 Hudson Street, New York, New York 10014.

To Lisa,

Almost twenty-five years ago we made a vow to walk through life together, hand in hand. And over the years, one thing continues to stand above all else—your radiant joy.

Through your constant encouragement, heartfelt love, and unconditional commitment, I have seen a portrait of what joy really is.

Everything written in these pages is a reflection of what I see in you each and every day. I thank you for saying yes to me all those years ago. I pray that I have answered with my own yes each day since.

CONTENTS

PART 3 WHO ARE YOU RUNNING WITH?

PART 4 WHY ARE YOU HERE?

PART 5 WHAT ARE YOU WORKING FOR?

ACKNOWLEDGMENTS

When someone sets out to write a book, they are attempting something that can only be completed with the assistance, guidance, and support of innumerable people. I want to recognize some of those people who played key roles in helping to mold and shape this book into what it is.

First and foremost, to Lisa—thank you for the positive and creative ideas you contributed to the manuscript at various stages. They helped give the book life. And thank you for giving me a daily example of what the joy I write about looks like on the rugged plains of reality.

I also want to thank several key people who had a direct hand in developing this book. To Cliff McNeely, Chris Mc-Gregor, Andy Boyd, and Katie Moon, thank you for your tireless dedication to helping me compose, write, and edit these pages. Without your help, this book would not have become a reality.

To Denise Silvestro, Joel Fotinos, Katie Day, and all of the people at Berkley Praise, thank you for providing me with the amazing opportunity to work with you. I hope that this is just the first of many projects together.

To Tom Winters, thanks for getting me connected with the folks at Berkley and for all your counsel along the way.

A big thanks to everyone who so openly shared their personal stories with me so that I could share them with others. Your willingness to let me in on a little piece of your lives allows this book to resonate on a meaningful, intimate level with everyone who reads it. I hope that your stories touch others' lives as much as they have touched mine.

And last but not least, my heartfelt appreciation goes out to the great people of Fellowship Church, who show me through your outrageous, contagious joy what "going deep" in the Christian life is all about.

INTRODUCTION

WHAT IF . . .

What if life were not just good, but *great*? What if there were more to life than you ever thought possible? What if your days and weeks consisted of more than just waiting for the next vacation, or next payday, or next boyfriend, or next fun fix, or next happy feeling, or next . . .

What if there were a way to live the life you've always wanted? A way to experience outrageous, contagious joy, regardless of your present circumstances?

This book is all about seizing a great life—a life of fulfillment, clarity, and joy. In the coming pages, you and I will take a journey together that will revolutionize your life, as you take some time to stop and think big thoughts about five big questions that will lead you to one great life.

Discovering the great life God wants for you is all about dreaming about what is possible by examining the big picture. So often we get stuck in the mud and the mundane issues of life rather than seeing what is truly possible. We feel like there's something more out there, but don't know how to get it. We know there's more to life, but we don't know where to turn.

If you've ever felt that way, I want you to know that you're not alone. We all crave a life that's bigger, a life that's greater, and a life that's more meaningful. In the coming pages, I'll show you why this isn't just a pipe dream. And we're going to get there by answering these five questions together:

1. *Does God want you to be happy?*
2. *Where are you headed?*
3. *Who are you running with?*
4. *Why are you here?*
5. *What are you working for?*

With so many things competing for our attention today, we need to think big more than ever. We need to take a step back and take a panoramic look at our lives—a life full of potential and possibilities. So many of us are stressed out, overcommitted, and burned out. Instead of simplifying our lives, we tend to add more and more to our already stuffed plates. We envy other people rather than enjoying our own lives. We spend our lives living in the past or dreaming about the future, but never enjoying the moment.

This book will help you slow down and look at life in a fresh, new way.

Each chapter will ask you to "Stop and Think" about what you've just read. These pages are specifically created to help you think about where you are and where you are going. This book will give you some very specific and practical action steps that will revolutionize the way you think about—and carry out—your life.

For each chapter, you'll be asked to:

- Follow the Signs (review the major truths of the chapter)
- Check the Map (listen to God)
- Take the Next Step (apply the truth to your own life)

Are you ready to think big and dream big? Are you ready to turn "What if?" into "What's next?" Are you ready to open the door to the opportunities and insights that can change the course of your life? A new life is waiting for you if you're willing to stop, think, and answer five big questions. When you do, you will discover the keys to one great life . . . a life of outrageous, contagious joy.

PART 1

DOES GOD WANT YOU TO BE HAPPY?

We all live with the objective of being happy,
our lives are all different and yet the same.
—ANNE FRANK

Everyone, without exception,
is searching for happiness.
—BLAISE PASCAL

1

BEYOND HAPPINESS

Happiness is not a goal; it is a by-product.
—ELEANOR ROOSEVELT

Everyone would rather be happy than miserable. If given a choice, we would choose gladness over sadness. We would choose a win over a loss. We would choose sun rather than rain. We would rather attend a wedding than a funeral. We would rather ride the crest of a wave than sink into the depths of despair. If given an option, we would rather sing, dance, and shout than moan, weep, and pout.

We have this happiness-seeking, happiness-hunting nature in all of us. I believe we choose friends, spouses, careers, even churches on the basis of the happy factor.

When you have a case of the blues you might say, *If I could only have a problem-free life, then I would experience happiness. If I could eliminate all of my problems, then I would have true satisfaction.*

But then reality sets in. Even the Fortune 500 CEO who is married to Miss Universe and driving the hottest sports car is going to have problems. The problem with life is that we all have problems. You can't get around them. You can't eliminate them. And you can't wash them away. They loom large everywhere we turn. In an attempt to chase our troubles away and get our happiness back, we may change jobs and spouses and even geographical locations. But we end up on a never-ending merry-go-round of dissatisfaction.

We also say to ourselves, *If I had millions in the bank, a house overlooking the ocean, and everything I wanted, I'd be happy.* So we acquire a lot of stuff. And then slowly but surely, all the stuff we have succumbs to the forces of rot, rust, deterioration, and depreciation.

I remember getting my first new car. I swore I'd keep it clean and shiny and "like new." I wanted to preserve that rush of having a new car, but it wasn't long before it was "just another car." There was mud caked on the fenders and papers scattered everywhere. Everything we have eventually loses its luster and its value. So we have to look to the next purchase to replace that "rush." We also find that the more we have, the more those things begin to trap us. Our bloated credit-card balance and sixty-month car payment for that car we just had to have are now eating up big chunks of our paycheck. Before long, we can feel trapped in a dead-end job because we have to keep pace with our impulsive financial commitments. In short, we are enslaved to our employers because we're trying to fill a God-sized hole with inanimate objects. Roy Rogers said it best: "Too many people spend money they haven't earned, to buy things they don't want, to impress people they don't like." Our possessions start possessing us. And we are left with emptiness when none of that stuff delivers us the happiness we were promised.

So we move to the next pursuit. We decide to jump on the

health bandwagon. We think that if we eat properly and look good, that will do it. So, we tan and train and lift and laser and liposuction our way into oblivion, thinking that health and happiness go hand in hand. Again, though, we find disappointment. Even the most buff and beautiful man or woman in the world can't escape the reality of life's aging process forever. We are all going to get a bunch of wrinkles, lose our teeth and our hair. Eventually "mirror, mirror, on the wall" will have to tell us the truth: we are far from the "fairest of them all." Even if you are married to a plastic surgeon, you are not going to be able to maintain your youthful appearance twenty, thirty, or forty years from now—at least not without looking like an alien. So while it's a good and right thing to live a healthy lifestyle, the health kick does not bring the happiness we seek. It's yet another formula for frustration.

Next we look to accomplishments. *If I can claw and climb my way to the top, to the corner office; become the quarterback, the captain, the manager, the president, that will do it. That will really bring me happiness.* So we work long and hard, giving up fun and free time in pursuit of our goals. We work to exhaustion, sometimes at the cost of our physical health, our mental well-being, and our relationships. Once we get to the top rung of the ladder of achievement, though, we look around and wonder if our sacrifices were worth it.

In the Oscar-winning film *Chariots of Fire*, the hundred-yard sprinter Harold Abrahams candidly captures this fear. "I will raise my eyes and look down that corridor; four feet wide, with ten lonely seconds to justify my whole existence. But *will I?*" With all that you've sacrificed to make it to the top, what if "the top" isn't what it was cracked up to be? Will you be happy? Ultimately, we discover—to our great disappointment—that there is no *top*. There is always someone a little faster, a little smarter, a little sharper, a little better looking, a little funnier, and a little younger. The climbing, the clawing, the chasing, never stops if we choose this path to happiness.

We take all these different routes to obtain happiness, but we never get there. So we turn to our friends and family, those armchair experts who seem to always have an answer for everything.

When we have a case of the blues, they may say things like, "Hey, let's go out tonight and get wasted! That will make you happy." Other friends may tell us to go to the mall and buy a new outfit. Or they say, "Snap out of it, man, smell the coffee. Get in the game. Get real, it'll blow over."

And we respond with frustration, "If I could get in the game, if I could snap out of it, I would. But there's just something missing in my life."

The armchair experts, our friends and family, mean well. They really do. But their advice is worth pretty much what you paid for it—nothing. Oftentimes, their suggestions are shallow and superficial. And superficial advice often leads us away from where we want to be. It's like taking an aspirin for a broken leg. It'll make you feel better for a few minutes, but it won't fix your problem. You might feel better after the rush of your shopping spree, but how long will that new dress or those shoes keep you going? And what do you do when the credit card bill comes in?

"GOD JUST WANTS ME TO BE HAPPY"

I've heard that statement many times over the years. But for some reason, on one particular day several years ago, it sparked something in me. It hit a nerve. And I began to really examine whether that statement was true or not.

It was during a conversation I had with a man who had decided to leave his wife and family. When I asked him why, he told me he had fallen in love with another woman. He said, "I know what I'm doing is wrong, but I am miserable in my marriage. I just want to be happy."

Then he added, "Surely, Ed, God just wants me to be happy."

Questions began to flood my mind. Does God really want us to be happy? And what exactly does it mean to be happy? Who gets to decide what happiness is and isn't? I guess it made that man feel good, at least initially, to leave his wife for another woman. Evidently this new woman gave him those "happy" feelings that were missing. But how long would these new feelings last? Would she get left behind when the feelings changed? And what about this man's wife? Did his leaving make her happy? What about the kids? What sort of happiness would his decision bring them over the course of their childhood?

Did God want that man to pursue his own particular definition of happiness? What's wrong with that? Is it wrong to want a little happiness in your life? What kind of God would *not* want you to be happy? Or to put it another way: What kind of God would want you to be unhappy?

And if God does not want me to be happy, what exactly *does* he want?

Those are all great questions. And ones that I want to unpack throughout the pages of this book.

But in this first installment of our journey together, I want to at least give the short answer to the initial question: Does God want you to be happy?

Recent surveys reveal that the religious and not so religious alike believe it's true that happiness is the ultimate goal of life. As noted in a recent article in *Time* magazine, happiness is a dominant theme in modern American culture.[1] Happiness, most people believe, is indeed a virtue. The "pursuit of happiness" has been and continues to be a national craze. It is not just some long-forgotten phrase in our Declaration of Independence. It is the search of every freedom-loving individual for some mysterious and elusive ideal. Most of us can't define exactly what the end result of "being happy" is, but we are certain we will know it when we find it.

We are all looking for that certain state of mind that says, "You've made it; you can relax now. You are finally happy."

Sadly, though, that state of mind never comes for most of us, and if it does, it certainly doesn't last. We experience fleeting moments of "happiness," when everything seems to be going our way. But more often than not, we struggle to find that feeling again, as the never-ending issues of life crowd in around us.

I suspect, if you picked up this book, you are searching for that feeling again (or perhaps for the very first time). Chances are, if the title of this book intrigued you, you are not experiencing feelings of happiness right now, let alone outrageous,

[1]David Van Biema, "Does God Want Us to Be Happy?" *Time*, p. A51.

contagious joy. If you were, you would have moved to the next title on the bookshelf. You would not even have ventured a second look at the cover.

If I were able to somehow jump out of the pages of this book at this very moment, look you square in the eye, and ask you this question: Are you happy? what would your answer be?

I'm willing to bet that your answer would be no.

You picked up this book because there is, at some level, a feeling of unhappiness. You can sense something missing way down deep inside, something that you can't quite put your finger on. You are not completely satisfied with your life. And you want more.

We all want more out of life. We all have that nagging sense that life could be better, happier, more exciting, and more rewarding. We are all searching for that something that can make us feel good about ourselves, about our relationships, about our work, about our future, and about life in general.

Maybe, though, too many of us are searching for the wrong thing. Is it possible that we've gotten our ladders out, laid them against the wall, and climbed up, only to discover that our ladder is on the wrong wall? Maybe, just maybe, we are searching for a state of mind that ultimately does not exist—at least in the way most of us imagine it.

You may be thinking about now, "Why is this guy writing a book about happiness if he doesn't believe happiness exists?" Well, I don't blame you for asking that. But don't close the book just yet, because the implications of what I'm going to be exploring in the pages to come can jump-start your journey to a deeper level of happiness in every area of your life. Remember: we're after real answers, not quick fixes.

Don't get me wrong, I believe that God is concerned about our state of mind, but what he wants for us is not happiness.

No, *God does not want you to be happy.*

In fact, I believe happiness misrepresents what God intended for our lives. Happiness, as we commonly know it, is a myth. Yet we have been told for so long that happiness is what God wants for us, it has become "gospel truth," part of the fabric of our culture. In short, it has become a universal pursuit.

You can relax now, though. You don't have to keep searching anymore for that elusive ideal, for those feelings that come and go. You can stop. What a relief, right? You are now free to live in contented misery for the rest of your days.

Not so fast.

God may not want you to be happy, but he also does not want you to be miserable. He is not some cosmic killjoy, raining down boatloads of heartache and disappointment on people.

More than anything, God wants to give you a much richer life. He wants to give you more than fleeting feelings of happiness. He wants to give you a life full of joy. Happiness is a cheap imitation. And God is not into cheap imitations. He is into things that are spectacular, real, and eternal.

The problem with pursuing happiness, as I see it, is happiness itself. Happiness comes from the Latin word *hap*, which means chance. Happiness, therefore, is based on happenings or circumstances. When all of my ducks line up in a row, when I'm on a roll, then I can be happy. It's that when-and-then thinking that always keeps the elusive happiness we seek one step ahead of us. We never arrive at happiness because our circumstances are never exactly what we want them to be. Just when we get one area of our life in order, something else happens to rock the boat. The happenings of our life are never hitting on all cylinders at exactly the same time. That's why happiness is a myth. It is something we can never attain because it is tied to the currents of changing circumstances.

So, I say God doesn't want us to be happy, because happiness by its very definition does not produce the long-term, deep-down peace, contentment, fulfillment, and joy we long for.

What if there was something out there much better than happiness? What if there was something so incredible, so mind blowing, so life altering, that it defied all of the popular thinking of today? Well, I believe there is. I believe God wants something for us so much greater than fleeting and shallow feelings of "happiness." I believe he wants us to find a deeper, more satisfying destination—a destination not of feelings, not of the mind, but of soul and spirit. A place of peace, contentment, and tranquility that defies our circumstances, that outlives the struggles of today and gives lasting hope for tomorrow.

Happy feelings will come from time to time, but those are only a by-product of the real deal—the ultimate destination God has in store for all of us. It's the great life you've always wanted.

Are you ready to move beyond happiness and find that better place, that place you've been looking for without even realizing it? Are you ready to change the course of your life? Are you ready to find the full, rich life God wants for you? If you are, the principles found in this book will set you in the right direction. There is no shortcut, but for those who really want to find it, there is a definite path laid out for us.

I want to help you discover that path.

As you read this book, keep an open mind and heart to God's plan for your life. Let's walk together beyond the happiness myth to a better place—the promise of outrageous and contagious joy.

STOP AND THINK

FOLLOW THE SIGNS: God wants you to move beyond happiness, to replace those fleeting and shallow feelings of happiness with a real and lasting foundation of joy.

CHECK THE MAP: "My purpose is to give life in all its fullness" (John 10:10, NLT).

TAKE THE NEXT STEP: Why did you pick up this book? Are you satisfied with your life right now? What are some ways you would like your life to change as a result of reading this book?

2

JOY RIDE

Many persons have the wrong idea of what constitutes true happiness. It is not attained through self-gratification but through fidelity to a worthy purpose.

—HELEN KELLER

Several years ago, a movie hit the big screen that portrayed the plight of three middle-aged men in the midst of their midlife crises. Mitch, Phil, and Ed had taken several extreme vacations together to escape their normal routines, to recapture their youth, and to search for the meaning of life. They'd gone skydiving and running with the bulls in Spain, and wound up on a cattle ranch in New Mexico. In the midst of their difficult adjustment from city slickers to cowboys, these adult adolescents meet Curly, a leathery cowboy with confidence and bravado to spare. Though Curly is distant, he is admired by these men, and particularly by Mitch, *City Slickers*'s main character. In the key moment of the film, Mitch sidles up to Curly and asks him about the meaning of life. The cowboy holds up one finger and says,

"The secret is this: one thing, just one thing." When Mitch asks for clarification, Curly says, "I can't tell you what it is. You have to figure it out for yourself."

Relational experts, psychologists, and psychiatrists have spent tens of thousands of hours on case studies and in interviews trying to find that "one thing" that gives us meaning and purpose in life. One of the primary thrusts of their research has been to understand what makes us happy.

Here is what three prominent twentieth-century social scientists have to say about happiness:

※ William Glasser, a psychologist and the founder of reality therapy, says that from birth to old age, we need to love and be loved. Our health and happiness depend on both. Glasser went on to say that the key to happiness is finding meaningful *relationships*. He was right, at least in part.

※ Viktor Frankl, a psychiatrist who was interned for nearly three years in Nazi concentration camps, took it a step further than Glasser. He said that striving to find *meaning* in one's life is the primary motivational force in man. Frankl believed that there is more to life than relationships. We have to have purpose and meaning beyond human relationships to truly make us happy. He was also right, at least in part.

※ The third person is Bruno Bettelheim, a psychologist who also survived internment in Nazi concentration camps. He said that man cannot have happiness without *hope*. As he looked at the prisoners in the horrific conditions of the death camp, he noticed that the moment they lost their hope they turned into living corpses. He therefore concluded that we must have hope to survive. Hope will bring us happiness. And he, too, was right, at least in part.

I think these men have served humanity well, but they have

fallen short in a major area. They have identified the problems we face, but they didn't really give us specific solutions. What is the answer to our relational deficit, to our lack of meaning, to our missing hope? Where does the love come from? How do we find our purpose for living? From what or whom do we derive our hope? No, none of these experts give us the complete answers.

But we left out one expert who has something significant to say about the subject of happiness. God. What does our Creator say about happiness?

First of all, he would tell us that if we're looking for happiness, we're searching for the wrong thing. We discovered in the first chapter that happiness is a mere shadow of the real thing. The real deal is joy—outrageous, contagious joy.

Regardless of what may or may not happen in the details of our day, God's priority is to produce *joy* in your life and mine. Jesus came into the world to bring us joy: "so that my joy may be in you and that your joy may be complete" (John 15:11). Joy is the second fruit of the Spirit listed in the Bible, right after love (Galatians 5:22–23). The Spirit of God, often referred to as the Holy Spirit, works from the inside out to change us, to mold us, to make us into people who produce outrageous, contagious joy. In fact, the Bible tells us that the joy of the Lord is our strength (Nehemiah 8:10). It's the fuel that moves and motivates us from the inside out.

Our God has put the production of joy at the top of his to-do list in your life and mine. In other words, it is God's priority to produce joy in our lives, to turn us from self-centered people into others-centered people, to turn us from sorrowful people into joyful people. He is totally committed to carrying out this work.

SO WHAT IS JOY?

One day, several years ago, an ice storm hit North Texas on Thanksgiving morning. I had to drive to the church that morning to pick up the manuscript I had dictated for the sermon I was going to preach that weekend. My oldest daughter, LeeBeth, was with me in our Suburban. As we were carefully navigating the icy streets leading to my office, we listened intently to the radio to get the latest traffic and weather reports. We heard the gloomy news: "The ice is terrible, treacherous, and dangerous. Don't go out if you don't absolutely have to. The driving conditions are hazardous." They were talking about falling trees and limbs, car accidents, freezing pipes, and all sorts of doom and gloom. I was starting to get a little depressed about this wintertime catastrophe.

Then I looked over at LeeBeth, who was seven years old at the time. She was bouncing around in her seat, hardly able to contain herself. "It's an ice storm, Daddy! Ice! We are going to go home and slide down the driveway! We're going to make snowmen! We're going to make snowballs and throw them at each other! EJ [her little brother] has never seen snow! It's incredible! It's beautiful!"

The radio deejays, meteorologists, and traffic reporters were bemoaning the weather, but my little seven-year-old daughter chose a different path. She chose joy. She chose to see the beauty and fun in the circumstances. LeeBeth's words didn't make the ice storm less dangerous. I didn't take the weather reports and advisories any less seriously. But she reminded me that I didn't have to focus just on the negative and get depressed. The amazing thing about joy is that it doesn't disappear because of the circumstances.

This is a simplistic example, but it's meant to show how joy is choosing to see the beauty and blessings no matter what comes our way in life.

You may be thinking, I like this idea of joy, but I'm not sure I understand what it is. What exactly is the difference between happiness and joy? Well, you're asking the right question.

✳ *Joy can be defined as the positive confidence I possess by knowing and trusting God regardless of the circumstances.*

Joy is inner delight derived from an intimate relationship with Christ. Happiness is circumstantial, but joy is relational. No matter what life brings my way, no matter what the circumstances, if I have this inner delight derived from an intimate relationship with Christ, joy will flood my soul. It's the peace that surpasses all understanding.

Now just for a second, let's try to get into the mind of God. God is the Creator; we are the creatures. God could have said that he wanted the prevailing attitude of his children to be one of solemnity. And, as a result, we would all walk around with solemn demeanors and somber attitudes. Remember Eeyore, that depressed donkey in *Winnie-the-Pooh*? Eeyore is the one who eats thistles and is always complaining about something breaking. He even lives somewhere called Gloomy Place. A lot of us live like Eeyore. We can't get excited about anything and find it difficult to have a positive outlook on life. But, despite the fact that many of us do live our lives like that, that's not what God wants for us. His plan has always been for the prevailing attitude of his children to be one of joy. Joy is woven into the very fabric and framework of who God is, and as he lives and works in our hearts, he wants to produce joy in our lives.

JOY JAMMERS

While joy ranks high on God's list of spiritual priorities, a major problem exists. There is a battle going on in our lives. The Holy Spirit wants to manufacture joy, but we spend major amounts of energy fighting against him. By listening to the myths about happiness, we end up blocking the joy the Spirit of God is trying to produce in us. Our attitudes and actions battle against him and tell him that we don't want joy.

The weapons we use to fight the Holy Spirit are what I call *joy jammers*. And there are three joy jammers we all use at various times in our lives.

Selfishness

Selfishness is the first of the three joy jammers, especially in the area of relationships. As God works to produce joy in our friendships, our dating relationships, our marriages, our professional relationships, we push against him with selfish desires. The Bible says, "Wherever there is jealousy or selfish ambition, there will be disorder and every other kind of evil" (James 3:16, NLT).

In our quest for individual rights, in our universal pursuit of happiness, we think to ourselves, *I have got the right to be happy*. And that is true. We do have that right. But if you are always focusing on your rights in a relationship, you are not going to meet the needs of the other person. Instead, you will end up pushing them away or, worse, tearing them apart.

We are all basically selfish people. I know I am. I constantly struggle with this, with my family, with my co-workers, and with other people in my life. We all have a tendency to think about me, myself, and I.

None of us have to be taught to think about ourselves; we're born with a "me first" mentality. It's very rare to think of the needs of others—even in our closest relationships. Let's say your four-year-old son wakes you from dreamland at 3:28A.M. because he has a stomachache. Your first thought probably isn't, "Oh, come here, buddy. Let Daddy fix it!" More likely, you are bemoaning your lack of sleep and biting a hole through your tongue as you escort your son back to his room. What do you do when you come home and your living room is a disaster? Do you sit down with your husband and say, "I'm sorry you lost the remote for the TV. How can I help you find it?" That would be nice, but I'm guessing that you'll either unleash some choice words or run outside, count to one hundred—and then count back down to one before reentering the nest. Thinking about others is not natural. Instead, we ask, "How does it affect me? What's in it for me?"

For example, what if you and I met one day and someone snapped a digital picture of the two of us? What do you think would happen when you looked at that picture on the camera's preview screen? What do you think your reaction would be? How do you think I would react? You would say that picture is good or bad based on how you look, and I in turn would judge the merit of that picture based on how I look. It's human nature. We focus on ourselves first. That picture would only look "good" in our estimation if we photographed well. The other person could have both eyes closed, his tongue sticking out, and his hair all mussed up, but as long as we look good, everything's all right. That is just a microcosm, a small illustration, of how self-centered, how selfish, we all tend to be in our relationships.

Bitterness

Another joy jammer is bitterness. "Watch out that no bitterness takes root among you, for as it springs up it causes deep trouble, hurting many in their spiritual lives" (Hebrews 12:15, TLB). We all deal with bitterness because it is impossible to be in any kind of relationship without being hurt at one time or another. There is no way you can go through life and not experience a little bit of bitterness.

The issue is not how to avoid bitterness; it is how to deal with it when it comes up. Too many relationships are torn apart because of bitterness. We get hurt and that pain turns to bitterness. Instead of reconciling a broken relationship, we turn the situation over and over on the rotisserie grill of our minds until it leads to bitterness. Many of us would rather plot revenge than spend energy to reconcile a relationship. We'd rather inflict pain than forgive the offender. Once bitterness takes root, it begins to eat away at all of our emotional and relational energy.

We burn so much energy dwelling on the meeting where the boss embarrassed us in front of our co-workers that we have nothing left to spend on our productivity, or to help a teammate through their nasty divorce. Once we spend the majority of our energy dwelling on our pain, it can quickly become a downward spiral that progressively isolates us from our closest friends and family. Let me encourage you to deal with pain as quickly as possible. In a close relationship like marriage, it is especially important to deal with each issue and move on. If the pain isn't dealt with, seeds of bitterness will take root and you will start to think, *I don't love him anymore. I don't know who this person is. We've grown apart, and I'm going to bail on this relationship.*

Pain is real. There are times we need the guidance of trained professionals to work through our complex web of emotions, but many times the path of least resistance will emerge from simply picking up the phone to say "I'm sorry" or "Why did you hurt me?"

Until you deal with the seeds of bitterness in your heart, you are not going to have joy. Those seeds will take root and jam the joy God wants to plant in your life. Is there someone who has hurt you? Forgive them. People think forgiveness is for other people. Actually, forgiveness is designed for you. Release them and, more importantly, release yourself so that you can once again find the joy that only comes when you have let go of bitterness.

Fear

The third joy jammer is fear. What is fear? It is *f*alse *e*vidence *a*ppearing *r*eal. It is when we put too much stock in the great unknowns of life and allow them to paralyze us. Several years ago, I wrote a book on fear, entitled *Know Fear*. The reason I wrote that book is because everyone deals with fear, including me. We all need help facing the common fears in life. The most common fears we deal with are the fear of death, the fear of loneliness, the fear of failure, and the fear of the future. Fear keeps us from taking risks. Fear keeps us from trying new stuff. Fear keeps us from investing in life. I truly believe that God wants us to experience a life of unbridled vitality. This kind of life emerges from dreaming big dreams and taking big chances. It's a high-stakes game of big risks and bigger rewards.

Fear stops dreams in its tracks. Fear grinds vitality and excitement to a ho-hum, so-so kind of life. God has bigger dreams for us than we often care to pursue (Jeremiah 29:11–13). God has spectacular plans for our lives that we can't even fathom. But fear—the opposite of faith—will tell you to believe in a small God, to dream smaller dreams, to accept the status quo and live a life on the sidelines.

Here's what God says about this joy jammer: "Fear always contains some of the torture of feeling guilty. The moment fear comes into a relationship, joy just jumps out. The man who lives in fear has not yet had his love perfected" (1 John 4:18). Fear causes us to build walls instead of bridges to other people. Because we are fearful, we don't open ourselves to others; we don't reveal our true selves. We worry that others won't like us or will judge us.

Fear keeps us from being vulnerable in relationships; it keeps us from revealing our hopes and dreams, pains and sorrows, to the significant people in our lives. In short, it jams the joy of living and connecting to others. It's hard to be confident, it's difficult to find inner peace and contentment, when you are dealing with large levels of fear.

CLEARING THE WAY FOR JOY

God wants to take you on a ride, a joy ride. Get in, buckle up, and push the pedal to the metal. We all may experience selfishness, bitterness, and fear from time to time—after all, we're human. But there are things we can do to make sure these joy jammers are just speed bumps and not roadblocks on our journey to joy.

Giving, Not Getting

First, God asks us to concentrate on giving, not getting. We live in a get-to-get world. We get money and things so we can get more money and more things. But that is not the way to true success in God's economy. If we want to experience real success and lasting joy, we need to convert our get-to-get mentality into a get-to-give lifestyle. I'll spend an entire chapter in this book talking about how to do this. The only reason God lets us have stuff is so that we can bless others with it. The more we try to hold on to it, the greater the hold *it* has on *us*. Material possessions can only bring you joy if you are able to let them go. I'm not saying that you should sell everything you have and give the money away. I'm not saying you shouldn't have possessions. But they shouldn't have you. It's a matter of perspective and focus. The moment your focus turns to getting and having rather than giving, you are on the wrong track.

No doubt you've heard many times that it is more blessed to give than to receive. Do you believe that? More importantly, do you live that out? What are you giving in relationships? What are you giving to your spouse? What are you giving to your children? What are you giving to all the people around you who desperately need this character quality called joy? The world is dying for it. God wants our joy to jolt the people we come in contact with. And if you are not joyful, it may be because your perspective on getting and giving is not in focus.

Healing, Not Hurting

God also wants us to concentrate on healing, not hurting. He says to us, "Bear with each other and forgive whatever grievances you may have against one another. Forgive as the Lord forgave you" (Colossians 3:13). Sadly, too many of us concentrate on hurting, don't we? We like to keep score. And the grudge builds and builds and builds inside of us until we are ready to explode at the other person. But that's not what God does. God is ready to forgive you and me. Are you ready to do the same, to forgive people who have hurt you? Just think about it. God simply forgives. He doesn't put conditions on it. He doesn't hold a grudge over us for the rest of our lives. He forgives and forgets. We should be ready to do the same. This readiness to forgive goes back to our focus on giving, because if you look closely at the word *forgive*, right there in it is the word *give*. Forgiveness is a gift. Healing is a gift. So concentrate on healing, not hurting.

God's Power, Not Your Problems

Finally, God wants us to concentrate on his power, not our problems. It is so easy to become enmeshed and ensnared in our problems, but the Bible says to trust God "at all times" (Psalm 62:8). It doesn't say, "Trust in God *some* of the time"; it says *all* of the time.

My mind goes back to the apostle Paul. In the first century, Paul spent a lot of time in prison because of his belief in Christ. But while he sat in a dark, dank, and dirty prison cell, he wasn't singing sad Johnny Cash songs. He wrote a letter to other believers, and this letter is known as the book of Philippians in the New Testament. And take a wild stab at what the theme of Philippians is. Joy. Nineteen times the words *joy* and *rejoice* are used. The apostle Paul was joyful even in prison. Isn't it great to know that God can use anything—bad times, good times, and mediocre times—to do wonderful things in our lives? He is able to use all things—good, bad, and in between—for our good and his glory. And because we know that, it should bring us joy in the middle of our trials and tribulations.

Throughout this book, we're going to learn how we can trust in God at all times. Pour out your heart to him. Be honest with God. You can express anger to God. You can express laughter to God. And through it all, regardless of the circumstances, your heart will be able to overflow with unimaginable, unthinkable, and unquenchable joy. God is offering your very own keys to the joy ride you've always dreamed about. Will you join him?

STOP AND THINK

FOLLOW THE SIGNS: Happiness is a myth. Happiness is not the overriding attitude God wants for us. Instead, God's priority is to produce joy in our lives. Joy is the positive confidence I possess by knowing and trusting God regardless of the circumstances.

CHECK THE MAP: "For the joy of the Lord is your strength" (Nehemiah 8:10).

TAKE THE NEXT STEP: Name the three joy jammers and the three antidotes that were mentioned in this chapter. Choose one of these antidotes that you feel is a particular weakness in your life. What can you do to develop this habit in your life?

3

IS IT IN YOU?

One filled with joy preaches without preaching.

—Mother Teresa

In 1901, a man named Luigi Bisera owned a manufacturing plant in Milan. He was tired of his workers taking long, drawn-out coffee breaks, so he figured out a way to hurry them up. He invented a rapid way to brew strong coffee that was served in little cups to shorten their coffee breaks. With his workers spending more time on the job, Luigi was able to make more money—not to mention the caffeinated edge it gave his employees. Thus, "espresso" was born, an express method to make very strong coffee.

I can identify with Luigi. I'm an espresso kind of guy. When most people are enjoying their morning cup of joe, I'm sipping my little cup of espresso. I like this particular coffee drink because it's small but powerful. Just two shots of espresso in a little cup are like two strong cups of coffee. Like I always say, life's too short to drink weak coffee.

Life's also too short to be negative.

Take a second to think about it. We only have about five or six decades to make a real difference in this one and only life. And the more time we spend focusing on the negative, the less time we have to make a positive influence on the people around us. The life that we have been given is simply too short and too precious to waste with negative words, thoughts, and actions.

Instead, we need to learn to be positive. But how do we make that happen? How do we turn the negative into the positive?

We do that by becoming espresso kinds of people, because one of the by-products of joy is a lot like espresso. I'm talking about that contagious, outrageous character quality called enthusiasm. It's small. It's concentrated. A little bit goes a long way. And it will caffeinate your life. It will also caffeinate the lives of people around you.

Conversely, negativity will decaffeinate your life. Negative people suck the life out of us and make even the best of circumstances seem dire and dismal. Negative people are like Chicken Little waiting for the sky to fall. Nothing about life is good, and they're always expecting the worst to happen—and it usually does.

Enthusiastic people, by contrast, are optimistic. Enthusiasm comes from two Greek terms, *en* and *theos*. *En theos* means "in God"; thus, enthusiasm is all about being connected to God. When we trust Christ for our life and salvation, God infuses his Spirit within us. Once God is in us, he'll replace negativity with enthusiasm. He'll replace old habits with new habits that will improve every area of our lives. The Bible tells us, "anyone who is in Christ is a new creature, old things have passed away, and new things have come" (2 Corinthians 5:17). That newness

"My Spirit Rejoices in God"

Mary, the mother of Jesus, was in her ninth month of pregnancy. She had to take a long journey on the back of a donkey, from Nazareth to Bethlehem. I got carsick on a tour bus two years ago taking that same journey. Can you imagine riding on the back of a donkey . . . nine months pregnant? And Mary is fourteen or fifteen years old, having a baby in a cave inhabited by livestock. This was no five-star honeymoon experience at the Ritz. No white picket fence or a dog named Rover. Yet she told God that she wanted to be used by him and be responsive to his will.

This is how Mary responded to her circumstances: "My soul glorifies the Lord and my spirit rejoices in God my Savior" (Luke 1:46–47). She was enthusiastic. Mary was enthusiastic because she was intimately connected with the living God of the universe, and she praised him for using her in such an incredible way. Have you thanked God today for being *your* God and for the opportunities he has given you to serve him?

of life transforms the past into a bright future. It brings inner joy that overflows into an enthusiastic and contagious attitude.

THE THREE PARTS OF ENTHUSIASM

For me, part of the pleasure of drinking espresso is making it. In trying to perfect my espresso-making technique, I've researched and compared coffee beans, experimented with the texture of the grinds, and taste-tested shot after shot of coffee. I've tried to learn as much as possible. For instance, did you know that when made right, espresso is made up of three parts? At the bottom of the cup is the heart, the middle is the body, and on top there should be a nice froth known as the crema.

You know enthusiasm is a lot like espresso. Enthusiasm also has three parts to it: heart, body, and crema.

Heart

Enthusiasm is an inward quality, an issue of heart and spirit. The moment we become followers of Christ, the moment we ask Jesus Christ to take over our lives, we become right with God vertically. When we are right with God vertically, we'll have the power to be enthusiastic horizontally in our relationships. Followers of Christ should be filled with excitement, purpose, and hope, which will impact every relationship around them. Instead of dragging people down, people will be drawn to those who have that positive outlook on life. It doesn't mean we're going to be perfect, but we'll have that quality that will allow us to positively influence the people around us.

Sadly, though, along life's journey, a lot of us develop enthusiasm spasms. These enthusiasm spasms dilute our enthusiasm.

The first spasm is *worry*. I define worry as an inordinate amount of anxiety about something that probably is not going to happen. But this anxiety consumes our thoughts and dominates our lives.

A couple of years ago, I put a battery in the back of my car. Unfortunately, some of the battery acid spilled on the carpet. I quickly got a towel and tried to get up the battery acid. Over the next few days, though, I watched in horror as the battery acid disintegrated a huge chunk of the carpet. Like battery acid, worry eats away at our spirit, killing our enthusiasm.

Jesus said, "Who of you by worrying can add a single hour to his life?" (Matthew 6:27). Worry serves no purpose. It doesn't change circumstances. It won't make things better. In fact it often makes them worse. Worry is a lot like bitterness. It steals time from the present to dwell on the past. I've heard it said that more than 90 percent of the things we worry about never transpire. That's a sobering statistic. Worry, like bitterness, takes energy away from problem solving to exacerbate the problems we're already facing.

Are you familiar with that spasm called worry? Do you spend inordinate amounts of time worrying about things that never take place? Is acid eating away at your insides because you just can't let go of things in your mind? Think about Jesus' words. Worry won't add an hour to your life, but it could very easily take hours away from your life when it escalates into stress. And that doesn't take much.

Stress, or worry on steroids, is another common enthusiasm spasm. Stress is an intense strain about something that is out of our control. The National Occupation Board of Health and Safety estimates that stress on the American workforce costs the country about $100 billion a year. Stress, according to a recent *Wall Street Journal* article, can wear down the immune system and increase the risk of disease, it can damage the brain and cause memory problems, it can interfere with sexual performance, and it can lead to heart attacks and premature death. Does that get your attention?

The Bible says this about stress: "Do not be anxious about anything, but in everything, by prayer and petition, with thanksgiving, present your requests to God" (Philippians 4:6).

We're warned not to be anxious, but the verse continues, "but in everything [not in *some* things, but in *every*thing], by prayer and petition, with thanksgiving, present your requests to God." The cure for stress is talking to God through prayer. When stress begins to stalk your spirit, when it surrounds you like a pack of hungry hyenas, take time to pray. Present your requests with thanksgiving to God, in *everything*. This isn't always easy to do. So many times I'll spend countless hours mulling over the problems in my life or ministry. I'll examine the problem from every conceivable angle. I'll burn valuable time and energy isolating myself from God, who has all the power I need to solve the problem. Sometimes I'll take it out on my family and friends. Because I've burned so much energy trying to solve problems on my own, my ability to help my wife and kids will be severely weakened. I'll come home in a sour or introspective mood and ignore the needs of my wife, Lisa. And my kids will find that their dad is emotionally unavailable to help them work through the minefield of issues that teenagers have to face today. When stress permeates a life, the only remedy is the peace and perspective that God provides through prayer. Prayer slows us down, allows us to ask for help, and lets us know that God is bigger than us and our problems. When we take stress to God, the stranglehold of stress will fall away.

These two enthusiasm spasms have some other bad byproducts, or sinister symptoms. You show me someone who is riddled with worry and stress, and I will show you someone who is critical, rude, and unappreciative. The reason that so many of us have a tendency to fall into these enthusiasm spasms is because we forget who we are, what we have, and where we are going.

Body

That's why the second part of enthusiasm is so important: the body. Enthusiasm starts in the heart and then it flows into the body. If you don't have it in the heart, you won't have it in the body. I'm not referring to your physical body here. I'm referring to what the Bible calls the Body of Christ, the Church. This is that spiritual and universal union of Christ-followers.

When God is "in" us, he changes us from the inside out. That's the heart. But he also binds us together with other Christ-followers. That's the body. As believers, because we are in God and God is in us, we should be the most enthusiastic people around. I need to remind myself constantly that I have been adopted into the family of God, the Body of Christ. I'm not on an island anymore. I'm not going through life confused and purposeless. The Bible says the moment I receive Christ, I am adopted into his family.

That reminds me of that classic pop song by Sister Sledge, "We Are Family." As Christ-followers, we can sing at the top of our lungs, "We are family." We are united together with people from every age group, ethnic background, and country around the world. We can share our struggles and our successes with our new family. And we have the comfort of knowing that we are not alone on our journey. When we realize we are a family, it should cause us to be caffeinated with enthusiasm.

When we embrace Christ, we're adopted into the family of God. *Adopted* is an important word. During biblical times, parents could legally disown a biological child, but they couldn't disown an adopted one. I believe that's why the word *adopted* is used to signify what it means to become a Christian. Once we become a Christian, God will never disown us or turn his back on us. We are permanently united to God and to his Church. That's a pretty good reason to be enthusiastic; our lives are secure in the hands of God.

But if you are like me, you sometimes allow those enthusiasm spasms to creep into your mind and heart. The reason we deal with these spasms is because we are basically forgetful. We forget we are permanently grafted into God's family.

In the face of obstacles, we often forget why enthusiasm is so important. I believe that this quality is what truly separates an outrageous, contagious life from the life for which most people settle. Enthusiasm is hope when problems overwhelm us. Enthusiasm is the passion for excellence when "good enough" isn't good enough. Enthusiasm provides endless energy and focus when most are willing to throw in the towel. Enthusiasm attracts other people. It excites them, energizes them, and gives them a reason to roll up their sleeves to join you. Enthusiastic people live an exciting and full life. But as a Christian, it is especially crucial that we maintain our enthusiasm, for it is our enthusiasm that enables us to reach out to others and share the glory of God.

When I think about enthusiasm, I think about the history of Fellowship Church. Our church began sixteen years ago with only 150 people in a small office complex. As we continued to expand, we moved from there to a little fine arts theater. When we outgrew that facility, we met in a high school. And we eventually grew into the five campuses we have today. In a real way, that small group of 150 committed Christ-followers cleared the path for others to hear the life-changing message of Jesus

Christ. How did they make such a huge impact? It was their un-bridled, outrageous, contagious enthusiasm. Because of the en-thusiasm of those early attendees, today we are seeing thousands of lives transformed from darkness to light as more than twenty thousand people attend our services every weekend and many more thousands hear and see us over TV and radio airwaves.

Don't ever underestimate the power of enthusiasm. As we experience the reality of God living in us and become an active part of a local body of believers, we have the power to impact the lives of thousands of people over the course of our lives. People are drawn to enthusiasm, and as we portray Christ as a person of enthusiasm and joy, we will attract countless people to him—people who will find, at last, the life they've been searching for.

Crema

The third layer of espresso is the crema. The crema imparts the nutty flavor. It gives it that little zing, that taste, that kick. It's also the sweetest part of espresso. And it's the sweetest part of en-thusiasm. The crema is that part of enthusiasm that we give to others—the part that other people see. Enthusiasm is caffeinated by the heart, flows into the body, and then is topped off by the sweet crema that we share with others.

In the New Testament, the apostle Paul tells a group of Christians, "Your enthusiasm has stirred most of them into ac-tion" (2 Corinthians 9:2). The Bible says that God wants our enthusiasm to turn the heads of others so that they look at you and me and ask, "Where does your enthusiasm come from? Where does your joy come from?" In other words, where does your crema come from?

Let me give you a tip about ordering espresso. There are two things you need to watch out for. One, you need to ask the barista this question: Do you pull your own shots? Equally important is how the espresso looks when it arrives at your table. Does it have a good head of crema on it? If it doesn't, send it back.

I could say the same thing about a Christ-follower. If you claim to be a Christian but don't exhibit that sweet crema in your life, the world is going to send you back. And if you are not pulling your shots from the source of all life, from the Creator of the universe, if your life is not the real deal powered by the Spirit of God, you'll have nothing to say and you won't impact anyone with the hope that Christ provides. If they don't see that passion, that sweetness, that java jolt of enthusiasm in your life, your message will go nowhere.

There may be times in your life when you wonder why you are not making an impact on others around you, why your words are not hitting the mark, or why others are pushing you away. It may be because you are missing this vital element in your walk with Christ: the crema of enthusiasm.

During my high school basketball days, we would have closed practices. Our coach didn't want our rival schools to figure out what we were doing, so no one could attend the practices except the players, the trainers, and the coaches. I remember checking out the horizon line in the gym during practices—the ground floor and the upper deck—and seeing no one in the stands. But when I looked at the two doors in the back of our gym, it was a different story. These doors had little windowpanes, and many times I would look up and see the silhouette of my father watching me play. No one in the gym knew that Dad was there except me. I recognized my father because I am his son. And just knowing that Dad was watching motivated me to play better.

As you live your life and I live mine, *our* Father is the same way. He is constantly looking down from the windowpanes of heaven, watching you and me. And that realization should motivate us to have this outrageous, contagious, and caffeinated enthusiasm and joy that begins in the heart and flows into the body. As believers in the Body of Christ, we should be the most enthusiastic people around because we have a constant companion we can relate to and talk to. This companion lived his life on planet Earth with all the junk and the funk that we have to deal with. He knows all about the highs and lows of life. His name is Jesus.

We can't fake him out or pretend he's not there. When we try to run away from him, we end up running right into him. And because God is our constant companion, we should talk to him and rely on his power.

So many times, when I choose not to enthuse the people around me, it is because I forget who I am, what I have, and where I am going. And I miss great opportunities to influence others with the enthusiasm that comes from my relationship with God. I am sometimes duped into thinking that enthusiasm is emotional, but it's so much more than emotions. It's relational and intentional. It comes through my relationship to Christ and through an intentional decision to express the joy within me. When I wake up in the morning and don't choose enthusiasm, I miss opportunities to make a positive impact in my family, my marriage, my career, and my friendships.

Jesus had some serious, infectious enthusiasm going on. Look at the account of how Jesus called the disciples Peter, Andrew, James, and John (Matthew 4). These guys were hard-core fishermen, working with tackle boxes, nets, lures, and all that stuff, when Jesus said simply, "Follow me." And what happened? They left all their stuff and they immediately followed him. They abandoned their careers and their way of life to follow Jesus. Why is that? I believe that core group of disciples followed Jesus so quickly because they realized something unique in him—they saw that rare and unique quality of enthusiasm. They sensed that he was different. He wasn't "just another man." As they would eventually discover, he was the incarnation of God himself—God in the flesh.

God is enthusiastic in his relationship with us. He does not speak to us with his arms folded and a scowl on his face. He communicates his love to us with his arms wide open. And his enthusiasm should fire us up and cause us to be enthusiastic, too.

In the same way, our enthusiasm can light a spark in the lives of others. There have been many weekends when I have walked into Fellowship Church and experienced an enthusiasm spasm. Maybe I was tired or stressed or both. Many times I feel inadequate to speak God's word. But something changes my whole demeanor. When I see smiling men and women serving in the parking crew, as ushers or greeters, and teaching kids in the children's ministry, it revs me up! Sometimes I'll receive a warm handshake and a word of encouragement that they are praying for me. Moments like that mark my life. In the midst of the intense pressures of leadership, many people have changed my week and my outlook because of their enthusiasm. Enthusiasm is contagious.

And enthusiasm doesn't just move people; it gives you and me an opportunity to move the heart of God. Have you ever thought that you could actually move the heart of God? As I give my enthusiasm to God, as I worship him with enthusiasm, it pleases him (Psalm 69:30–31).

The Bible tells us, "Whatever your hand finds to do, do it with all your might" (Ecclesiastes 9:10, NKJV). Whether you are washing dishes, changing diapers, staring at the computer screen, pulling shots of espresso at Starbucks, or carpooling the neighborhood kids to soccer practice . . . whatever you do, do it with all your might. And do it for your Creator, who is watching you with a smile on his face.

Espresso. You have to have three things for it to be a great shot of espresso: the heart, the body, and the crema. If we are going to be constructive people, if we are going to be respectful people, if we are going to be appreciative people, if we are going to be enthusiastic people, it starts with the heart and exudes to the body—the Body of Christ. Then we give that crema to others. And that's the sweetest part of espresso.

Espresso. It's small. It's concentrated. It has a caffeine kick.

Enthusiasm. It's small. It's concentrated. It has a caffeine kick.

When we are right vertically with God and we are right horizontally with others, we'll have that authentic enthusiasm— the true caffeine—for a life of joy.

STOP AND THINK

FOLLOW THE SIGNS: I compared enthusiasm to espresso in this chapter. Both of them require the heart, the body, and the crema to function the way they were intended. Enthusiasm is a contagious quality that starts with a connection to our Creator and flows out from our heart to infect others with energy, encouragement, and excitement.

CHECK THE MAP: "So it is right for me to be enthusiastic about all Christ Jesus has done through me in my service to God" (Romans 15:17, NLT).

TAKE THE NEXT STEP: When you think of the word *negative*, who comes to mind? When you think of the word *enthusiasm*, who comes to mind? Would your friends and family classify you as negative or enthusiastic? What principles from this chapter can you begin to apply this week to caffeinate your enthusiasm?

4

I'VE GOT A FEELING

*You cannot make yourself feel something you do not feel,
but you can make yourself do right in spite of your feelings.*

—PEARL BUCK

"If it feels good, do it!" was a mantra of the 1960s. And out of that popular expression, a host of other feel-good statements emerged over the ensuing years: "Go with your gut." "Explore your feelings." "If it feels right, it can't be wrong." And the list goes on and on.

We still live by our feelings, don't we? Feelings, more often than not, rule our lives in twenty-first-century America. If something feels good, we do it. If it doesn't, we don't. That's why the idea of happiness continues to be such a big deal to the vast majority of us. We crave that good feeling we get when things are going our way, when everything "just feels right."

The problem is that just because something feels good doesn't necessarily mean it's right. In fact, many times, if it feels good, that means I shouldn't do it. Feelings often betray us, and when it comes right down to it, feelings don't always have our best interests at heart. Feelings can actually keep us from finding the life we've been searching for. They can keep us from finding that better place God wants for each of our lives.

So, as we move further into this journey toward joy, we have to put feelings in their proper perspective. If we're going to understand what it means to live a life of deep satisfaction and joy, we must first establish some emotional boundaries. Or, to put it another way, we have to install a feelings filter to determine when our emotions start to get away from us. To do that, I want to unpack several statements regarding our feelings that will explain where they come from and what role they play in our lives.

FEELINGS COME FROM GOD

Our Creator has given us our feelings, and we should thank him for that. Did you know that God has feelings, too? Feelings of joy, gladness, anger, and jealousy are just a few that describe God's emotions in the pages of the Bible. We can make God smile. We can make his heart beat fast. We can also make him angry. Think about Jesus, the Son of God, when he lived on this earth as a man. He got tired, he was lonely, he cried, he got angry. He was perfect in his emotional expression. Since we are made in God's image, we express the same feelings. All of our feelings, all of our emotions, come from God. And that should make us respond, "Yea, God! Thank you for the opportunity, for the ability to feel things."

We should thank God regularly for our feelings. Think about all of the feelings you displayed just in the last twenty-four hours. We have a wide variety of emotions layered into the very fabric of our being, and they are all given to us by God himself.

FEELINGS OFTEN LIE TO US

Despite the fact that God gives us our emotional capacity, feelings often lie to us. I know my feelings have lied to me! Have your feelings lied to you? If you're being honest with yourself, the answer is yes. I was talking with a Christian psychologist one day, and he told me something very important. He said that when we get too tired, too lonely, or too hungry, we tend to make bad decisions and set ourselves up for failure. These are prime times to allow our feelings to derail us. When you are missing sleep, you become irritable and can easily get overwhelmed with your family and work responsibilities. You might feel like quitting. During those times when you are busting it to get a project done, your feelings can be your enemy. Because you are both tired and isolated from your relational network, an affair with an attractive co-worker might feel right. Your feelings will tell you that you deserve it. Feelings are only part of the equation, so when we give them too much power and control in our lives, they end up leading us astray.

Right now, you may be in the throes of making a decision, and your decision is feelings focused. You're saying things like, "I'm going to do this because I *feel* like it." Or, "I'm not going to do that because it won't *feel* good."

You may be thinking of quitting your job because you feel underappreciated. Or you're going to break up with your boyfriend or girlfriend because you feel jealous or angry or both. Or maybe you've stopped talking to your best friend because you feel betrayed or taken for granted. You're not feeling good about some situation, so you're taking action. This would be fine, but what if you're actually well liked and well respected at work? What if there's no reason to be jealous, and your perception of being betrayed is actually based on a misunderstanding? You see, feelings are based on your perception of a situation, and sometimes our perceptions can be way off base.

So, although feelings are from God, they must be tethered to the truth. God is the source of our feelings, but most importantly, he is also the source of all truth. Feelings apart from truth will always, always, lead us astray.

Whenever I think of feelings, my mind rushes to the 1975 song by Morris Albert. Do you remember the lyrics: "Feelings, wo-oh-oh, feelings . . ."? That song is a classic because it played beautifully to our feelings-driven culture. But pop songs, as great as they are, should not dictate how we negotiate our emotions. Instead of singing "Wo-oh-oh, feelings," a better way to ensure that our feelings are tethered to the truth is to slow down and say, "Whoa, feelings!" When those feelings begin to surface and pull in one direction or another, we need to quickly respond, "Whoa!" I'm talking about reining in those freaky feelings until we've had time to process everything and make a decision grounded in truth.

My wife, Lisa, and I have had an opportunity to counsel a number of people over the years. And recently we were talking to a couple whose marriage was hanging by a thread. As we began to discuss a source of conflict in their relationship, I decided to start at square one. I said, "Now tell me, have the two of you sought forgiveness from one another over this issue?"

They both looked at me like deer caught in headlights and finally responded quietly, "We haven't."

I said, "Now wait a minute. You have this issue that is tearing your marriage apart, you both say you're Christ-followers who have been greatly forgiven by God—something you don't deserve, something I don't deserve, and none of us deserve—and you're telling me you have not sought forgiveness from one another?"

They looked at me again. "Right."

I said, "Can I ask you why, because this is kind of hard for me to process. Why haven't you done the forgiveness thing?"

And here's what they said to me: "We're waiting to *feel* it."

"Feel it?!" I said. "You're never going to feel it!"

You want to mess up your marriage? Then just let your feelings be the guide in your marital relationship. If you let your feelings dictate when you feel like taking out the trash, or putting your spouse's needs ahead of your own, you'll wait a very long time. You want to mess up your life? Give emotion free rein in your day-to-day decisions.

I've been married for twenty-four years, and very rarely did I feel like offering forgiveness to Lisa before I decided to forgive her for something. Forgiveness is a decision, not a feeling. It flows from our marital commitment to love one another without condition. The reality is that she's had to forgive me a lot more than I've had to forgive her, and I know she'd say the same thing: she didn't feel like forgiving me all those times, either. The feelings came later but not before we made the commitment to forgive one another.

The same is true when I go to seek forgiveness from her. When I say, "Lisa, I blew it. I'm sorry. I messed up. I was wrong. Will you forgive me?" I don't *feel* like walking up to her with my tail between my legs and admitting my guilt. And I've had to do it hundreds of times in our marriage. If I

waited to feel like it—"Okay, I *feel* it now; 'Honey, I'm sorry,
will you forgive me?' "—it would never happen. Most of the
time, I feel the opposite. I don't want to offer or seek forgiveness from Lisa, or anyone else for that matter. My feelings
usually lead me to make it easier on myself. And that's when I
have to say, "Whoa-oh-oh, feelings. I'm not going to be led
by you."

I'm not indicating that forgiveness is merely lip service. It's
not a license to say "I forgive you" without really meaning it.
The point is that, even if you don't feel like forgiving, you can
make a decision to forgive. God will give you the power to follow through with that commitment, and in time, the feelings associated with forgiveness will come.

I don't feel like releasing other people who have wronged
me. Do you? No. You don't. But you know you have to do it
anyway because it's the right thing to do, and it's the right thing
to do because that's what God did for us. We are simply mirroring what has already been done for us through Christ.

Feelings will lie to us, so we have to be very, very careful
how we handle them. Feelings can be a great tool and an awesome companion in our lives, but we must always keep them
tethered to truth—truth that helps us follow through with the
commitments we make in every area of our lives.

FEELINGS FLOW FROM COMMITMENTS

Life is all about commitments. Commitment is pledging yourself
to a position no matter what the cost. Within the context of
commitments, we will have feelings. But we can't feel our way

"That's How I Feel About Chocolate"

For many years, Dean has been counseling people who are new to our church. As he talks to people every week, he tells them what our church is all about, what we believe, and how they can be involved. Most importantly, he shares what it means to enter into a committed relationship with Jesus Christ.

One morning he was counseling a woman who had been attending the church for a while and wanted to join. When Dean asked about her relationship with Christ, she told him that she always felt better when she came to church. When she was sad, God comforted her and made her feel good. In a loving and direct way, Dean responded as only he can: "That's how I feel about chocolate. Let's talk about Jesus."

Commitment isn't about what makes you feel good. It's about pledging yourself to a position no matter what the cost.

into a commitment. For instance, when it comes to taking care of your body, you can't wait until you feel like eating healthy and working out regularly. You do it whether you feel like it or not because it's good for you. That's the whole point of making a commitment—deciding ahead of time that we will follow through with something whether we feel like it or not.

Nowhere is this contentious relationship between feelings and commitments more apparent than in the scenario of people "playing house." Why do people live together? They are duped into thinking that shacking up with a guy or girl will help them feel their way through sex into the commitment of marriage. People play house thinking that one day something inside will click and they'll really feel it—"Okay, now I'm ready to make a commitment. Will you marry me?"

But the reality is that, especially for men (I can pick on them because I am one), it's the best of both worlds—free sex with no commitment. "Well, Ed, you don't know my man." Oh, yes, I do. If you don't believe me, let me challenge you to try an experiment: stop having sex for three weeks and see what happens. I'm willing to bet that if you are living together outside the commitment of marriage, he'll be gone within seven days. It's just like my grandmother from Laurel, Mississippi, said, "Why buy the cow if the milk is free?"

I have never felt my way into a commitment. Feelings come and go. Commitments do not. The deep feelings of satisfaction and joy come after I've pledged myself to a position and followed through no matter what the cost.

I'm going to make two statements that may surprise you. Number one: I do not always feel feelings of love for Lisa. Number two: I don't always feel feelings of love for God.

"Pastor, what did you say?! I can't believe you said that!"

If that was your reaction, you may have a limited definition of love. Love is not about feelings. I said I don't always *feel* feelings of love. When Lisa and I had two kids at home and she was pregnant with twins, there wasn't a whole lot of romance in the Young home. There were dolls and G.I. Joes and blankets and diapers everywhere. There were work responsibilities and errands and household chores. There was a lot of time and energy being given to the daily demands of life. But there wasn't a lot of energy left for the practice that created those kids—if you catch my drift. I wasn't feeling those same happy, butterfly-in-your-stomach feelings that we had had on our honeymoon. I just wasn't feeling it the same way. That's why commitment in marriage is so important. During those times when life is tough and love is even tougher, we can't feel our way into love. True love is commitment on steroids, so we have to love our way into feelings. Feelings flow from commitment, not the other way around. I love Lisa (in the true essence of love) more today than I did over two decades ago when I first met her. I love God today more than I did when I first gave my life to him as a child. But that doesn't mean that I always have an emotional experience of love in my relationship to my wife or my God.

In the true sense of the word, love is decision driven. It's all about commitment. Yes, there are feelings involved. Yes, wonderful feelings, passionate feelings, feelings like you're on fire; feelings of happiness and all that good stuff often go hand-in-hand with love. But true love in both human and divine relationships flows from commitment.

Examine God's definition of love and see if you can find the part about feelings:

"Love is patient. Love is kind. It does not envy, it does not boast, it is not proud. It is not rude, it is not self-seeking . . ."

I know feelings are in here somewhere. They've got to be.

"It is not easily angered, it keeps no record of wrongs . . ."

Where are those feelings? I'm looking.

"Love does not delight in evil, but rejoices with the truth. It always protects, always trusts, always hopes, always perseveres" (1 Corinthians 13:6–7).

Do you see anything in there about mushy, gushy feelings? You don't see it because it's not there. Love is about commitment. It's about a decision.

The *C* word—*commitment*—has become a dirty word today. It's hard to embrace that word in a culture that exalts two other words beginning with the letter *c*: *comfort* and *convenience*. We live in a culture of comfort and convenience, and following through with commitments is neither comfortable nor convenient most of the time. Is it comfortable to love your spouse as yourself? Is it convenient to live a healthy lifestyle?

I keep a journal of my thoughts and prayers, and recently I wrote down some things I don't always feel like doing. I wrote in my journal that I do not feel like getting up at 6:00 A.M. every day. I don't feel like driving to the office, praying, and studying for a message I have to deliver every weekend for twenty thousand people.

I travel around the country and speak at different conferences throughout the year, and I often don't feel like preparing for those talks. I don't always feel like working on the books that I write. I didn't always feel like sitting down and working on this book.

I don't feel like eating a turkey sandwich on whole wheat bread with a side of brussels sprouts for lunch. I don't feel like lifting weights and spending forty-five minutes on the treadmill at least three times a week. Sometimes I don't even feel like going home early and spending time with my family.

I don't feel like following through on most of my commitments before I do them. But after I do, I'm always glad! Feelings follow commitments. I've made commitments in all of these areas before God. And because of these commitments, I'm glad I put the time into the messages I give and the books I write. I'm feeling it now! I'm glad I eat healthy. I'm glad I exercise. I'm glad I go home early to spend time with Lisa and the kids. I'm glad, because the feelings have followed. But when

I'm in the thick of doing what I know to be the right thing to do, I don't always feel it.

There is a powerful scene in the movie *The Passion of the Christ* that reveals the struggle Jesus had with his own emotions. As he thought about going to the cross to die for your sins and mine, he didn't feel like doing what he was about to do. What did Jesus pray in the Garden of Gethsemane? "Father, if this cup can pass from me, if this suffering can pass, let it be." But then he said, "Not my will, but your will be done" (Luke 22:42, author's paraphrase). Feelings flow from commitments. Jesus didn't feel like giving his life, but he did because he had pledged himself to a position no matter what the cost.

How about you? What commitments have you made relationally, professionally, or spiritually? Are you following through with those commitments no matter what the cost? Or are you allowing feelings and emotions to trick you into flaking out on the promises you've made?

Over the course of this book, this journey toward joy, I'm going to give you an opportunity to rethink, reprioritize, and rededicate yourself to those major areas of commitment in your life. We're going to look at making the right choices in our priorities, our relationships, our worship, and our work.

Jesus said that if we love him, we will keep his commandments. Then he told us what the two most important commandments were: first, love God with your whole being, and second, love others as you love yourself. Every other commandment hinges on these two. We have many choices to make every day that relate to these two great priorities, these two great commandments that Jesus gave us. Will our lives be marked by decisions that reflect our love for God and our love for others? Every decision, in every area of our lives, should be an outward reflection of the inward connection we have with our Creator.

As we dive deeper into the practical issues related to priorities, relationships, work, and worship, we will get intentional about infusing our lives with joy. Remember, joy is not based on feelings; it is based on a relationship with God. So allow God to work in these major areas of your life and show you a higher road toward the better life you've been searching for.

The Bible says that we are to enter through the narrow gate. The wide gate is the road that leads to destruction, and many enter through it (Matthew 7:13–14). The wide gate (and the easy road) is to do what feels good in the moment. That is the comfortable and convenient way to go, but it will bring you emptiness and destruction. Deep, lasting joy comes by pledging yourself to a position and following through no matter how you feel and no matter what the cost. Remember the example of Jesus when you are battling some funky feelings. We're told that Jesus endured the shame and the pain of the cross for the joy set before him (Hebrews 12:2). He pledged himself to his position in advance to enjoy the rewards that were waiting. And because of his obedience, he was rewarded with unprecedented glory and honor.

STOP AND THINK

FOLLOW THE SIGNS: Feelings can betray us. Feelings must be tethered to the truth, and they must flow from our commitments.

CHECK THE MAP: "Commit your way to the Lord, Trust also in Him, and He will do it" (Psalm 37:5, NASB).

TAKE THE NEXT STEP:

- Circle the feelings below that you've felt just in the past twenty-four hours:

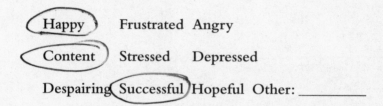

Happy   Frustrated Angry

Content   Stressed   Depressed

Despairing Successful Hopeful Other: _____

- List some things you have made a commitment to— relationally, professionally, and spiritually—that you need to follow through with regardless of how you feel from day to day. Pray for God to give you the strength to be true to those major areas of commitment.

PART 2

WHERE ARE YOU HEADED?

But what is happiness except the simple harmony
between a man and the life he leads?
—Albert Camus

Plans are only good intentions unless they
immediately degenerate into hard work.
—Peter Drucker

5

STRUGGLING WITH JUGGLING

The first step to getting the things you want
out of life is this: Decide what you want.
—Ben Stein

Let's go retro for a second, back to 1967. Back to beehives and bell bottoms; back to psychedelic shirts; back to Greenville Memorial Auditorium, where my mother took me to see "the Greatest Show on Earth."

I was mesmerized by the circus. I'm talking about sensory overload, even for a kid like me, who struggled with ADD. The ringmaster was the one setting the pace for the entire show. "Welcome to Ringling Brothers and Barnum & Bailey Circus. In ring one . . . In ring two . . . And in ring three . . ." And I saw the people juggling, and the acrobats flying, and those on the tightrope, and the contortionists and the clowns and the elephants and tigers and Gunther Gable Williams (remember that guy, with the golden tan and the blond hair?). I loved that stuff!

When I got home, my mom said I was so excited I made a beeline to our refrigerator, pulled out three eggs, and said, "Mom, watch me juggle these eggs!" And then the predictable happened: *splat, splat, splat!*

Does your life feel like a three-ring circus these days? Are you struggling with juggling? Do you have a bunch of balls in the air, desperately trying to keep them all in play—the carpool and the kids and the work and the household chores and the shopping and the church activities and on and on? Do you feel as though it's just a matter of time before all the balls in your life are just going to go *splat, splat, splat!*?

I've often felt that my schedule was so stretched that I felt like a juggler desperately trying to keep my life in balance.

Over sixteen years ago, as the pastor of a brand-new church, I was a master juggler. There was a vision and there was excitement, but not much else. No staff, no building, no reputation to fall back on, not even a typewriter. There were people to meet, a vision to cast, sermons to prepare and deliver. If there was something that needed to be done, I was probably the one doing it. It was an exciting time. There was so much potential. I saw it, and my closest friends saw it. It was this potential that fueled my fire every morning. We knew what we wanted, and we were working tirelessly toward that end. The sky was the limit. It was definitely an exciting time.

Only a few miles away, Lisa was also a master juggler. Her mission was even more critical than my own. As the mother of four high-energy kids, she certainly had her hands full. There were futures to shape, diapers to change, rooms to clean, parental laws to lay down, and meals to prepare. She was the chauffeur, cook, judge and jury, sanitary engineer, and resident therapist. If there was something that needed to be done, she was the officer on deck. But she saw the potential in her children. Her firstborn daughter was a great helper. Her son was always quick with a hug. Her twin daughters were full of life. She knew in her heart of hearts that her kids could do some great things, and all her work was worth the sacrifices.

Adding more fuel to the fire was the fact that these two master jugglers were married. Two important commitments. Two hardworking leaders. Two different perspectives. You get the picture—and I'll bet you can relate.

In case you missed the memo, we're busy. All of us. What are we supposed to do about it? Sell our possessions, move to the country, and start farming? Picture yourself and your partner with the pitchfork and the overalls. Remember that famous portrait? You could be *that* family! Doesn't that sound exciting? Wouldn't it be great to simplify your life by moving to the farm so you can relax and put your feet up? I mean, it's not like farmers struggle with a lot of work, a lack of time, or have a problem with priorities. You know I'm kidding. From the farm to the factory, the corner store to the New York Stock Exchange, we all deal with unique loads of busyness and stress. There is no such thing as the stress-free life—only the stress-managed life. Some of us are just better at stress management than others.

Rewind with me back to my situation. A young church and a young family. I was seriously stressed out. Eighteen months into my little project, I was on the verge of burnout. How do you think my wife felt? Rosy? Not likely. She was stressed, too. Not only was she managing her own juggling, but she was also trying to care for her overworked husband.

One day, my wife showed up at the office with the kids. I guess she figured it would be the only way she could get us all together for a few minutes. She managed to pull me away from my office for a little walk. I have to admit that I wasn't there mentally. I had a message to deliver the next day and had two meetings scheduled that same afternoon. Trying to manage all those pressures in my mind, I tried to concentrate on this time with my family. It was then that something got my attention, wresting me from my thoughts of work. Here we were, walking down this road around my office complex, with my wife next to my oldest daughter, LeeBeth, and pushing our twins in a double-wide stroller while I walked beside my son, EJ. It was quite a sight. It was then that "that something" hit me like a ton of bricks.

Reality finally set in. This was it. This was my life. I realized more clearly and profoundly than I ever had before that my life had changed. I was not only a husband but a father of four.

In the shadows of that office complex, God got my attention. He allowed me to see my family, and only my family, for the first time in quite a while. I was there in mind and body. I felt the warmth and strength of my son's hand. I saw the independence of LeeBeth as she walked alongside us. I saw the dependence of Laurie and Landra as they slept in their stroller. And I saw the absolute beauty of Lisa, my wife and high school sweetheart. God showed me all of this and allowed me a little glimpse into the future. I saw a future that included my four young kids growing into teenagers and then getting married and leaving home.

My thoughts went something like this: "Just think, fifteen or twenty years from now I'll perform the wedding for each child, and I'll be wishing that I had truly savored this precious time with them. I've got to capitalize on this time, and I have to do it now! They'll only be this age for a short amount of time, and then they'll move away and out of our home. I've got to be a great father for them. They need me now!"

IT'S ALL ABOUT PRIORITIES

It was an emotional few minutes to say the least. To call this experience a wake-up call is an understatement. It was like a big slap across the face. I decided then and there that I would never compromise my family for my work again. Never again would the needs of my congregation come before the needs of my family. As you can imagine, this is a tough challenge for a pastor. Souls are hanging in the balance. No doubt, I was doing some good things. I was trying to really help change our community. I was working tirelessly to help people who were emotionally broken, those who were addicted, and those who were just lost. All of these things were really good things. But I was still missing it. Even though I was working hard to build a church, my wife and kids were missing me and I was missing out. And if I kept going at that pace, I'd miss everything.

To gain victory over these sometimes competing commitments, I asked myself one simple question. "What are my priorities?" I knew I couldn't do it all, and I knew that my life was out of balance. This started me on a journey that I still battle today. It's a common struggle for all of us. It's all about priorities.

If we're going to find the lasting joy we long for, we have to practice what we preach. We have to put first things first on the rugged plains of reality.

The question that I asked myself sixteen years ago is the same question that I ask myself today to keep me accountable to my ultimate priorities in life. *What are my priorities?* It's been a great way for me to keep my busy life on track. When we're unsure about where our lives are headed, we can quickly get off track. Our priorities should govern the way we live. Ultimately, they should free us to be the people we were made to be.

You might be a little fuzzy about the word *priorities*. What are priorities all about anyway? Notice that the word *priority* has the word *prior* in it. There's a past time element. It's also an exercise in advance decision making, so there's a future element to it as well. According to *Webster's*, it has to do with "superiority in rank, position, or privilege." It's about rank and order. It means ascribing value to the best things in your life and saying yes to those things.

Remember my experience as a young leader and young father? I was saying yes to a lot of good things, but missing out on the best: cherishing my wife and raising my children. If we really long to say yes to the best, we'll have to say no to a lot of good stuff. But so often, because we aren't saying no enough, the good eclipses the best.

You might be wondering what those best things are. What should our major priorities be? The good news is that these major priorities really aren't hard to determine. The word *priorities* sounds intimidating, but they aren't something that we need to freak out about. They've already been settled. They're in stone. God has talked about them for thousands of years.

God has established many principles for life found in the pages of the Bible. You'll find that God places a premium on interpersonal relationships. God created man with the innate need for relationships. Man and woman were created for a relationship with their Creator. The Bible says that Adam and Eve got to walk with God in the garden. From the very beginning, God has pursued a relationship with his children. We not only crave a connection with our Creator, but we crave family and social relationships as well. The most basic building block of our society is the family (Deuteronomy 6). A husband is in covenant to his wife and vice versa. They are asked to train up children so they will be able to live independently, love God, and love others. Those who are single are to care for their own family as well as pursue other relationships that enable them to grow and weather the storms in life. The relational priority is huge in God's economy.

Another major priority is worship. God tells us that every thought and every action is an opportunity for us to worship, or celebrate God's goodness. But we are also asked to join our worship with others. We will live the way we were intended to live when we are tethered to a local community of other believers. Church is the place where we can find encouraging relationships, find opportunities to serve others, and grow together while worshipping our Creator (Hebrews 10:25).

Finally, we spend so much of our time and energy working because God has wired us to work. The first man and woman were asked to work (Genesis 1 and 2). Work was not given as a punishment; work was given as a gift to his children. There is, however, an important paradigm shift for our work-crazed culture. Work is to be an act of worship, not an avenue to seek power or riches at the expense of God or others.

You may wonder, "Okay. I get this. Relationships, worship, and work are my top three priorities. But what's number four? And what about five . . . and six?" This is exactly where most of us get into trouble. We think we don't have limits. If you really want to be joyful, to live the life you were meant to live, just say no to all the other stuff.

It's really very simple. God has already taken the guesswork out of the situation. We don't have to come up with some brilliant list or mission statement. We simply say, "God, since you created me, I agree with your rank order of priorities for my life. I know that your plans are far greater than my plans. I will follow your blueprint and let your timeless principles become the priorities that I live out."

Our priorities should reflect God's principles. There is a simple decision to make regarding the principles that God has laid out for us in the Bible. Just a simple answer to a simple question will tell you all you need to know about God's principles. Do you agree with them or not? Will you choose to sync your life with the principles of your Creator, or will you choose to go your own way? When you go with God, you have the confidence of knowing that you are living according to his plan for your life. When you go your own way, it all falls on you to pull your way through life.

Here's the really interesting paradox. Those who go their own way, turning their back on God's priorities, end up in the bondage of uncertainty. Those who submit to God's principles by making them their priorities actually experience the freedom of knowing their life is on track.

It all comes down to whether you are willing to follow God's principles or not. Our priorities emerge from God's principles. God's principles are found throughout the Bible and are made so that all of us can enjoy an amazing life. I'm talking about the sweet spot that God wants for us. We get all messed up when we rank ourselves and our priorities above our Creator. An ancient prophet warned us all about the danger of rebelling against the plans of the master designer. He compared God to a potter and his creation to clay (Isaiah 45:9). When the

"He Was Preparing Us for What Was to Come"
TRACY'S STORY

"God is always working in us, whether we realize it or not. That's what happened with us—God was working in amazing ways, but we didn't know it yet. We were the typical suburban family with a husband and wife, an eight-year-old daughter, and a six-year-old son. Our schedule consisted of my husband working and traveling a lot. I was involved with several different activities and responsibilities in addition to being a 'stay-at-home mom' (who was never 'home'). And our kids were involved in many activities outside of school, plus friends, extended family, and so on. We had always 'struggled' with our priorities—choosing God's best over just the good.

"Over the years, though, I started saying no to things—even activities that I really enjoyed.

"I was trying to simplify our schedule so I could be the wife and mother that God called me to be. I was much less stressed out and able to meet the needs of my family. We were still busy and running around, but it was better.

"And then a diagnosis of leukemia stopped us in our tracks. Our son was a healthy, happy, flag-football-playing kind of kid. Why did he get leukemia?

"Our world changed. Now I realized why God wanted me to say no and decrease our activities. He was preparing us for what was to come. We had to say no to so many good things. But God's best for us at that point was family time. We were shut in because of our son's illness, but we were able to make the best of it. We took one day at a time and didn't worry about tomorrow, appreciating each other and growing closer as a family."

clay tries to form itself, it makes a mess. Only in the hands of the designer can it become a masterpiece.

Why does God care about our priorities anyway? Is God some kind of management consultant, trying to make his created beings more efficient and concerned about mission statements? Yes and no. Like a consultant, he is concerned about keeping the main thing the main thing. He is intimately concerned about us following the path he has mapped out for our lives. The major difference between this master designer and a consultant is that he not only maps out our direction but also empowers us to accomplish this direction.

The Bible warns us to live wisely because time is always up for grabs (Ephesians 5:15–21). God knows we need wisdom to battle our tendency to mismanage our priorities in life. We need the ability to choose the best option among many good options. Throughout time, men and women have always had to choose wisely among a buffet of choices. There are many good choices, but only a few are really worth pursuing.

GIVING CONTROL TO THE RINGMASTER

How do we bring the circus of our lives under control? When we feel as though a hundred different circus rings are all vying for our attention at the same time, what do we do? How do we find focus and direction with the dizzying pace of action all around us?

The best decision we can make when it come to priorities is to give the microphone, the top hat, and the ringmaster suit to God. You see, God is the Ringmaster. But instead of letting him have control of our lives, a lot of us are trying to run the show. A lot of us are trying to pace our own circus. A lot of us are trying to be the ringmaster, and we're not wired to do it. It's a formula for frustration. We're trying to say, "Okay, I'll do what I want to do. I'll call the shots. I'll tell you how my life should be run." That's a great way to mess up your life. Until we give control to the one who created us, allowing him to call the shots, our lives will never be the greatest show on earth.

So that's the first decision we've got to make when it comes to priorities. And once we give our lives to the Ringmaster, once we allow him to run the show, he'll give us focus and direction. He'll take the dozens of rings that dominate our lives and direct our attention to just three major priorities. These flow from the basic life principles that God gave us thousands of years ago in the Bible.

Give Him Your Relationships

God has made each of us relational creatures. When Adam was alone, God created Eve for companionship. God then told them to be "fruitful and multiply" (Genesis 1:28, NASB). And so the institution of the family began. Sharing joy with someone else is better than being joyful alone. Sharing difficult times with close friends is also better than trying to go it alone. There's no doubt that life is better when we are connected to family and friends. On the other hand, life can be miserable without close friends and family to help us through.

However, our number one relationship has got to be our relationship with the Ringmaster himself. Knowing that he created you (and the entire universe) is reason enough. It's even more exciting that this Creator desires a relationship with you. He is not someone who sits on a faraway throne in heaven, away from all the action. The Bible tells us that he is intimately involved in all the details of our lives. Can you believe that he is personally available to you? You are wired to have a relationship with your Creator. Christ called that the greatest commandment: to love God with all your heart, soul, mind, and strength (Matthew 22:37–38).

Relationships on the human plane are also huge. That relates to what Jesus called the second greatest commandment: to love others as we love ourselves (Matthew 22:39). There are family relationships, which are essential. They are designed to provide love, security, and self-esteem. That's why it is most devastating when those who are supposed to build us up leave us hurting and lonely. A family that does it the right way can provide a foundation that lasts a lifetime. A misguided family unit, on the other hand, can minimize one's potential for a lifetime. Many other human relationships also influence and impact our lives. Dating relationships provide excitement and companionship. Friendships encourage and sharpen us. Even those in authority over us are given by God to guide and help us.

The bottom line is that God has wired us for relationships. God is relational, and we are made in his image. We cannot neglect other people by pretending that we live alone on an island. We especially need to work hard to maintain those relationships that encourage us and help us with the joys and challenges of life. I'm talking about your family and closest friends. Married partners must strive to ensure that their relationship is number one, even above the parent-child relationship. Did you catch that? The marriage comes before the kids. The best gift parents can give their children is a great marriage. Mothers and fathers have a responsibility to provide a home for their sons and daughters that is built on a strong and vibrant marriage. Single adults need to orbit their lives around a deep community of other people who love and challenge them. We're in this together, and we cannot be who God made us to be without the positive, life-giving influence of a close-knit community of family and friends.

Give Him Your Worship

We all worship something. It might be the worship of a rock band, the warmth of the sun, or even another person. The Bible says that we're wired to worship. (This is the point of Romans 1:18–23.) The question is not: Do you worship? The question is: How do you worship?

For many people, the local church seems totally out of touch with the real world. They think that going to church is great for the religious types, or maybe on special occasions, but certainly a waste of time to go every week. I know where this type of thinking comes from. It took an experience in college for me to understand how people who have not grown up in the church view the whole church scene.

When I attended Florida State University as a basketball player, my safe little world got a rude awakening. Looking back, I was more than a little naive. The lifestyle of my team-mates was radically different from mine. My dorm had a full bar in the basement and offered happy hour every day. It was pretty wheels off to say the least. Of the fifteen hundred stu-dents in that dorm, fewer than ten attended church on a regu-lar basis.

One Sunday, I took a risk and invited some of my team-mates to join me at a local church I was attending. As we started singing the second verse of one of my favorite hymns, I looked over at my buddies. You should have seen their faces. It was so foreign to them. They had no idea what a "diadem" or an "Ebenezer" was. (Come to think of it, neither did I!) I saw church through their eyes. It did not connect with them. The hymns that we sang that morning may have been contempo-rary a few hundred years ago, but they held no meaning for this group of modern-day college ball players. A lot of pastors and church leaders could use a wake-up call like the one I experi-enced that morning.

The local church is compared to the bride in a wedding (2 Corinthians 11:2). She is beautiful. She is magnetic. At a wed-ding, all eyes are fixated on the bride. Unfortunately, though, many churches are not beautiful and magnetic the way they are described by Jesus. Some of these brides are stuck in the last century and are totally irrelevant to the day-to-day challenges of life. Others are seen as a place of condemnation, with a big index finger wagging in your face. Many of these brides are totally self-absorbed and don't care enough about the outsiders who are looking in.

Maybe you attended church when you were younger. Your parents dragged you every Sunday, and once you hit high school, you were out of there. For you, the church is maybe a good place to learn about morality, but it's not really worth your time. Maybe you have been burned by a local church. Have shady finances, poor leadership, or scandal and accusations eroded your faith in the church? For the handful of church leaders who are messing it up, there are thousands who are doing church right. These pastors and leaders truly care about people. They are making a difference in their communities. Have you checked out these difference makers? Just because you've had a bad meal at one restaurant doesn't mean you stop eating out. And just because you've had a bad experience at one church shouldn't mean you give up on the whole church experience.

So many people are missing the benefits of being connected to a local church. First of all, God asks us to continue to meet together as a community of faith. The church is the one community relationship Jesus set up before leaving this earth. If your Maker asks you to do something, you know it is for your benefit. There's got to be something to it. Another reason is for those relational realities. So many people have fragmented and superficial relationships these days. The church is supposed to be a place where one can find encouragement, hope, and grace by connecting with a community of people who genuinely care about one another.

Give Him Your Work

We love it at certain times and hate it at others, but we can't deny that our work demands an overwhelming amount of our time and attention. We are all made in the image of God, and because of that, work is a good thing. God is a working God. God gave us the ability to work before sin ever entered into the equation. So work is good. And the feeling of accomplishment is a good thing. You know that feeling, don't you?

Teachers know that sense of accomplishment when the last school bell of the day rings and they can say, "I think my class actually got what I was trying to say today!" Or the business-woman who just closed a crucial deal might say, "Wow, I can't believe I did it! That's a huge client for us!" Professional ath-letes feel it when they score a touchdown in the fourth quarter or pitch a shutout to win a pivotal game. The police officer who captures a key drug dealer in his district knows that his diligence will make his streets safer for everyone. When I finish our weekend services, there is a great sense of accomplishment when I drive home to be with my family on Sunday afternoon. There's nothing like the feeling that you've achieved something worthwhile in the work world.

Is it bad to feel that way? No. It's a good thing because it's a God thing. God himself worked for six days in the story of creation. Then after that, he looked back on his work and an-nounced that it was "good." God experienced work satisfaction in creation.

Work is good, and we're all unique. We all bring different skills and abilities and aptitudes to the table. We've been wired not only for worship but also for work. Retirement is not mentioned in the Bible. You're not going to find it there. We should always be producing something, because every time we work—if we are doing it God's way—it is an opportunity to worship our Creator. Whether you preach sermons, close real estate deals, raise children, perform life-saving operations, or score touchdowns, do it for God. "*Whatever* you do," the Bible says, do it for the glory of God (Colossians 3:23).

So let me ask you a question. Is your work an act of worship to God? Or has your work become the object of your worship? In other words, has it become an obsession—the most important thing in your life? Work is important, but it must not eclipse the worship or relational priorities of life.

I CAN SEE CLEARLY NOW

Recently, I purchased a brand-new pair of glasses. And while it didn't take me very long to pick out the glasses, it did take the salesperson what seemed like an eternity to explain to me, in meticulous detail, the care that these lenses would require. She showed me how to hold the glasses and sold me special cleaning solution to spray on both the front and back side of the lenses. Then she brought out a high-tech cleaning cloth that would never scratch the lenses. Finally, after a thorough lesson in the proper care of these lenses, I made my way out of the store with my new glasses.

Why was this lens care professional going through all this? She took the time to explain the care of glasses to me because, for optimal vision, you've got to regularly clean your lenses. Glasses have a way of picking up tiny particles of dirt and grime that can obscure your vision. Any one who wears glasses will tell you, if you want to have optimal vision, you've got to have pristine lenses. You have to clean your glasses regularly.

Life is a lot like those glasses. If we don't clean the lenses of our mind and heart regularly, our vision will be blurred. And when our vision is blurred, we can't see where we're headed. We don't know where we're going or how to get there. That's why we have to spend time rethinking and reevaluating our vision and how we're following that vision on the rugged plains of reality every day. The vision God has given you and me relates directly to his plan to give us a better and brighter future. Without guidance, the Bible says, we perish (Proverbs 29:18). We may not literally die, but our spirit languishes and our passion fades when vision is absent from our lives. If our vision is fogged and blurry, our decision-making ability becomes hazy.

Joy is tied directly into building God's vision into our lives. How do we sync up with his vision for our lives? Supernatural vision comes from accepting the priorities God has laid out for us in the Bible. Very simply, the priorities we choose in life determine where we're headed. Priorities help us make the right decisions in the present based on where we've come from and where we want to go. After all, we cannot discover the path to joy if we don't know where we're headed. And we can't know where we're headed if we don't, first, have vision and, second, choose life's major priorities based on that vision. *Joy is fueled and formed through a relationship with God, and then it is reinforced and built as we make wise decisions every day based on the vision and priorities he has given us.*

Can you see clearly now? Are you following God's vision for your life based on the big three priorities of relationships, worship, and work? Do your daily commitments match your priorities? How are you doing with these big three areas of your life?

Are they competing with one another or are they functioning harmoniously together?

You might be wondering about now, "What about other things? What about money and entertainment? What about exercise and nutrition?" Don't get me wrong—all of those play a crucial role. But, as we address these various aspects of life throughout this book, you need to understand that all these good things are there to support the main things. All of these other things in life should complement, not compromise, our ability to maintain the big three. They should fit into and contribute to the success of those major life priorities. God has wired us for relationships, worship, and work.

How's your vision? Are you concentrating on the three major areas of life, or is your vision blurred by too many distracting and competing activities? Is there something you need to add or subtract? Let me challenge you to do some serious self-examination right now. Look at your calendar. When you look at how you spend your time, are you giving proper attention to relationships, worship, and work, in that order? Now take out your checkbook. Is your money being used wisely to support the importance of these three priorities, or is your bank account being stretched in a hundred different directions?

We are all in a juggling game. It's not easy living in our fast-paced society with all the responsibilities on our plates. But we need to slow down. We can only handle so much stuff. We aren't made to be machines; we are human and need to start acting like it. That doesn't mean that we are free to be lazy. God wants us to maximize the time and resources we've been given to pursue the things in life that really matter. Fortunately,

God has already laid these all out for us. We don't have to spend a lifetime trying to figure out these priorities.

God has made us for relationships, for worship, and for work. Anything that falls out of these three categories is not a major priority. So, before moving to the next chapter, take some time today to consider how to begin to make changes that will help you orbit your life around these major life priorities.

STOP AND THINK

FOLLOW THE SIGNS: In a world that often feels like a circus, life is all about priorities. We need to give ourselves to the Ringmaster and orient our lives around his three priorities to gain the freedom to be the people he created us to be.

CHECK THE MAP: "Be very careful, then, how you live—not as unwise but as wise, making the most of every opportunity, because the days are evil. Therefore do not be foolish, but understand what the Lord's will is" (Ephesians 5:15–17).

TAKE THE NEXT STEP: Compare your schedule right now to God's three major priorities. How are you doing? Are you placing a premium on relationships, worship, and work? What changes might you need to make?

6

IT'S ABOUT TIME

Time is what we want most, but . . . what we use worst.

—WILLIAM PENN

I don't think anyone would deny that we live in a fast-paced world. We weave our supercharged SUVs through crowded freeways, sipping our triple-shot lattes with one hand, while simultaneously talking through our wireless headsets, straining to hear the daily news and weather from our car stereo, and checking our PDAs for our daily appointments with our "free" hand. And that's just the drive in to work. Once we get to our desks, we have e-mails to answer, voice mails to return, faxes to send, meetings to attend, and on and on. At the end of our ten-hour work marathon, we race home for another late dinner to squeeze out a few quality moments with our spouse and kids.

We long for the weekend, when we plan to relax, but there's housework that needs to be done, and there are baseball games and dance recitals and sleepovers. Even a date with your spouse requires so much energy coordinating babysitters and eating schedules that you wonder if it's really worth it. Midway through another crazy weekend, you long for the slower pace of the work week.

It's no wonder we feel overcommitted, stressed out, and out of control. Do you ever get the feeling that there's more to life than trying to survive your weekly routine? The way most of us are going these days, you'd think there was an Olympic gold medal at stake for "most ink on the pages of a calendar." Who are we trying to kid? Is there hope for something better in life, or should we just grin and bear it?

Technology works to support our frenetic pace. There are new gadgets released every quarter that are designed to "simplify" our lives, from wireless e-mail and wireless PDAs to Bluetooth mobile phones, more sophisticated computers, and satellite television and radio. Just when we think we have all the latest innovations, something else comes along that promises to save us time, but inevitably adds even more to our already stuffed full plates.

We live in a time when we want to be able to get ahold of anyone at any time in any place. We have more information at our fingertips than anytime in history, but less time to process this wealth of knowledge. We have more options than ever to occupy our time, but less focused time to devote to the things that really matter to us.

The question is: why can't we slow down? What's wrong with us? Why do we constantly feel like we're trying to keep our heads above water? If technology is supposed to help us, why do we end up drowning in it? Why can't we find the balance, the sweet spot in the midst of our hectic schedules?

Even our mundane tasks seem like timed events. When my wife and I are making a run to the grocery store, I have a hard time slowing down enough to see the people around me.

Somewhere between our hunt for whole wheat bread, yogurt, and those oatmeal raisin cookies my son loves, I usually run into a neighbor or friend from church. The conversation is usually rushed. The standard response to the "How are you?" question is usually, "I've been busy. *Real* busy."

Seems like we're all busy these days, and proud of it. Being busy is a badge of honor. "How am I? I'm busy, busy, busy. I haven't had a vacation in two years. I'm always working overtime. I'm an executive during the week and a chauffeur on the weekends . . . blah, blah, blah."

Okay, so you're busy. Me too. But why has that become our standard response?

I think part of the answer is because we haven't figured out one very simple principle. Can you guess what it is? Time is limited, and so are we. There is a fixed amount of time for each one of us, a certain number of years, months, days, and minutes that each of us has been given. There is no arcade operator we can find to buy more minutes for our playing card. There is no fountain of youth or Holy Grail we can find to extend our lives.

We are also personally limited. We have a limited amount of time and energy each day to accomplish our daily grind. Even if we have enough energy and time to add something new, it doesn't mean that we can handle the additional emotional or spiritual pressure. We all know that there is a "tipping point" in all of us. As much as we'd like to be Superman or Superwoman, we've experienced enough frustration and failure to know that we don't have superpowers. Even though we love to wear a lot of different hats and excel at all of our roles, the truth is that we simply cannot excel at anything when we are trying to do everything.

Our culture bows to busyness. As much as we like to deny it, we reward hard work and the hard worker. We reward those who can do it all. It's not enough to be a great mom anymore. Now we reward the mom who is a great mom—and a great executive. We applaud the dad who not only brings home the bacon but also cooks it up for his family each morning. This great value of hard work should be encouraged, but when it affects your children, your marriage, or your health, you must reexamine this value against the backdrop of all your priorities. With so many things at our fingertips these days, it is easy to OD on opportunities. We can surf millions of websites, chase hundreds of channels, and choose from a buffet of activities to overfill our bulging calendars.

Nobody is immune to this challenge, and it is certainly nothing new on the human scene. Over two thousand years ago, the Bible addressed this struggle of busyness and the difficulty of choosing the very best in life (Luke 10:38–42).

A GOOD CHOICE OR THE BEST CHOICE?

Jesus was invited to a dinner party with two female hosts. Sounds pretty simple, but the story reveals that a simple dinner party escalated into an ancient cat fight. Two sisters were going at it, and Jesus had ringside seats.

Fighting out of the red corner was Mary the Magnificent. And out of the blue corner was Manic Martha. The place was Bethany, about two miles from Jerusalem. Here's how it all went down.

It begins pretty simply. Jesus and his students were walking into a village, where an invitation came for dinner. Martha, the host of the party, received the RSVPs from her guests and began the preparations to entertain these esteemed guests. She pulled out her favorite cookbooks and most elegant decorations to pull off the event of the year.

But here's where the plot clots. In the midst of all her preparations, Martha turned manic. She was running around in a thousand different directions trying to prepare her home and the meal for her guests. The food needed cooking, the table needed setting, and the house needed decorating. And her partner in crime, her party cohost, was just hanging out with Jesus. Instead of helping to prepare the meal, set the table, and serve the guests, Mary was resting. She was simply sitting at the feet of this great teacher, while her sister took care of all the details. Can you feel Martha's anger growing?

The scenario may have played out like this. After a few minutes, Martha is talking to herself: "It's okay; she's just being a good host and making sure he feels welcome. I'm sure she'll come here any minute to help me with this salad."

While trying to rescue the bread from the oven, she inadvertently burns her hand and gets a little more upset. "Alright, she's had twenty minutes with him. Surely she's coming now."

When she scurries over to the other room to see where her precious sister is, she discovers that Mary the Magnificent hasn't moved. "It's like she's never seen a teacher before," she mutters under her breath.

Now the pressure is really on. The lamb is ready, but the vegetables need to be seasoned. The salad needs a bowl and some serving pieces, the bread is starting to get cold, and the table hasn't even been set.

Just as she's recapping all these important details, she really loses it. "What in the world is she doing?! I thought she said she wanted to throw this party, and I'm stuck in the kitchen doing all the work! Some sister she is. Oh, just let Martha do it. She'll take care of it," she says to herself. Well, Martha has had enough. She decides to plead her case to this famous teacher. Maybe she can use this moment to embarrass her sister for being so lazy.

"Teacher, can you tell my sister to help me out? Dinner is nearly ready, but she hasn't lifted a finger yet. We're in this together, but she hasn't helped me cook, clean, or decorate. She has spent this entire time with you, and hasn't done one thing to help me. Think about how I feel. I'd love to sit and chat with you like Mary, but someone has to get things done around here! I mean, do you think it's fair that she left me all alone so she could sit on her lazy rear end listening to you this whole time?"

You might think that Jesus told Mary to get busy, to go to work and help her sister. But Jesus had an interesting answer to Martha's problem. His response was to tell her to relax, to chill out. He said that she was worried about all those little details, but her sister, Mary, chose the most important thing.

Mary the Magnificent had won again. Even though it looked like she was lazy and inconsiderate, she was actually being very wise in the eyes of this teacher. She knew it was better to show him honor by listening to his teachings than it was to serve him dinner with an ugly attitude.

Martha was truly manic. She was so distracted with all her preparations that she lost focus on the purpose of the party: to honor this man. She spent her time on all the superfluous details and missed out on a significant relationship. Her energy was so focused on the details of a task, she lost track of the person. She forgot that the highest form of honor is listening to someone.

We see a number of things at work in this story. Obviously, Martha was doing some really good things—even some great things. She was working hard at being a thoughtful host. Details such as making sure the food was tasty, the house was clean, the presentation was appealing—all these elements take energy and planning. Jesus even commends his followers to be hospitable, so we know that this was not her problem. Was she wrong for being frustrated that her sister had bailed on her in the hour of need? I don't think so. I think anyone in Martha's situation would have done the same thing. We've all been on the losing end of a "team effort." We know how frustrating it can be when a teammate disappears when the hour is at hand. Certainly her big party would have been much more successful if she had an equal partner sharing the load.

Perhaps her problem was trying to do too much. Was she guilty of trying too hard to do too many things? The key to her problem is found in the words of this teacher from Nazareth. He summarized the struggle by telling Manic Martha that she was troubled about all the details of the party, but her sister Mary chose one thing—the best thing.

Mary had a choice: She could focus on the arrangements of the party, or she could sit and listen to Jesus. Her decision seems strange to us, doesn't it? From our limited perspective, it seems like Mary was neglecting her responsibilities and alienating her closest friends and family. Why would she neglect the duties necessary to throw a great party? Why would she leave her sister hanging like that? What was Jesus driving at?

Time.

Time is limited, and so are we. Even as I write this I'm

"Now We Have a New Routine"
DENISE'S STORY

"Most people don't think of stay-at-home moms as being overcommitted. But I had a problem with saying no to all of the opportunities and activities that came my way. I definitely suffered from 'hurried woman syndrome.' I was heavily involved in various good opportunities, as well as activities with my kids, but it was too much. I wanted to move farther out of the city because I felt like where we lived contributed to my overcommitted lifestyle. I was going nonstop. Everywhere I turned, there was an opportunity to do something else. We actually thought about moving to Colorado to find what we thought would be a slower pace, fresh air, and beautiful scenery. It sounded so peaceful. But God shut that door and, instead, expanded my husband's business into the heart of the metropolitan area where we lived. We actually ended up moving farther into the city.

"In preparation for the move, I began to cut activities out of my life. And after we moved, I was very careful about adding things back into my schedule.

"Now we have a new routine, a much slower, peaceful pace. What's so funny to me is that God gave me the peace and slower pace I desired even further into the hustle and bustle of the city.

"I don't regret any good thing I've given up because God's best is always more than I could hope for. I am willing to do whatever it takes to keep us closer to God, closer as a family, and at a slower pace in the midst of a busy place."

thinking about my sermon this weekend, the direction of my church, the well-being of my wife and four kids, and a myriad of other things on my plate. It's gotten to the point that it's sometimes scary just to look at my to-do list, let alone actually get it all done.

But this story about Mary and Martha helps me put things in perspective. If we know that we are limited, that we can only get so much done, we are well on our way to the solution. The question then becomes, What are you going to do with your limited amount of time? How are you going to invest your life? Martha chased what was good. Mary pursued the best. Is your "good" eclipsing the best?

Sounds to me like people were battling busyness back then, too. Sounds to me like these people struggled with too many opportunities and too little time to get the job done. Sounds like we've always had this struggle.

THE TIME OF YOUR LIFE

Are you satisfied with your life right now? Even if life is going great, I'd be willing to bet that things could be better. One of the easiest ways to experience pressure and dissatisfaction with life is to overdose on good things and miss the best things.

In a perfect world, we'd have unlimited time to do everything we wanted to do. In the real world, we know that we have to make smart choices when it comes to prioritizing our lives. You might try to do it all, and you might succeed for a while—even a long while—but eventually all those balls you're trying to juggle are going to crash. When, not if, these balls crash, there will be serious consequences. You won't be talking about juggling balls falling harmlessly to the floor. You'll be talking about broken marriages, kids in rebellion, losing your career, and experiencing anxiety and despair. The stakes are sky high. We aren't meant to carry the world on our shoulders. We are all guilty of adding too much to our lives—from work to leisure to spending and eating, we love the buffet mentality. "The more the better" is the mantra we follow.

Priorities are easy to come up with, but hard to keep. Anyone could come up with a list of three, four, or five priorities that supersede everything else. If you're like most people, you have journals full of New Year's commitments that have gone sour. Anybody can spend a few hours of reflection, but few take that good work to the next level. Whether it is a spouse and kids, a dating relationship, a career, traveling the world, or helping the poor, adding to our to-do list doesn't take too much time or energy. The real deal is when it comes to elimination. Subtraction is always more difficult than addition. The challenge is deciding what you need to give up in order to concentrate on the best. Hard decisions are always ahead when you need to cut the excess to focus on the excellent.

Let me close this chapter with a few questions. First, what are the best things for you to do? I'm not asking you about the good things; I'm talking about the filet mignon of life. Second, are you a Mary or a Martha? Do you have trouble seeing the big picture in life like Martha? Maybe you're missing out by trying to do it all. Think about all your activities this past month. What are your nonnegotiables, and what can be cut? Take some time to consider your top priorities in life. What are those best things that you absolutely need to accomplish? What should you spend your time doing, knowing that your time is short?

STOP AND THINK

FOLLOW THE SIGNS: Time is limited, and so are we. And so often, the good things eclipse the best. Pursuing outrageous, contagious joy God's way is seeing the big picture like Mary did. It's all about following his game plan for our life.

CHECK THE MAP: "Martha, Martha," the Lord answered, "you are worried and upset about many things, but only one thing is needed. Mary has chosen what is better, and it will not be taken away from her" (Luke 10:41–42).

TAKE THE NEXT STEP: Look through your calendar for the past month. Where are you spending your time? Based on these activities, what are your *actual* priorities? How do your actual priorities compare with your desired priorities—the way you wish your life could be? Do you think you are a Mary or a Martha?

7

CLOSING THE GAP

The future is something which everyone reaches at the rate of
sixty minutes an hour,
whatever he does, whoever he is.

—C. S. Lewis

Several years ago, my son and I strategically packed up my truck for an overnight camping trip. Actually, I was the master packer; my son "helped" in other areas. As I loaded our gear, I was telling my son, "Get that flashlight and that green sleeping bag, but forget about the video games and the basketball. There won't be too many hoops where we're going, EJ."

We drove south down I-45 from Dallas, with all of our stuff strapped down. We drove to Fairfield, then from there, twenty-five miles out into the middle of nowhere down a series of dirt roads. It was just me, my son, and my truck on the open plains of Texas. As I was driving, I saw a little ravine in front of us. This ravine had a sparkling spring trickling through it. Getting closer, I saw the tracks of a few other cars that had crossed over the gap. Suddenly a rush of excitement coursed through my veins as I decided to relive my adolescent days by going extreme. The ravine looked a little shaky, but I was undaunted. I turned to my son and said, "EJ, you're going to see what off-roading is all about! You're going to see what a four-wheel drive can really do!"

I switched over to four-wheel drive, mashed on the accelerator, and aimed my assault vehicle toward the tiny gap. The adrenaline was pumping and we had a white-knuckled grip on the dashboard. I hit the hole and we stopped cold. Turns out it was a *huge* hole, and the entire front end of my Ford began to sink in the muck and mire of that "tiny" ravine.

I did what all of you would do in such a predicament. I just pressed the accelerator harder. And you know what happened? The more I pressed, the more mud started flying everywhere, including into the truck!

This little off-road excursion was definitely not one of my best decisions. We piled out of the truck and realized we were in serious trouble. We were twenty-five miles outside of civilization, and darkness was creeping in.

I learned something that day. I learned something about ravines and the limits of off-road driving. And my son learned to watch out for that crazed look in my eyes when I'm about to do something stupid. What went wrong? I misjudged the ravine.

So often we misjudge the ravines in our lives. We misjudge the gaps. Almost all of us misjudge the gap between our priorities and our commitments. In this section, I have outlined the three priorities that God has laid out for our lives. These priorities are already set in stone. But how do we ensure that our priorities are on the right track? We carry out our priorities through our commitments—in relationships, in worship, and in work. And anyone who has spent any time evaluating their calendar or checkbook knows that there is often a variance, or gap, between what we do and what we say we do.

Many of us are missing it. We have these great plans for the future, but we often get lost in the here and now. Instead of planning for a bright future, we sacrifice our plans for instant gratification. And when that happens on a regular basis, we can quickly lose our direction. Most of us know (at least in our heads) the most important things in life. We've already journeyed through the top three priorities in life in an earlier chapter. But even when we do know these top-shelf priorities, often our schedules do not reinforce these values.

When we have a gap between our big priorities and our day-to-day commitments, we set ourselves up for failure. When there is a gap, it leads us into the mud and leaves us with our wheels spinning. It leads us into bondage. Freedom doesn't come from a freewheeling lifestyle. Freedom comes from advanced planning. That's the ironic thing about those people who exalt the freewheeling and spontaneous life. They think they're living a life full of opportunities and possibilities, but when you get close enough, you realize that their lifestyle is actually preventing them from achieving anything significant in their life. And even if they believe they're doing all right, there is often someone or something that is suffering from this lifestyle. It could be a family member or a close friend. It could be their health.

As much as we would like to think otherwise, a fruitful life requires discipline and advanced planning. We'll never finance our retirement without disciplined savings. We'll never enjoy life the way we were meant to enjoy it without an exercise routine and a planned, healthy diet. Without that discipline, we fall into bondage to inevitable crises. The urgency of the day always seems to trump the future. By closing the gap between our priorities and our commitments, we can experience freedom and true joy in our lives.

PRINCIPLES, PRIORITIES, AND COMMITMENTS

God's principles are my priorities, and they're carried out through my commitments.

God's principles, found throughout Scripture, form guardrails for living. They are the instructions he has left us so we can live on the superhighway of a fulfilling and adventurous life (John 10:10). Our priorities for life should be governed by God's principles. When our priorities reflect the order our Creator intended, we will be set up for success. To put it simply, our priorities should agree with God's principles. He is our Creator, and we are his creation. You come to realize that it is far better to lean on the author of life during life's trials rather than leaning on yourself in dark days (Proverbs 3:5–6).

Our priorities are actually carried out by our *commitments*. Have you realized that? Have you looked at your bank account to see where your money is *actually* going? Maybe you noticed that your weekly schedule is tilted too heavily toward work, eating away time from your family. When you go through this difficult evaluation process, you are able to see how you're doing. Are you meeting your goals? Are your priorities truly your priorities, or are they being eclipsed by less-valuable pursuits?

You might say that it's a good idea to be physically healthy. I would agree. I think that part of our worship to God is taking care of our bodies through exercise and healthy eating, so much so that I'll spend an entire chapter in this book dealing with that issue. But how do you know if your priority of physical health is being met? A good place to start is to examine your exercise routine. If you have been exercising regularly, then you are off to a good start. How about your diet? Are you jamming junk food into your system, or are you eating high-octane meals? Once you are really serious about self-evaluation, it won't be difficult to determine how you're doing.

The real problem is that most of us don't have the courage to evaluate ourselves honestly. We would rather drift along and assume everything is going well. I think we all know where this hands-off strategy takes us.

If you place a premium on physical health, but never exercise or eat healthy food, there is a ravine-sized gap between your priority and your commitment. If you value financial stability, but never set up a budget or set aside savings, there is a gap. The reality is that your priorities must be matched with your commitments. If you aren't exercising or living on a budget, those priorities will never become a reality in your life.

Priorities Are Played Out Through Commitments

What are your commitments? Your commitments are what make or break you. They are what you do on a daily basis. And what you do should reflect what is really important to you. Sometimes we'll look at our calendar and realize that our commitments are out of whack with our priorities. Some of us are in denial when it comes to synching up our commitments with our priorities. However, when you go deep, when you get specific by logging the way you spend your time, you'll see some surprising and disturbing trends. I know this because I do it regularly. Most often, there is a gap, even a ravine, separating your priorities from your commitments.

There are two important principles to realize about time. First, time is limited, but we act like it is unlimited. Only God knows how much of it we have left. Second, we will use all of the time allotted to us, no matter how we decide to use it. We can't "bank" time, or turn back the clock. Once it's gone, it's gone. You can't talk about priorities without talking about the context of time. Time is fluid and always marches on. But you do have the opportunity to leverage your time wisely.

To do this, evaluate your priorities based on your commitments. Examine the way you allocated your time yesterday. How did those tasks and commitments line up with your priorities? When we look in the past, even the near past, it will help us be better prepared to respond in the present. And when we respond wisely in the present, it will give us a great trajectory for the future.

As you evaluate the best thing to do with your time, ask yourself this question: "Knowing that my time is limited and that God is ultimately in control of how much time I have on earth, what is the best way to use my time?"

You know what? If you ask yourself this question and answer it honestly, you can make the wise move right now. You can decide to act in a way that mirrors your priorities.

When you hear the word *priorities*, what do you think about? You should think about rank and order. You should think about saying yes to the very best and no to those merely good options that are outside of your major priorities. Here's a key to success in every part of your life: You will have to say no more than yes if you really want to succeed. You will have to strip away those things—even though some of them may be good—that are not about pursuing the best. What does that look like for you? It might mean that you'll have to resign from the PTA leadership (a good thing) to devote more time to your family (the best thing). Maybe it'll mean skipping your dream European vacation for a more financially feasible vacation. You might have to cut some of your kids' activities on the weekend to ensure that you can worship together as a family.

"But Ed, what about things that I enjoy, things that make me feel good? Those things are important to me. Surely God wouldn't want me to give up those things."

Well, think about those things. Do they serve your three big priorities—relationships, worship, and work? Anything that doesn't feed those priorities actually robs from them. Any time that you spend on other pursuits is time you can't spend on the three priorities that God has deemed most important for us.

Rest assured, God doesn't want to take away from your life. He wants to add to it. God says that the devil comes to steal and kill and destroy, but God comes to give the abundant life for all of us (John 10:10). That word *abundant* in the Greek means "overflowing." Picture waves continuously crashing on the seashore. It's like filling your cup full of water, and the water just keeps coming and coming until it spills over into your hands and all over the table. It never stops coming. That's the kind of life that God wants for us. But we can't get it ourselves. We've got to leverage this gift, this amazing gift called time, and use it to truly savor this life God has given us. Elsewhere in the Bible, God tells us that time is up for grabs, and we need to exercise wisdom to use time properly (Ephesians 5:15–20).

Most of us have been given a fair amount of wisdom, but we act unwisely when we chase after things that are not important or, worse, chase after things that lead us nowhere. Spending our time and energy on pursuits that make us feel good now but have no future payoff is a bad investment. Hanging out and partying might seem like something you want on your calendar; you have to relax sometimes, right?

Sure, you need to take care of yourself. As I stated earlier, keeping healthy is a way you can worship God—respecting the body he has given you. Relaxing and rejuvenating yourself also serves your relationships (you can give so much more to your spouse and kids when you're not stressed, anxious, and a bundle of nerves) and your work (I know I always do my best work when I'm refreshed). But when your "relaxing" entails all-night parties, that's just wasted time—not to mention the time you will need the next day to recover.

Ambition is not a problem for most of us. If you're anything like me, you want the very best out of life. And you are probably going after it to the best of your ability. For a lot of us, though, it's this ambition for something bigger and better that gets us into trouble. In our attempt to get the most out of life, we lose control because we don't want to miss out on anything. We'll add a fourth big priority, then a fifth, and a sixth, and on and on. We want a great house, so we emulate Martha Stewart and try to be a domestic goddess. We want to be hip and cool—up on the newest bands, trying to be seen at the right places, wearing the right clothes. We work hard trying to be perfect at all things. Eventually, we get so overloaded, juggling so many balls, that we drop them all. We simply have to remember that according to God's blueprint for our lives, when we focus on the big things, everything else will fall into place.

His principles become our three priorities, and these are

"I Was Trying to Please Others and Not God"
PHILIP'S STORY

Philip was constantly frustrated with life because it seemed like everyone else "had it all together" but he didn't. He lived his life trying to gain others' acceptance. In his attempt to keep up with everyone else, he filled his schedule with every activity that came along. They were all good activities, but it was just all too much. He just wanted that acceptance and feeling of accomplishment.

But Philip soon came to realize that he couldn't keep up with his madding pace of life. It became apparent that, as he puts it, he was "trying to please others and not God." He was doing it all to make himself feel good and to look good in front of others. But he was not joyful and content with life. And he desperately wanted that. One day, he sensed very clearly that God wanted him to be still, to feel his presence and love. He began to slow down and seek God's best for his life—in his relationships, his church activities, and his work.

Philip has learned that God's acceptance is what ultimately matters. In everything he does in life, he is working for God's approval. "At the end of the day," he says, "I can truly rest in what I have accomplished because I have learned to say no to some good things so I can say yes to God's best."

carried out through our commitments. When we live this life and agree with God, we have the clarity to really understand what life's all about. Our lives will be fulfilled and free from the anxiety and pressures that come with undisciplined living. We'll be more productive, and God will be pleased with us. That's what I call a win-win.

Managing Priorities Leads to Freedom

The smaller the gap between your priorities and your commitments, the greater liberty you will have. On the other hand, the bigger the gap, the more enslaved you will be by your schedule.

Do you know what will happen in your life when your commitments and priorities sync up? You'll finally have breathing room. When you live by these three priorities, when you give every moment to the one who knows all about time (after all, he invented it), you won't have to worry about what you're doing with your life because you'll be doing exactly what you should. And what can you do with all that time that you used to spend worrying? Do you just sit there and twiddle your thumbs? No. This is time to get to know God better. It's time to get to know your spouse better, to grow that dating relationship, to build friendships in a deeper way, to enjoy your work more, and on and on. You'll finally be living in the sweet spot, right in the middle of where you're supposed to be—really enjoying the present and also preparing for a bright future.

So why does God care about our priorities and commitments? Why did he put his principles into the Bible? He did it because he is the ultimate Ringmaster, and he wants our lives to be the Greatest Show on Earth. He knows all about the juggling balls, and all about the circus that our busy lives can become. If we give our lives to this Ringmaster, he will help us sort through our commitments and our pressures so that we can live a blessed and productive life.

I left you hanging at the beginning of the chapter about my off-road excursion. Did I ever make it out of Fairfield, Texas? Well, yes, I did; but it wasn't easy. EJ and I walked two miles in the blistering Texas heat. We were on a dirt road that I've driven on many times. I've only seen maybe three or four cars come down this dirt road in my whole life in all my trips down to this area. So I was not feeling too confident about finding someone to help us. I thought that EJ and I were going to have to walk the full twenty-five miles to the nearest town to get help.

All of a sudden, we heard a car. I could hardly contain my surprise and my excitement. Not wanting to endanger my son any further, I told him to wait at the side while I got in the middle of the road and yelled, "Hey! Please stop!" I had mud all over me and I'm sure the elderly lady who was driving the car thought I was crazy.

I said, "Ma'am, my name is Ed, and this is my son, EJ. I am stuck way down in that ravine, way, way, way down there. I know you can't see the truck. But we climbed our way out." Here's where being a pastor has its benefits. "And I'm a pastor in the Dallas–Fort Worth area."

Not believing this mud-soaked pedestrian, she muttered, "Right. Uh-huh."

I said, "Really! In fifteen minutes my radio show's going to be on. We can listen to it. Would you please take us to town? I've got to get a tow truck to get us out."

She sat there for a while, asked me some more questions, and I guess I finally won her trust. "Okay, come in. I'll give you a ride," she offered.

So we got in the car and, sure enough, fifteen minutes later we turned on the radio. "See? That's me." And she said, "Yeah, it is you!" She could hardly believe that this muddy thrill seeker could really pastor a church.

So then we drove to one tow truck service. "Hey, would you please pull us out?" The guy said, "No way, man! I'm not going there." Strike one.

I went to another place, and I was even more pathetic. But he said the same thing. "Please, sir. My son and I are from Dallas," I begged.

"I can't help you. It's real bad where you're stuck, and I just can't risk our equipment. Sorry." Strike two.

Attempt number three was equally unsuccessful. "It's just too sandy." At this point I'm thinking I should really choose my ravines more carefully.

Finally, I met a young man who agreed to do it. So we hopped in his truck and drove twenty-five miles back to the scene of the crime, and he looked at us and said, "Man, you've really got yourself stuck! You don't go off-roading very much, do you?"

Not feeling very masculine, I replied, "No, I don't." But thankfully, this guy pulled me out. I was so relieved and so appreciative that I still carry his card in my wallet. What a great feeling to finally be free from the giant-sized ravine.

A lot of us are stuck in the muck and mire of a zillion commitments. Many of you are probably saying, "Ed, I'm stuck bad.

I'm stepping on the accelerator, but it's not working. I'm trying to get out of this, and I'm just getting further and further into trouble. And it's too late to realize that this gap is too wide and I've got too much stuff on my vehicle weighing me down." You've gone to your co-worker and pleaded, "Hey, get me out!" You've gone to your parents—"Get me out!" You tried to buy this or that to numb the pain—"Get me out!" But none of it is working. There's only one person who can get us out and free us up. And that is the Ringmaster.

So lay your calendar before him and ask him for wisdom so you can get back on track. Ask him to look at your bank statement to see if you are spending money wisely. Set some goals based on your three priorities for the future. Ask yourself, "Where do I want to be in five, ten, or twenty years?" Once you map out the destination, all it takes is a little discipline to get there. So what are you waiting for?

STOP AND THINK

FOLLOW THE SIGNS: When you begin to orient your life around God's priorities, you'll experience freedom in your life. Living outside these parameters will lead you into frustration and failure.

CHECK THE MAP: "Be very careful, then, how you live—not as unwise but as wise, making the most of every opportunity, because the days are evil" (Ephesians 5:15–16).

TAKE THE NEXT STEP: Now that you've had some time to review your daily commitments against the three major priorities, let me challenge you to set some goals. Spend some time setting some short- and long-term goals (relationally, spiritually, professionally) that will help you make the necessary changes this year to gain the freedom that comes from following the blueprint of your Creator.

8

MULTIPLE CHOICE

Decisions determine destiny.

—Frederick Speakman

The teacher weaves her way through the aisles as the students sit anxiously on the edges of their wooden chairs with freshly sharpened No. 2 pencils in hand. The answers from the previous day's test review are swirling in their heads. Some students are having trouble just holding on to their pencils, as beads of sweat begin to form on their foreheads. Others are more prepared for the inevitable event. Then the dreaded computerized-test answer sheets arrive. There will be no more studying now. No more last-second cramming. It's time to take the multiple-choice test!

When I think about that scene, images of sweaty palms, all-nighters, and red-pen marks from my own academic career flash across my brain. The premise of a multiple-choice test is simple—each question on the test is followed by a series of possible answers. The only thing that the test taker has to do is eliminate the wrong choices and select the right one. But actually taking the test is never that simple. In order to choose the right answer, you have to actually *know* it (or at least be able to make an educated guess). As a last resort, if you have absolutely no clue, random selection is your only hope.

Multiple-choice tests always brought a certain amount of anxiety and intimidation into my life. I remember the feeling of utter relief that came over me when I turned in what I thought would be my last multiple-choice test ever. But I failed to realize something then that I have since learned.

Life is one big multiple-choice test.

And the answers that we select in this test—what we decide to do every day, whether trivial or momentous—determine who we are. What we chose yesterday makes up who we are today; what we choose today will make up who we will be tomorrow. In effect, we are the sum total of our decisions. The problem is that most of us have some stupid, unexplainable, "What was I thinking?" decisions tangled up in our makeup. We have selected the wrong answers to many of the questions in life's multiple-choice test.

True, you may have made some great decisions. You may still be reaping the benefits of those wise choices. But the chances are high that not every decision you made was a wise one. And you may even be paying the consequences of some of those poor choices today. Your vision may be temporarily impaired because those poor decisions are fogging up the lenses of your life. But don't think that your vision will be impaired forever. There is hope of changing your decision-making ability so that you will be able to select the right answers in life's multiple-choice test.

We've seen so far that joy is not based on feelings. It rises above circumstances. Joy, evidenced by enthusiasm, is about being in God and having God in you; it is relational and intentional. And it is directly related to the priorities we choose to orient our life around. Joy, we will find in this chapter, is also about building vision into your life. It is about making the right decisions in the present based on where you've come from and where you want to go. It is fueled and formed through a relationship with God, and then it is reinforced and built as we make wise decisions every day.

Throughout the rest of this book, we're going to look at making the right choices in every area of life: our relationships, our worship, and our work. But first I want to give you a basis for making those right choices, a filter of sorts through which you can run all of your decisions, large and small.

DECISIONS BIG AND SMALL

Now, people don't strategically plan to make bad decisions. A new husband doesn't look at his wife on their honeymoon and plan to have an affair on her in about ten years and blow their marriage out of the water.

No new parent cradles his or her five-day-old baby and says, "I'm going to smother your dreams. I'm going to live my life through you and push you to do what I always wanted to do. And you'll need counseling for the rest of your life to sort it all out."

No one says, "Hey, I am going to get myself addicted to drugs and alcohol. Then I'm going to drop out of rehab after rehab. My ultimate goal is to make a mess of my life through substance abuse."

No one intentionally decides, "I'm going to let adult websites, topless bars, and pornography rule my world. I'm going to let them ruin my family, my friendships, and my life."

No one says or thinks those things. They just happen.

But do they really *just happen*?

As a pastor, I have had the opportunity to talk to a countless number of people who have made decisions that range from one end of the board to the other—good and bad. As I have uncovered some of the bad decisions over the years, I have laid them out on the table and dissected them with the very people who made them. And here is what I have discovered: in life, there are macro decisions and there are micro decisions.

Macro Decisions

It's easy for us to understand that the major decisions in life will have major implications. I'm referring to decisions like: Who should you choose as your closest friends? What kind of person should you marry? Should family take priority over your work? How should you take care of the body God has given you? What place should God and his Church have in your life? How should you budget your money? And when we are faced with these macro decisions, we should ask ourselves some macro questions.

First, we need to ask, "Is it written?" In other words, is the decision that I am making in sync with what God tells me in his Word, the Bible?

The next macro question our decision needs to face is, "Is it based in love? Does the choice that I am selecting reflect God's love for me? Will it express love to the people around me?"

And finally, the third macro question that we should ask is,

"Does it fit with God's vision for my life?" If I can answer yes to all three of these, then I am free to go for it. If not, then I need to put the brakes on the decision-making process and re-assess the choices.

Micro Decisions

The macro decisions loom large in our lives, and we tend to give them a lot of thought and attention. But there is another kind of decision that can easily slip past us without much fanfare. I'm referring to the micro decisions, like: Should you attend that party or event this weekend? Should you go out on a date with that person you're attracted to? Should you buy that item you've had your eye on? Should you work late again tonight for the third night in a row? Micro decisions like these are often not given as much significance because we simply don't understand how important these choices are in our everyday lives.

There is one common thread that I have found among the poor decisions that have led people into the deep weeds. The people who have to live with the consequences of poor decision making all say that their macro mistake was the result of a series of micro, seemingly insignificant, bad calls. And those micro decisions created a domino effect in these people's lives that pushed them over the edge. Decision making is not just an event, it's a process. And the daily process of making poor micro decisions leads to macro implications. Those dumb, "What was I thinking?" decisions, which seem minor by themselves, will lead to a macro mess and cast a major cloud over your life.

RENEWING YOUR MIND

Oftentimes, the micro decisions in life are not specifically covered in the Bible. So, what do we do when the choices that are in front of us are not expressly addressed in Scripture?

I believe that the Bible, God's definitive Word to you and me, covers any case that may come up. It says, "Do not conform any longer to the pattern of this world, but be transformed . . ." How are we to be transformed? ". . . [B]y the renewing of your mind. Then you will be able to test and approve what God's will is—his good, pleasing, and perfect will" (Romans 12:2).

Well, how do you do that? How do you renew your mind? By making great decisions. How do you make great decisions? By thinking the way God wants you to think. It may sound a little confusing, a little like a catch-22 situation, but hang in there.

I mentioned earlier that we have all, at one time or another, looked back at some of the choices we have made and asked ourselves, "What was I thinking?" That question is usually looked at in a negative light. But let's look at that question from a different angle. Let's ask the question, "What *should* I be thinking?" When we ask that question, when we make up our minds to start thinking right, when we decide to follow God's Word and think like we should, then we will have the mind-set to make the wise decisions in life. We will then be able to decipher the line between morality and immorality, good and bad, right and wrong. We will have the clear *vision* to know which side of the line we need to be on—and we will make the kinds of choices that will keep us there.

It's all about becoming insightful in our decision-making process. When we gain insight from God, we are able to comprehend the things that are obscure to the rest of the world. Every one of us has that potential. With insight, we can discover the great decision-making ability that God has for us all. You may be asking, "But just what is insight, and how do I get it?" Let's find out.

The Bible says, "And this I pray, that your love may abound still more and more in real knowledge and all discernment, so that you may approve the things that are excellent, in order to be sincere and blameless until the day of Christ" (Philippians 1:9–10, NASB). The knowledge that the writer is talking about is information. And discernment is application of that knowledge; it is the ability to see what is obscure to others. If we have both of those, if we know what to do (knowledge) and then we do it (discernment), then we have gained insight.

BECOMING IN-TENSE

To get to where the rubber meets the road, to get to where we can understand all this talk about knowledge, discernment, and insight, we have to ask ourselves an "in-tense" question: "In light of my past experiences, considering my present circumstances, and looking forward to my future dreams and aspirations, what is the most knowledgeable, most discerning, most insightful thing for me to do?" Every time we face a decision in life's multiple-choice test, we should consider its past, present, and future tense.

We are going to discover, through the rest of this chapter, just how to become in-tense in our decision making and ask the right questions. Because once we learn to be in-tense, we will fall in line with God and uncover the amazing vision that God has for us.

If we don't become in-tense, if we don't learn to ask those important micro questions, we will spend an insane amount of time swimming laps in the Olympic-sized pool of regret. We will find ourselves asking that regrettable question, "What was I thinking?" far too often. So how do we learn to ask these micro questions? Through insight.

The Past

First, let's discover how our past can help us determine what decisions to make. We have all made poor choices and done things we regret in the past. But so often, we allow our past failures to set us up for poor decision making today. The past can make us vulnerable to certain temptations in the present. For some, it may be lust. For others, money may be a temptation. Still others may find food to be a stumbling block. Or it may be a tendency to make poor relational choices.

Whatever the present temptation may be, here is how to make a decision based on your past. Look back at the last time you were faced with that same situation and mentally recite what happened: *The last time I went there, I did such and such. The last time I logged on to that website . . . The last time I drank that . . . The last time I hung out with that person . . .* Remember and realize the consequences of those past decisions. Be honest with yourself and admit that doing those things really got you sideways. They really took you over the line of right and wrong. So, you need to make a commitment to yourself before God: "Because of my past experiences, I'm not going there anymore. I'm not going to make the same mistake again."

For example, let's say you are freshly divorced. The ink on your divorce papers is not even dry yet, and you have decided to make a macro decision: *From now on, I'm going to date God's way. God says I should only hook up with believers (2 Corinthians 6:14–18), so that's what I'll do. I messed up before, but I'm going to do it God's way this time. In fact, I'm going to dive right into the dating scene. I'm not going to wait because I'm so confident that I have learned from my mistake.*

No, no, no. Don't do it. You're not ready. If you do that, then you are going to make some dumb micro decisions that will cause a destructive domino effect that will lead you to a macro mess. Don't go there. I would strongly suggest waiting a year before you begin to date again. Let God heal and restore you first. Get involved in a singles program at church. Learn just what it is that God has in store for you. Grow deeper in your relationship with him. And then, after a year, you can start to contemplate dating again. But in light of your past, take some time to reassess the decisions that you are going to make in your present relational world.

The Present

How do your present-day circumstances help determine your decisions? To find out, we'll put a hypothetical financial opportunity under our scope. Imagine that someone came to you and told you that if you invested a certain amount of money, he or she could guarantee that you would quadruple your money within eight years. What would you say at that exact moment? If you are in debt, if you are leveraged to the hilt, the best response would probably not be, "I just can't resist! I'll do it." Yes, that investment might be a great idea in a few years. But considering your present financial circumstance, it may not be the most insightful decision to make. Decide, considering today's circumstances, what the wise thing is to do. How will it affect your family's financial security? If the investment doesn't pan out, can you afford to lose that money?

Let's say you are offered a new position at work with more money—a lot more money. But there is a catch. You will have to travel extensively every week. You will be away from your spouse and children more than you will be with them. To make the right choice in that situation, to select the right answer to that test question, you must take into consideration your present circumstances. If you have a new marriage or young children, you may need to say no to that opportunity in order to be around your family more. You have to decide what the discerning thing to do is, given your life circumstances.

The Future

The future is another micro aspect that we need to consider when making decisions. If you want to take your marriage to a certain level in the future, what decisions should you make in the present? If you want your friendships to really soar tomorrow, what relational choices do you need to make today? Based on your long-term financial goals, how should you spend your money in the short term?

I can't answer those questions for you. You will have to answer them yourself. Look at each decision and ask yourself, "In order to get to that level, should I choose yes or no?" If you look to the future and you see your children in a certain place,

"It Just Wasn't Worth It"
GARY'S STORY

Gary was struggling professionally. He had owned his own business for years but had to close it down because sales had been declining steadily. But he was unsure of where to go next. He took a sales job that would require a lot of overtime, but he felt this would be a good move financially for his family's sake. Month after weary month went by as he racked up seventy-plus-hour work-weeks. He and his wife barely saw each other. His son wondered why Daddy didn't live at home anymore. He wasn't able to attend church with his family because he often had to work weekends.

On one of the rare Sunday mornings that Gary was able to attend church, he and his wife heard a message about priorities and decision making. "It felt like God was talking directly to me," he said. He realized that, based on God's priority structure of relationships, worship, and work, he had to make a tough call about his job. The next week he turned in his resignation. It took him several weeks to reconnect with his family and to recover physically from the exhausting schedule he had been keeping. After making that decision to put his family first, he found a job he loves with much better hours. When he looks back now on that period in his life, he says, "It just wasn't worth it. I was working so much because I thought it was best for my family, but I was missing out on the most important things in life."

your marriage in a certain place, your finances or relationships in a certain place, make decisions now that will lead you to reach the goals you've set for yourself and your family. Don't sabotage your future plans by making a regretful decision today that will only cause you to ask later on, "What was I thinking?"

Instead, ask yourself that in-tense question before each decision: "In light of my past experiences, considering my present circumstances, and looking forward to my future dreams and aspirations, what is the most knowledgeable, most discerning, most insightful thing for me to do?"

WALKING ABOVE THE LINE

As we think about this decision-making process, both the macro decisions and the micro decisions, we need to realize that God wants the very best for our lives. He wants us to achieve great things, to hit on all cylinders as we make our decisions. Mediocrity is when we walk on the edge of the line that separates morality from immorality, ethical from unethical, good decisions from bad decisions. Excellence is when we walk *above* the line; it's when we draw a new line not based on what is merely good but on what is the best.

Remember again what the apostle Paul wrote: "And this is my prayer: that your love may abound more and more in knowledge and depth of insight, so that you may be able to discern what is best and may be pure and blameless until the day of Christ" (Philippians 1:9–10). That is God's plan for you and me: to walk above the line of compromise by discerning what is *best* and living lives of excellence.

We do that, of course, by asking the macro questions we addressed earlier. Is it in line with Scripture? Is it in line with God's love? Is it in line with God's vision? And by asking the in-tense micro question: "In light of my past experiences, considering my present circumstances, and looking forward to my future dreams and aspirations, what is the most knowledgeable, most discerning, most insightful thing for me to do?" But how exactly do those questions play out in reality as we try to discern God's best for our lives?

In the chapters to come, we're going to delve deeper into the practical issues related to our relationships, our worship, and our work. I want to look at how we can establish some excellent guidelines in each of those crucial areas.

To make the right decisions in life, we must become in-tense. Understand that the micro decisions that we face will compound daily and result in macro consequences down the road. As you answer question after question in life's multiple-choice test, don't rely on whatever emotion you're feeling at the time. Instead, use the knowledge, discernment, and insight that God has provided through his written truth, his love, and his vision for our lives. And then recognize that the past, the present, and the future all play a part in helping you experience the in-tense life of joy God wants for you.

As we do that, we will begin to get intentional about infusing our lives with joy. Remember, joy is not based on feelings; it is based on a relationship with God. So allow God to work in these major areas of your life and show you a higher road toward the better life you've been searching for.

STOP AND THINK

FOLLOW THE SIGNS: Many of us are in tune with the big decisions we need to make in life. But most of us ignore the secondary decisions that can easily derail us. We need to compare our impulses with the truth of God's Word and our own past, present, and future to navigate through a life full of multiple-choice tests.

CHECK THE MAP: "And this is my prayer: that your love may abound more and more in knowledge and depth of insight, so that you may be able to discern what is best and may be pure and blameless until the day of Christ, filled with the fruit of righteousness that comes through Jesus Christ—to the glory and praise of God" (Philippians 1:9–11).

TAKE THE NEXT STEP: How did this chapter challenge you in the area of decision making? Circle the following area or areas that you feel are off track in your life right now.

Relationships   Worship   Work

What do you hope will happen as you examine these areas more deeply?

PART 3

WHO ARE YOU RUNNING WITH?

We must rapidly begin the shift from a "thing-oriented" society
to a "person-oriented" society. When machines and computers,
profit motives and property rights are considered more important
than people, the giant triplets of racism, materialism,
and militarism are incapable of being conquered.
—MARTIN LUTHER KING, JR.

The best way to cheer yourself up is to
try to cheer somebody else up.
—MARK TWAIN

9

ONE IS THE LONELIEST NUMBER

We cannot live only for ourselves. A thousand fibers
connect us with our fellow men.
—HERMAN MELVILLE

I remember the first time I experienced the pain of loneliness. I was in the fifth grade. My family and I had lived in the tiny town of Taylor, South Carolina. I attended Taylor Elementary School, a model for any parent who wanted the best for their "little Einstein." It was the kind of school where Keith Partridge or Jan Brady would feel right at home. During my fifth-grade year, my family moved from tiny Taylor to Columbia, South Carolina. I transferred from Taylor Elementary School to Lonnie B. Nelson Elementary School in Columbia, which was the equivalent of moving from a playpen to the state pen. The students at Lonnie B. Nelson were tough. It was a rough school with characters you would not believe.

To make matters worse, I had to transfer schools in the

middle of the school year. I will never forget the day my parents escorted me to Mrs. Blackwell's class at my new school. Mrs. Blackwell reminded me of Olive Oyl from the Popeye cartoon. She pretty much survived on caffeine and nicotine.

When I first walked in, she said to me, "Welcome to the class, Edwin."

Sheepishly I replied, "That's Ed, please."

I peered around Mrs. Blackwell and looked for a place to hide. I wanted to walk back to Taylor Elementary. At least it was safe there. Mrs. Blackwell's students were out of control. Despite my objection, she persisted in introducing me as "Edwin, a new student from Taylor, South Carolina." It would have been much quicker if she'd just painted a red bull's-eye on my shirt. She pointed out my desk, and I shuffled over to put my books down. When Mrs. Blackwell turned her back to write something on the blackboard, a kid walked up to me, took my books, and threw them against the wall.

He said, "What are you doing in my desk?"

When Mrs. Blackwell heard that, she halfheartedly disciplined my new enemy. "John, don't treat Edwin like that on his first day."

I remember praying and counting the ticks on the large plastic wall clock until the recess bell rang. Saved by the bell, I was hoping to put the "incident" from the classroom behind me so I could hit the playground with purpose. I figured I could win some new friends with my athletic prowess. Not seeing any basketballs lying around, I wandered up to a group of guys playing marbles. I had never seen this strange game before. Though it wasn't the most riveting event, I watched them for a while until a big kid stood up and cussed me out. He threatened to mess me up if I didn't stop hanging around them. Strike two.

I left the marble incident and began to circle the perimeter of the playground, whimpering to myself and wondering why my parents had ever left me in such an awful place. I can still feel the sting of the pain from that day. I can remember it like it was yesterday. I missed my friends in Taylor. I was angry. I was confused. And I was lonely.

Loneliness is real; it cuts deep, and it hurts.

AN AGE-OLD PROBLEM

We are relational beings, made in the image of a relational God. God the Father, God the Son, and God the Holy Spirit exist in perfect harmony together. Their relationship is flawless. Their roles are different, but they are each equal and eternal. Understanding the essence of the Trinity is an important first step we must take when we talk about relationships. It sets the tone for our own relationships.

Want to know something that will blow your mind? He didn't have to create us. We are only here because of his will. It is said that the first act of God's grace was man's creation. God gave us the opportunity to breathe, to talk, to walk, and to live in relationship with one another and with him. Some respond in humility and gratitude to his relational invitation; others, on the other hand, ignore and even slander him. God didn't need any of us to make him better or to somehow complete him. God is perfect; always has been and always will be. He extends his hand to us in friendship for our own benefit.

You probably know the creation story from the Bible, but let me highlight a few important thoughts related to God's relational agenda for our lives. We are made in the image, nature, and character of God. We know that God is a relational being. He models this through the relationships found in the Trinity in addition to his creation of each one of us. In the book of Genesis, we learn that God created everything—light, darkness, the sun and moon; the waters and the lands; plants, animals, and my personal favorite, all the fish I can catch. Marlin, tarpon, largemouth bass—you name the fish, and I will go after it. Sorry, I got a little excited there.

When God created all these things, he said to himself, "It is good" (Genesis 1:1–25). Everything he created was perfect, and it was so good that even God had to admire his work! But when God created man, he said something a little different. He called it "*very* good" (Genesis 1:31). These are the words God used when he formed Adam. It was very good, but something was missing.

Not too long after Adam's creation, God saw something that was "*not* good" (Genesis 2:18). Adam, who had an intimate relationship with his Creator, the beauty of a pristine garden, and the company of the most amazing animals, was alone. He was lonely. He had no equal. He had no human companion. There was no other person to walk with, talk with, and laugh with. The first something in our world that was "not good" was a description of something we all know very well: loneliness.

Mother Teresa, who spent most of her ministry in the slums caring for the sick and unwanted, called loneliness a disease. "The greatest disease," she said, "is not TB or leprosy, but the feeling of being uncared for, unwanted, deserted by everyone. The greatest disease is the lack of love. The unwanted are hungry—not for food—but for love."

Princess Diana, inspired by Mother Teresa, used her high profile to bring comfort to AIDS victims and sick children. She witnessed firsthand the pain of loneliness.

Billy Graham, widely believed to be one of the most re-spected and influential men of the twentieth century, described it as man's greatest problem.

We've all been stung by the pain of loneliness. Just ask a member of our military about this pain, as he serves his country halfway across the world, away from his family and friends and the comforts of home. Ask the divorcée and mother of three as she spends her first Christmas alone. Ask the husband who re-cently buried his wife. Ask the parents whose arms still ache, awaiting the return of a missing child. Ask the single adult who spends yet another Saturday night alone.

Most of us are dealing with layers and layers of loneliness. We sometimes deny our own loneliness on the surface, but we know that deep down in our core it's still there. So how can we deal with it? Is there a cure for this perennial problem? Yes. And I want to share a few things about the two layers of loneliness and how we can meet each one's different relational needs.

Outer Layer Loneliness

The first layer I want to peel back is called outer layer loneli-ness. The outer core is the human relationship level. Isn't it great that we are made as relational beings? We are made in the image, nature, and character of God. Since God is a relational being and we are made in his image, we crave relationships.

At no other time of year is that craving, that longing, for re-lationships more apparent than the holiday season. For those who have lost loved ones or gone through a divorce, the pain of loneliness can ruin these celebrations entirely. I'm talking about the widow going through her first Christmas without her life-long lover. The freshman, hundreds of miles away from home, may feel its sting as his family gathers together to celebrate without him.

Feeling left out is painfully real. And just like an aching back or twisted ankle, the pain demands attention. Some seek the assistance of alcohol or drugs to numb the pain. Some seek relief through the abuse or the neglect of food. Some seek attention from others through drastic and often dangerous measures. Others completely deny their relational DNA by deliberately shunning the companionship of other people.

Whatever the method, the pain of loneliness is something we've all experienced. Whether it comes about by moving to a new school, a death in the family, or a myriad of other reasons, we cannot deny that human loneliness is real.

Calling this the outer layer of loneliness doesn't imply shallowness. We are wired for relationships, and our lives would be incomplete without the input of close friends and family. We all need to grow, and there is no better way to do that than with the influence of people in our lives.

But this outer layer loneliness isn't our most significant problem. Yes, it's real, and yes, it's painful. Too many people, though, spend their whole life focusing on the surface and miss the inner core.

Inner Core Loneliness

Is it possible for the mom who is president of the PTA to be as lonely as the elderly shut-in? Can the college student who joined a fraternity searching for deep relationships still struggle with a nagging sense of loneliness? What about someone who has had several strong, supportive, and lifelong friends? Can this person still feel lonely?

"All the Emptiness I'd Felt for So Long Started to Melt Away"
AMY'S STORY

"Even though I became a Christian as a little girl and knew that God was always a part of my life, I felt empty a lot of the time. I had drifted away from a meaningful relationship with God, and I wasn't involved in a local church.

"This past year has been especially difficult for me. First, my father passed away in February. That alone was devastating and brought even more emptiness to my already lonely world. On top of losing my dad, I was betrayed by my two best friends. The people I turned to for help and strength when I needed it the most let me down. Everything in my life felt utterly empty.

"By August, I had given up and began wishing I was no longer alive. It's not necessarily that I wanted to die; I just longed for my new life in heaven. I just didn't want to experience any more hurt on this earth.

"After two months of battling a deep depression, a close friend of mine mentioned a church he thought I might enjoy. Nearly hopeless, I attended the church the following Sunday. I felt at home as soon as I walked through the doors. All the emptiness I'd felt for so long started to melt away. I had never felt the presence of God as much as when I walked through the doors of this church. That was the day that started something new and great for me. It was a whirlwind after that.

"In a matter of three weeks, I had gone through the newcomers' class, gotten baptized, joined the church, signed up for a small group Bible study, and volunteered in the preschool and homeless ministries at the church.

"I am so thankful for being led to this church. I'm so thankful to God for the way he's changed my life, and for the amazing friends he's put around me. My life has changed completely."

The answer to all of those questions is yes.

Inner core loneliness is that spiritual layer that is often ignored when diagnosing the common problem of loneliness. The Bible says that we are born lonely. We are born separated from our Creator, from our God. An Old Testament prophet said: "Your sins have separated you from your God" (Isaiah 59:2).

Everyone, at some point in life, has a gnawing sense that something is missing in life. There's a relational hole in the very core of our being. But so many are oblivious to this inner layer of loneliness and try to plug holes with things that were never meant to fill our soul. They try to fill their inner core emptiness with other people or material things.

We think, "Hey, once I make my first million, that will do it." But that doesn't work.

"Once I get into the corner office, that will do it." No.

"Once I drive that certain car . . ." Try again.

"Once I find Mr. or Ms. Right . . ." Nope.

None of those work; none will cure our inner core loneliness.

We are made in the image of God, and only God can fill the

God-sized vacuum that exists deep within us. When we feel the pain of loneliness, it is an opportunity for us to turn to God.

God has made it possible to enter into a relationship with him and to fill that spiritual void in our hearts. Because God saw that we were facing an eternal loneliness, he commissioned his only Son, Jesus Christ, to die on a Roman cross for the sins of all mankind. He cured, once and for all, our inner core loneliness. But we have to respond to this work of Jesus. When we do respond to his work, he will adopt us as sons and daughters, giving us freedom from our sin nature (Galatians 4:3–7). Once we make the decision to trust Jesus, we become his followers and his friends.

Weight Limits

Living in Texas, I see a lot of trucks on the roads. I'd say it's pretty much the automobile of choice around here. There are 4×4 trucks; V-6 and V-8 trucks; quarter-ton, half-ton, and one-ton trucks on the roads. These descriptions tell you how much the truck can haul. Essentially, the truck manufacturer is warning you not to dump fifty tons of material into a one-ton truck. The axles would collapse and leave you stranded.

It's too bad we don't have those labels for our relationships. We often try to dump God-sized pressures on human relationships. We try to fill inner core needs with outer layer people and things. We try to fill our lonely hearts with a new car or a new boyfriend. Or we'll try a new career or move to a new city. We think, maybe a change in scenery will do it.

No wonder so many marriages don't work. No wonder so many relationships end up broken. We are trying to put inner core weight and pressure on other people, and that will fail every time. There is no way, relationally speaking, you can take fifty thousand pounds of baggage and expectations and put it on a relationship that can only bear two thousand pounds. The pressure will quickly overwhelm the relationship, shattering it under the heavy load. Our earthly relationships are not meant to shoulder the pressure of our spiritual condition.

Handling that kind of pressure is God's job. He can handle any amount of pressure we can give him. He is more than capable of solving our inner core problem and then allowing it to transcend our outer layer condition.

In one of the most significant verses in the Bible, Jesus captures the solution to our lonely condition (Matthew 22:37–40). He tells us to love God first—with all of our heart, soul, and mind. In other words, we are asked to love God with everything we have. That is a vertical relationship, where we experience a connection with our Creator. This connection was always meant to fill our deepest longings. And when we have that vertical relationship going, everything else can fall into place. When we are connected to God, we can experience peace, joy, hope, and healing from the pain of loneliness.

The second part of the verse is a horizontal dimension. Jesus tells us to love our neighbor as we love ourselves. When we love God with all of our being, we will be given a supernatural capacity to meet the relational needs of others. It is not natural to think of others first, but when we are connected with our Creator, we will be given the octane to lay aside our self-centered desires to focus on the needs of other people. And that's when your life will go on a higher trajectory to the life God intended for you and me.

Inner core loneliness is a low-grade, gnawing sensation that something is missing. You'll feel like something is not right in your life. Let me tell you that the itch that you can't quite scratch is a spiritual issue. You are separated from your Maker, and it is upsetting everything else in your life. Please don't turn your back on the core issue of loneliness. Only God can fill the void in your life, so let him fulfill your basic need at the deepest level.

Many times I run into people who are clueless about the God-gap in their lives. Because Christ has not filled that gap in their lives, they're trying to fill it by putting God-type pressure on other relationships. They think, "If I could just hook up with him . . . He's rich like Bill Gates and he kind of looks like Brad Pitt. He will solve all of my loneliness, all of my relational needs."

No, he won't! He's not God. It's not going to happen.

Or guys think, "She looks incredible! If I hook up with her, I'll never be lonely again, and I . . ." But she's not God either.

It begins with the real God, our all-powerful and relational God. Once we get to know God, then we'll get to know what relationships are all about. We'll understand the vertical relationship with our Creator. That's the most important relationship and the first one we have to get right. Once this is going, we can live out our friendships on the horizontal level. Our relationships will be fueled through our connection with God.

The surface layer and the inner core layer both demand decisions. The first decision is simply this: Have you come to a point in your life where you will admit the truth about your lonely condition? Will you accept the fact that your sins have separated you from God? If so, you need to fall on your knees and give your life to him. Ask him to fulfill you from the inside out and make you whole.

The Bible says that when Jesus was dying on the cross for our sins, he experienced utter loneliness (Matthew 27:46). We can't even imagine how it must have felt for the Son of God to be betrayed by his friends and also abandoned by his own Father. In that moment, because he was carrying the sin of the world on his shoulders, he was totally separated from that dynamic relationship he always enjoyed with God the Father. The Jewish nation—his own people—turned its back on him. His best friends and closest followers deserted him at his hour of need. But, despite his own suffering and loneliness, Jesus had our lonely condition on his mind as he hung on that cross for you and me.

Jesus went through all that suffering and loneliness so we could have his companionship today. Being a follower of Christ is having a friend who "sticks closer than a brother" (Proverbs 18:24). Have you made that inner core decision? Have you trusted Jesus to cure your deepest longing for relationship?

We are all made in the image of God. We are relational beings. Our first priority is to let God heal our inner core reality of loneliness. From there, God will give us the octane and the resources to work on forming relationships that sharpen and encourage us to be the people God designed us to be. To put it plainly, we need God and we need other people. And in the next chapter, we'll shift our focus to how we can increase both the quantity and the quality of our friendships here on earth.

STOP AND THINK

FOLLOW THE SIGNS: We are relational people that were created to enjoy a connection with God and other people. We need God and other people for our journey through life.

CHECK THE MAP: "Two are better than one, because they have a good reward for their labor. For if they fall, one will lift up his companion. But woe to him who *is* alone when he falls, for he has no one to help him up. Again, if two lie down together, they will keep warm; but how can one be warm alone? Though one may be overpowered by another, two can withstand him. And a threefold cord is not quickly broken" (Ecclesiastes 4:9–12, NKJV).

TAKE THE NEXT STEP: Do you feel connected to God right now? Rate your relationship with God from 1 to 10 right now, with 1 being the lowest and 10 the highest. How would you rate your interpersonal relationships using the same scale of 1 to 10?

What relationships in your life are you putting too much pressure on, instead of allowing Christ to bear that load?

10

RELATIONAL REALITIES

Only a life lived for others is a life worthwhile.

—ALBERT EINSTEIN

"He did not let anyone follow him except Peter, James and John" (Mark 5:37).

"When he arrived at the house of Jairus, he did not let anyone go in with him except Peter, John and James" (Luke 8:51).

"Jesus . . . took Peter, John and James with him and went up onto a mountain to pray" (Luke 9:28).

"They went to a place called Gethsemane, and Jesus said to his disciples, 'Sit here while I pray.' He took Peter, James and John along with him, and he began to be deeply distressed and troubled" (Mark 14:32–33).

Notice a trend here?

Those are all accounts from the Gospels related to the interaction Jesus had with his closest companions.

Jesus needed friends, too.

Peter, John, and James were Jesus' posse. They were his buddies, his homeboys, his friends. It's hard for us to imagine that the Son of God had human relationships. It's even harder for us to imagine that he needed them.

But since Jesus was both fully human and fully divine, he too was wired for relationships. He craved friends with whom he could share the highest highs as well as the burdens that weighed him down. The friends of Jesus comforted him. They made him laugh. And cry. Life was better with them. Jesus loved his friends. And if Jesus, the second person in the Trinity, needed friends, we do, too.

As we saw in the last chapter, God graciously cured one of our deepest emotional problems. He cured the problem of inner core loneliness when God sent his Son, Jesus, to die on a cross and then rise again for all of us. He rebuilt the God–man relationship that was fractured by Adam and Eve.

However, loneliness is still an ongoing issue for many of us. Even those who follow Jesus can feel the sting of loneliness. There is another hole that can only be filled through human relationships. Even if Christ has filled the God-gap in our lives, we are incomplete without a close friend and a community in which we belong. That's where this chapter comes in. We'll address the question of how we can increase both the quality and the quantity of our friendships. Because quality relationships are an integral part of a life of joy and fulfillment, I want to unpack three statements in the pages to come that will help all of us develop better and more strategic friendships. God truly wants the best for us relationally. He has some incredible people in store for us that will help us along the journey toward joy.

DEVELOPING QUALITY FRIENDSHIPS IS INTENTIONAL, NOT ACCIDENTAL

We don't just fall into friendships. Building quality friendships requires intentionality. The good news is that we have the freedom to choose our friends. But careless choices will yield big trouble because our friends influence us in a huge way. So as we make decisions about the people we want in our inner circle, we need to discern whether a person is going to help us along our journey toward a better life or hinder us.

If I could just talk to your best friends, I'd know all about you. And that's without ever meeting you. The friends you choose says a lot about the kind of person you are. Choosing friends is like looking in a mirror. I would guess that you looked in the mirror this morning before you started your day. You wouldn't want to have any parsley hanging between your teeth or miss a button on your shirt—or even worse, a button on your pants—before you walked into a meeting. A mirror lets you know if you have those things going on. A mirror is limited, though; it is meant to reflect physical reality. Your friends, on the other hand, do not let you off the hook quite so easily. Your character, your true nature, is revealed by the friends you choose.

Do you ever wonder, "Who am I? I mean, who am I *really*?"

Do you want to see who you are and where your life is headed? All you have to do is take a look at your friends. When you examine your relationships, you'll see your character plainly. We can know who we really are by the friends we choose. The great news is that we have choices when it comes to our friends, and God wants to help us choose the best relationally.

For those of us who are parents, one of the greatest opportunities we have to shape the direction of our children is the ability to help them select great friends. I believe we have the responsibility of monitoring our children's relationships. We can guide them and help them set relational patterns today that will influence them for a lifetime. We can do this whether our kids are five, fifteen, or even twenty-five. Do you know what your kids are doing and who they're with? Let me challenge you to keep your parental radar on high alert when it comes to your child's friends. You have tremendous power to shape the future of your kids' lives just by helping them choose great friends who will build them up and help them in this game called life.

And don't ignore the fact that your kids will examine the kind of friends *you* choose. They'll test you at times to make sure you practice what you preach. My oldest daughter is in college, and I know that LeeBeth's best friends, as she emerges into adulthood, will mirror my best friends. So parents, who do *you* run with? Who are your best friends? How are you guiding your children by example?

What do you look for in a friend? As I have thought about my own friendships, I have come up with the qualities that make up a positive friendship. These qualities all begin with the letter *d*, so I call these friendships "3-D Friendships." (If nothing else, you've got to give me credit for making it easy to remember.)

First, God wants us to be able to share relationships on the *deepest* level with our friends. He wants us to be able to share our deepest joys and our deepest pain. He wants us to be able to enjoy intimacy the way he designed it to be. The friends I look for have a love for God. They love their wives and children. They share their goals with me as well as their frustrations. I don't look for shallow relationships. The people that I spend most of my time with share a commitment for a deep and lasting friendship.

The next important quality to look for is *direction*. God wants our closest friendships to have a definite purpose and direction. Our friends need to know that we're going somewhere together. All of us are on a relational freeway. Some are heading in the wrong direction. Some are moving too slowly. Some are swerving all over the place. Others are getting off at the wrong exits. Those who are trying to follow Jesus need to hook up with people who are heading in the same direction, to the same destination. Christianity is an event followed by a process. It's a journey that is better taken with other people to encourage us and keep us focused on the goal. Our friends need to be reading the same playbook as we are—the Bible. If our friends are getting their most fundamental direction for living from a different source, that's a sign of relational trouble.

The third *d* stands for *development*. We want friends who will sharpen and improve our lives somehow. God wants us to develop one another, to help one another, to challenge one another, to encourage one another and sharpen one another. One well-known proverb emphasizes the impact that close friends can have on one another: "As iron sharpens iron, so one man sharpens another" (Proverbs 27:17). That is an important function of any relationship. The Bible doesn't say plastic sharpens iron. Some of your friends right now might be plastic. Do you have friends who are cheap plastic when you need the strength that only iron provides? Plastic cannot improve iron, but it can make it dull and ineffective. Who's causing you to compromise?

Once again, God's relational priorities are basic. Intellectually, everyone will say, "Oh, yeah, I sign off on that." But where should this play out?

You might be thinking, "Ed, I see where you're going. I understand that friendships are a force to be reckoned with. And we serve a relational God. And we are wired to relate with others. But where do I meet these right people? Where do I meet these high-octane friends? In what context, in what venue, do you see this happening? Does it happen around the neighborhood? Does it happen on the soccer field? Does it happen in the classroom? Does it happen in the boardroom? Where do you find these people? Where can you see this stuff exhibited?"

A good place to start is the local church.

I laugh when people tell me that the church is just too social. That's the point! What better place is there for Christ-followers to meet quality friends than the local church? When it comes to selecting people with similar goals and values, the place you worship is a natural place. We're supposed to be social. Just check out the early church in the Bible. The early church met in large gatherings and also in intimate settings. It provided strength, encouragement, and hope for thousands who were oppressed. It taught people how to be the people of God. The church has always been built on relationships—first, on our personal relationship with God, and second, with others.

The church mirrors the great commandment: a love for God first, which is then demonstrated by a love for others (Matthew 22:39–40). Churches should be a gateway to your best relationships. Churches should be the most inviting, most accepting, and friendliest places around. Unfortunately, that is not always the case. But the example of the early church shows us how it could be. Let me urge you to get involved in a local church. It might take you a few tries, but I believe that God will direct you to a place where you can worship him in a community filled with people who love God and love other people. That's what the church is all about.

What about other places? We need to keep our eyes open for people who will give us depth, direction, and development. You might find a close confidant at work. It might happen at the gym. Maybe there's a mom in your neighborhood play-group that is trying to go in the same direction that you are, spiritually and relationally.

Wherever you find people with similar values who can build you up, take the initiative. Remember, replenishing relationships don't just happen. The best relationships I've ever had took initiative on my part. And when we take the initiative, we are mimicking the character of God. He took the initiative with us when he sent his son, Jesus, to cure our sin, which separated us from him. Just be sure to surround yourself with people who will influence you positively and encourage you regularly.

Do you have trouble forming solid friendships? If you have a bunch of people getting next to you and then backing away, then maybe the problem is you. That's a pretty good sign that there's something funky going on that you need to change. Go home, hit your knees, and say, "God, what quality about me is keeping people from me? What quality is keeping me from the depth, direction, and development that you want for me relationally?"

And this is where it can be really tough. Step up and ask one of those quality people, "Okay, what is it about me that keeps you from hanging out with me?"

If you take this challenge, you will grow. If you ignore

these warning signs, you are handicapping your relational potential and character development. If you want to have an exciting, adventurous life, look for ways to grow, and increase the
quantity and quality of the people in your life.

You might wonder about people who don't fall into the
3-D category. What about people who aren't ready for a deep
relationship or aren't heading in the same direction? What
about people who might drag us down? We have to walk
wisely in this area. The solution is to build bridges of integrity with those people. In other words, we meet them in
areas that don't cause us to compromise. We meet them on a
neutral playing field. If you are trying to honor your commitment to marriage, don't spend time in a singles bar with
an acquaintance. Don't agree to play golf on Sunday morning
with your neighbor if you've made a commitment with your
family to be in church.

Again, it takes wisdom to know how to handle situations
like these. Relationships like these have to be driven by love.
We should love everybody because they matter to God. That's
what the Christian life is all about—attracting people to Christ
by being a living demonstration of his love. Just because they
don't fall into the 3-D category doesn't mean we shouldn't talk
to them, socialize with them, help them, and love them.

But while you are developing those kinds of friendships,
beware the strong forces of negative peer pressure, which can
bring down even the best of us. That brings us to the second
statement about friendships.

THE KIND OF FRIEND YOU ARE IS THE KIND OF FRIEND YOU'LL ATTRACT

Who are you? What kind of person are you? It's important to know, because you're going to attract that same kind of person as a friend. You want to attract high-quality people? Be a high-quality person. Real friends support, help, and encourage you when times are tough. They've got your back. What kind of friend are you? Do you have your friends' backs? Are you there when they need you most? The kind of friend you are is the kind of friend you'll attract.

Just as we spoke of 3-D friendships, now I want to talk about the three *C*s of being a friend.

The first *c* is *commitment*. I've got to be committed to my friends. And I've got to look for that in others as I choose my friendships. It's great to have a dozen acquaintances, but God says that it's much better to have one quality friend that treats you like a brother (Proverbs 18:24).

People love to talk about investments these days: "I'm going to invest in that new company or that hot deal." But before I put my hard-earned money somewhere, I always do some research on the company. I'm going to find out about it before I drop any money down.

Investing relational capital is no different. Before you invest relational capital, you'd better research the person. What kind of commitment does he or she have?

If you're not sure whether or not a person has a high commitment quotient, that individual probably hasn't got it. You'll see it pretty easily. If the person is committed, it'll be like a neon

Las Vegas sign blinking. Committed people make regular decisions that reinforce their priorities. It won't take you long to recognize the people who orient their lives around the three major priorities we addressed earlier.

Committed people will block out time for their spouse and kids. They won't miss a lot of dance recitals or basketball games. Committed people will make it to church rather than making excuses each weekend. Committed people will be recognized at the office as hardworking and focused employees who add value to their company. Trust me: you'll just see it. The telltale signs of a committed person are obvious.

Here's the second *c*: *confidentiality*. Can your friends keep secrets? Can *you* keep secrets? Have you ever had a radio friend? You tell them something that you are dealing with or struggling with, and then you find that your trusted confidant is broadcasting your secrets to anyone in the world who'll listen.

Sometimes I go to Barnes and Noble and down a few shots of espresso at its café. Once I'm all wired with caffeine, I'll start to weave through the rows and rows of books. Inevitably, I'll find myself in the aisle of those kiss-and-tell books. These books are the big thing now. Celebrities and wanna-be celebrities are being paid exorbitant wads of cash to betray confidences and expose some dirt.

Why are we attracted to that trash? Why are we attracted to tabloid television? It's because we like getting the lowdown on other people, don't we? Gossip has become an amateur sport! We just don't want others to find out about our own dirt.

But a real, true friend doesn't do that. You can't say the word *gossip* without that "sss" sound—the sound of a snake. Gossssip. Ssslander. The Bible says that friends keep secrets, but gossipers betray us.

"I Wish I Could Do It All Over Again"
SABRINA'S STORY

In early September 2001, Randy was diagnosed with kidney disease. Dialysis and the necessity of a transplant were very real possibilities in Randy's future. And in a new town, far from the security of family and friends, the bad got worse. In the aftermath of 9/11, Randy and his wife, Judy, both lost their jobs and came face-to-face with some uncertain times in an uncertain world.

Then Judy met Sabrina at church. Their two families quickly became close friends, and Judy told Sabrina about Randy's failing kidneys.

After a lot of prayer and talking it over with her husband, Sabrina decided to get tested to see if she was a possible match for Randy. After a battery of tests, Sabrina learned that she had the perfect match and donated one of her kidneys to him.

Since the surgery in 2004, Randy's health has improved dramatically. He now lives an active and vibrant life.

Seeing the difference she was able to make for Randy and his family has only fueled Sabrina's desire to make an impact on the world. She understands what commitment, love, and friendship are all about. And she prays that God will continue to provide opportunities for her to make a difference.

She says now, "Just thinking about all that God has done brings tears to my eyes. I am so humbled to have been chosen to give this gift to Randy. I wish I could do it all over again."

So let me ask you: Are you confidential? If you are a gossip, you won't win trustworthy friends. You'll find that your junk is being broadcast via satellite through your "friends," too. Is that what you want? Confidentiality in friendship is huge.

The third *c* is *constructive*. Are you a constructive person? Or are you a destructive person? Do the people with whom you've initiated relationships build you up? Do they add to your life? Or are they leeches? Do they help you and grow you? Or do they tear you down?

I believe there is already far too much negativity going on in the world today to have a negative person in my inner circle. I've got to have friends in my life who are encouragers. I need people who will pray for me and hold me accountable when I'm wrestling with decisions about my family. I need friends who will make me laugh when I've had a stressful day. I don't want a bunch of whiners in my life. I love them and minister to them, but they aren't my closest friends.

The kind of friend you are is the kind of friend you'll attract. Are you a committed friend who will be there no matter what? Are you a confidential person who tenaciously guards your friends' secrets? What about constructive?

If you are like me, you could probably stand to improve on at least one of those characteristics of true friendship. Let me challenge you to go to your spouse or your closest friends and ask them for an honest evaluation. Where do you need to improve in the friendship department? What do you do well? The answers may surprise you.

ME, MYSELF, AND I

We often hear people talk about the Golden Rule: treat others as you would have others treat you. It is a concept that comes right from the mouth of Jesus (Matthew 22:39). He never asks us to love ourselves. We're born with this gift, and we don't need any help doing it. It's natural for us to look out for our needs, our desires, and our own happiness, but we don't naturally look out for the needs of other people. It's hard to put another's needs ahead of our own.

Loneliness is common for people who haven't learned to put their own needs aside for other people. They spend so much time worrying about what they need that they leave no room for others. For people like this, relationships are few and far between. If we want to find positive relationships, we need to stop obsessing about ourselves—"What about *my* needs? What about *my* feelings? What about *my* wants and desires? What about *my* family? What about me, myself, and mine?"

That kind of preoccupation with self prevents us from connecting with others. If we're going to get beyond ourselves and enter into real, satisfying relationships, we need to make an effort to think about the needs of others.

God wants us to be relational. He took the first step by creating Eve for Adam, and then bridged the chasm of sin by providing Jesus for us. Sadly, a lot of us miss out on the relational world that God has for us. We're too self-focused. Is it merely selfishness that causes people to be so self-centered? Maybe. But for some, their lack of connection with others is because of fear. They might be fearful because of bad relationships in the past. Maybe they were rejected when they stepped out and got burned for it. Their memories from the past prevent them from enjoying the present. Don't let this fear cripple the incredible relationships God has in store for you. Take the risk and reach out to others. You'll be glad you took the chance.

Instead of moaning about your lack of friends, take some relational risks. Don't complain about people you think are snobby; walk up and talk to them. Find out for yourself. You might find that they aren't snobby; maybe they're just shy. Don't assume that someone is a one-dimensional caricature of your imagination. Take a chance. Be a friend to someone. Help them out. Listen to their problems. Smile more. Invite them over for coffee or iced tea. One of the least talked about commands in the Bible is to be hospitable (1 Peter 4:9). I rarely hear anyone talk about hospitality today, but I think it's crucial to forming great relationships.

People sometimes complain about the size of the church I pastor. They complain about finding good relationships with thousands of people all around them. They say it's too big and too hard to get to know people. These are usually the same people who won't go up to talk to anybody in the lobby between services. They won't check out our small group ministry to meet other people. They won't volunteer to help others. They won't even go to the café to meet someone new. And they wonder why they struggle with relational loneliness.

You can't be lazy relationally, or in any realm of life for that matter, if you are in the pursuit of outrageous, contagious joy. God has some incredible relationships in store for you. He wants people around you who will build you up, who will make you laugh and, sometimes, make you cry. He wants to give you friends who will help you in the brightest and the darkest moments in life. These quality people will reflect the character and nature of God in how they live and how they treat you as a friend. Since each one of us is made in God's image, we'll have a better glimpse of our Creator when we surround ourselves with the kind of people that are aligning their lives with God and his principles.

Don't let the evil one discourage you from sharing your life with others. Don't let him keep you on the sidelines as the game of life is going on all around you. Take the initiative to be a friend and be hospitable. God has allowed these principles to bring me great friends and win the victory over loneliness, and I know they will help you, too.

Every time I have busted through a barrier of fear in relationships, I've been rewarded. I will receive a new friendship or a deeper friendship. Sometimes, when the relationship doesn't work out, I'll learn something important about my own character that will help make me a better person. I remember how nervous I was to express my feelings to a crush I had in high school. I rehearsed it over and over in my mind. I practiced my Shakespearean speech in the mirror. Then I finally met up with her in person. All of my rehearsals went out the window as I looked at this girl in the eyes. Though I didn't say it as I had written it, or come off as cool as I wanted, I rolled the dice, and twenty-five years of marriage later, I'm proud to tell you that the gamble paid off.

We are built for community. We have got to step out and take relational risks. When we take those risks and make hospitality happen, we can expect some great results.

First of all, it will *mature us and deepen our faith*. Maturing in the Christian life is not about sitting and examining the lint in your navel. No. It is about thinking of others. The Bible says to serve one another, help one another, pray for one another, and the list goes on and on. Growing spiritually is all about learning to live with a "one another" mentality. Our human nature and our culture tell us to think about ourselves first. Look out for number one. But that is not the path to true joy. In one passage, often referred to as the "one another" chapter, we are told that we can't profess to love God if we don't love others (1 John 4:7–12).

Taking relational risks will also *broaden our horizons*. If we are not careful, we can end up saying to ourselves, "I'm just going to spend time doing *my* deal, with *my* friends; this is *my* little huddle of people and that's it."

But people who broaden their relational horizons notice, "There are some people who didn't go to *my* school. There are some people who don't have *my* skin color. There are some people who don't live in *my* neighborhood and go to *my* church. And some of those people are really cool."

You will not believe the relational opportunities available if we will just open our minds, our hearts, and our eyes to what's all around us. God created a beautiful world for us to enjoy that is rich with diversity. And I believe that embracing diversity will develop you in amazing ways. For some of you, your best friends and closest relationships aren't even in your life yet. They are yet to be discovered. I cannot force you to reach out to others relationally, and God is not going to do that, either. But I'm telling you that God has something great for you. He has a plan to enrich your life through other people.

STOP AND THINK

FOLLOW THE SIGNS: Even Jesus, the Son of God, needed friends. The best way to discover good friends is to *be* a good friend.

CHECK THE MAP: "Jesus replied: 'Love the Lord your God with all your heart and with all your soul and with all your mind.' This is the first and greatest commandment. And the second is like it: 'Love your neighbor as yourself.' All the Law and the Prophets hang on these two commandments" (Matthew 22:37–40).

TAKE THE NEXT STEP: Do something today that expresses your love to one of your friends.

11

I HAD THESE FRIENDS...

Without friends no one would choose to live,
though he had all other goods.

—ARISTOTLE

I went to high school with this guy named Larry. Larry and I played a lot of sports together. And though we were not close friends, we ended up spending quite a bit of time hanging out because of our mutual interest in sports. If there was a sport to be played, I wanted Larry on my team. We seemed to get along really well, and we often dreamed about playing college basketball together.

But after my junior year in high school, my family and I moved again. This time, we moved from Columbia, South Carolina, all the way to Houston, Texas—1,004 miles away from my friend Larry. I pretty much lost contact with him for about six years.

Then one night I got a phone call from one of my best friends. He said, "Ed, do you remember Larry?"

"Yeah, of course I remember Larry!"

"Are you sitting down?"

"Yeah, man."

With a slight hesitation, I heard him say, "Larry just murdered someone. Ed, he's in the state penitentiary! Can you believe that?"

"Are you kidding me? Larry? I know he was having some problems back in high school, but I didn't realize things were that bad! What happened to him?"

Two weeks later I found myself sitting across a picnic table from my friend Larry in a prison yard. With tears streaming down his face, he began to tell me his story. I finally said, "Larry, where did the wheels come off, man? When did these problems begin?"

And he told me a four-word phrase I'll never forget. He said, "I had these friends . . ."

I had these friends. If I could tell you how many times I've heard that four-word phrase, it would break your heart. Whenever I talk to someone in the midst of a serious tailspin, that phrase comes up over and over again. Whether the person is in junior high or college, is single or married, drives a Porsche or a pickup truck, comes from a good family or a dysfunctional one, the common theme is bad friends who derailed the person's life. So often we fail to realize the sheer force—the power and influence—of our friends. Many of the problems we deal with can be traced back to poor choices in the relational realm, to giving in to the power of peer pressure.

THE PEER PRESSURE PRESS

Let's talk straight. I've been there in the thick of the peer pressure press. I understand how painful peer pressure can be. It can circle you like a school of tiger sharks. This pressure is a real and powerful force in our lives, especially when we're young. We want to run with the herd; we feel that cross pull. Deep down, we all know what's right, but there's a strong pull from the opposite direction.

Every friendship we choose is a critical decision that will affect the rest of our lives. You may be setting yourself up for a fall simply because of the people you're hooked up with. Don't take the bait. Don't compromise. Do it God's way. God's way is not the easiest, but it's always the best. I'm telling you from experience, it's the best. Just ask Larry.

In junior high and high school, I wasn't part of the popular group. I felt the pressure to compromise and run with the wrong crowd. But I was able to withstand that peer pressure and keep my principles and integrity intact. When I got to college, the pressure intensified.

Florida State University, a thousand miles away from Mom and Dad, was rated as the number one party school in America at the time by Mr. Hugh Hefner, the creator of *Playboy*. FSU had some crazy stuff going on. The school had a three-to-one ratio of girls to guys. Gulp. I was in a dormitory named Cash Hall, an athletic dorm housing one thousand five hundred students—though only about fifty of us were actually athletes. This coed dorm boasted private rooms for each of the athletes, maid service, and a full bar in the basement. Cash Hall was party central.

And the first Sunday I was there, only three of us got up for church. Three out of fifteen hundred! Yes, I was one of them. The rest were enjoying a nice Sunday morning hangover, I guess. The next Sunday, the same three went to church. And so on and so on.

I really felt lonely. I felt misunderstood and just plain uncool. I definitely felt like the odd man out with my basketball teammates and those I lived with. It was difficult to keep my priorities straight and my life on track God's way in the midst of this pressure. No one was checking up on me. I could have done anything I wanted. But I knew God had a bigger plan for me. And more than anything, God gave me the strength to persevere.

God leveraged that loneliness in my life to drive me closer to him and enabled me to see the funky, self-centered relationships of the others who lived in the dorm. I learned what *not* to do just by watching the relational wreckage all around me. I saw the shallowness of ungodly relationships. I saw the pain that was caused by envy, greed, and wheels-off living. I believe God used all those experiences to make me a stronger and, ultimately, a more complete person. He showed me some hard stuff, there's no doubt about it. But I'm so thankful that I remained faithful during those years. And I'm also thankful that God had some incredible friendships waiting for me when I got beyond this lonely time in my life.

Right now I have the most amazing friends a guy could have. But let me tell you something: I see the same problems in my church as I did at Florida State years ago. It's almost as if God were giving me a preview of what I'd be dealing with in the ministry. As a pastor, I have the privilege of helping people work through the junk in their lives. God used those years in college to prepare me to help others who would face the same relational, personal, and spiritual issues. It's amazing how God works. His plan was flawless. And I'm so glad that he held me to it.

If you stay with it, if you build your life around God's principles and people who love him, the pressure will subside. It really will. When I graduated from high school and then college, I looked back and realized, "I was worried about *those* people accepting me? *Those* people? What was I doing worrying about *them*?" You'll realize the same thing when you go to your own ten-year reunion!

I'm here to tell you that God's way works. Choosing friends God's way is the best way—not just some of the time, but all of the time. So who do you need to cut from your herd? Who are you compromising with? Who's slowing you down?

We know that Jesus told his disciples to love people, but did you know that he also told them that there is a time and place to turn your back on certain people? He told his followers to do just that with those who stubbornly opposed their mission and values (Luke 10:11).

The apostle Paul compared the Christian life to a race. And he warned his runners not to let anyone trip them up (Galatians 5:7). We should never be hostile to anyone, but we need to realize that other people can derail us. They can influence our behavior, and our behavior *today* influences our *tomorrow*.

We need to be more careful about the people we allow to influence our behavior. We should never disrespect or belittle anyone, but we need the right people in the inner circle of our lives to keep us moving in the right direction. I'm talking about moving with the kinds of people who will challenge you, not the people who just make you feel comfortable. Life is too

"I Have These Friends"

ALAN AND KELLY'S STORY

"Kelly and I were having a lot of problems when we came to the church for the first time. Our marriage was hanging by a thread. I was failing miserably in the one thing that I wanted to be the best at, which was being married to my wife. Six months into our marriage, things started to get really rocky. We realized that our closest friends were dragging us down. When we were single, we had a lot of fun together as a group. But things change when you get married. And our marriage priority was suffering as a result of the people we were spending so much time with. They were just living different lives.

"Then one day at church we heard this sermon about how friends can drag you down. As we listened to that talk, my wife and I looked at each other and knew it was all about us. This talk could not have come at a better time in our lives. We knew that a lot of our problems stemmed from the people we were associating with. But all that began to change when we went to our first small Bible study group.

"Even though we sat in the car for a while and debated even going in, we eventually got up the courage to step into that room. Our marriage improved immediately.

"Plugging into that small group has played a huge role in saving our marriage and has also given us some incredible new relationships. I truly believe that our marriage would have ended if it wasn't for the friends we met through that Bible study.

"Now, rather than struggling to hold it together on our own, we have people who love us, support us in our marriage, and help us keep our priorities in line. And instead of regretting the fact that 'I had these friends,' I'm grateful to be able to say, 'I *have* these friends.'"

short to be comfortable. We need some challenging people in our lives who will tell us the truth when we're heading the wrong way. We need friends just as Jesus needed friends. We need friends like Peter, James, and John, who energized Jesus and lightened the load of his heavy mission. Those of us who are following Christ are tasked with a similar mission. So let me ask you an important but difficult question: Who do you need to cut from your relational herd?

Samson: A He-Man with a She-Weakness

Samson was the biblical body builder. He had all the potential in the world. He was handsome, supernaturally strong, and even his name was strong. *Samson* means "strong and daring one." Samson was so strong that he killed a roaring lion with his bare hands. He even killed three thousand of his enemies with a donkey's jawbone. Samson was empowered by God himself and had everything in the world going for him. He was set apart to be the deliverer for an entire nation, and all he had to do was follow a few simple rules that were a part of the Nazarite vow.

This vow he had taken prohibited him from eating and drinking anything that came from grapes, and he wasn't allowed to touch anything dead or to cut his hair. By dedicating himself as a Nazarite before God, these rules would protect Samson and allow him to accomplish God's purposes for his life.

However, Samson began a slow, treacherous journey down the slippery slope of compromise. Though he was set apart to deliver Israel from the enemy Philistines, he married a Philistine girl. God warned the Israelites that they should only marry other Israelites because the surrounding nations worshipped pagan gods, a practice strictly forbidden for the Jews. But Samson married this girl simply because he was attracted to her physically. He made this life-changing decision with his hormones. He lusted after this idol-worshipping girl from a foreign land, and that was just the beginning of Samson's slide.

Sadly, there's no record of Samson surrounding himself with wise friends who could keep him on the right path. There's no record of his Israelite buddies warning him about his problem with shady women. And that lack of quality friends was a big part of Samson's downfall. He not only thumbed his nose at God's rules, but also at his parents. The Bible says that Samson's choice of a Philistine wife greatly displeased them. But he did it anyway.

Samson then defiled himself and broke his promise to God when he reached inside a dead lion to get some honey to satisfy his sweet tooth. Though God had set him aside for a specific purpose, Samson abandoned God's plans and chose instant gratification instead. During his pagan wedding feast, the wine was flowing, and Samson, already laying aside his vow to God, was surrounded by people who lived in direct opposition to the way God had set him apart. Though there is no record of it, Samson most likely continued his rebellion by sipping some Merlot during the feast. Surrounded by the enemy Philistines, Samson had no one to help him through the peer pressure. So he broke vow after vow. Now he was falling fast down the slope of despair and depravity.

Samson then committed strike three when he divulged the secret of his strength: his long hair. His pagan wife betrayed him for seven hundred pieces of silver. She cooed the mighty man to sleep, then shaved off the visible symbol of his vow to God; the Bible says that at this very moment, "the Lord had left him" (Judges 16:20). What a tragic statement.

Samson broke his vows, abandoned his potential, and spent the rest of his life in a Philistine prison. He was ridiculed and his eyes were gouged out. If only Samson had had some good friends pulling him in the right direction. Instead of publicly delivering his nation from the Philistines, he was publicly humiliated. Samson was supposed to be the deliverer of Israel from its enemy, but his victories recorded in Scripture are private, personal battles that did little to deliver his nation.

What went wrong? For Larry, it was four simple yet profound words. For Samson, it was the same four simple yet profound words. For both of these tragic characters, one small phrase derailed their lives: *I had these friends . . .*

And don't think any of us today are exempt from the same kind of destiny Samson experienced. We may not be imprisoned by pagans and sentenced to hard labor. But if we surround ourselves with shady people, we'll miss the potential that God has for us and end up incarcerated by our own bad decisions.

God wants to save you from the deep weeds by allowing you

to learn from biblical examples like Samson. He wants to give you the very best relationally. In all my years, I've never seen anyone beat the system. The wrong people will take you to the wrong places, not just some of the time . . . every time. They'll lead you to break God's principles for your life . . . every time. And they will cause you to remove the guardrails that he's placed in your life for protection . . . every time.

David: The Hebrew Hillbilly

Once upon a time there was a Hebrew hillbilly named David. He was a precocious teenager who had more guts than brains. The Bible says he had a ruddy complexion. It means he had red hair, freckles, and pimples all over his face. And one day, this young shepherd boy hears about a battle about to go down.

David leaves his sheep to get in on the action and runs into King Saul. Saul was probably about six feet six, with long, flowing, and beautiful black hair. Saul, as King of Israel, was supposed to fight this giant named Goliath, but he didn't want any part of it. Goliath was the undefeated and undisputed heavyweight champion of the world. So what was ruddy little David going to do?

David, the unknown and untested shepherd boy turned warrior, said, "Bring him on!" Miraculously, David struck Goliath right between the eyes with a smooth little pebble from his sling. He dropped Goliath like a bad habit, and David became an instant celebrity. He was walking the red carpet, doing the celebrity wave, eating at the finest restaurants, and signing autographs for every pimple-faced teenage girl. David was the toast of the town.

As he made his way through the city, women were coming

out of the houses screaming, "Saul has slain his thousands, but David has slain tens of thousands. Oh, David, you go, David! You the man, David. The man of the hour. Too sweet to be sour. The tower of Hebrew power!" They loved their new hero. And this didn't sit too well with the reigning king.

Saul started giving David the evil eye. You know, the eye of envy. As the jealousy and paranoia intensified, Saul literally went psycho. That's what jealousy and envy can do to you. It'll make you crazy.

Through all this tension, David met Saul's son, Jonathan. He was the heir to Saul's throne. When they met, there was an instant connection. They each made a covenant to commit to the other's well-being. They decided to hold each other accountable to God and his plans for their lives. They supported one another. They watched each other's back.

When Jonathan's father, psycho Saul, was trying to kill David, Jonathan would warn David. Despite the power of his own father, Jonathan put his own life on the line for his friend David. They shared secrets with each other that they shared with no one else. And they built one another up.

Even though Jonathan was the heir to the throne, God had other plans. He anointed David as the new king. Instead of being jealous or angry, Jonathan celebrated this news with his buddy. He lost power and inordinate wealth, but his response was true friendship. He was a committed, confidential, and constructive friend. (That was a review from the last chapter, in case you missed it.)

Real friends applaud one another when they close the deal, when they make the big score. A real friend says, "Way to go! That's incredible! You went out with him? You bought that car? You graduated at the top of your class? Congratulations!"

And real friends also support you and encourage you when times are tough. They've got your back in the good and the bad times.

David, unlike Samson, surrounded himself with great friends—not just good friends, but great friends. David wasn't perfect, but he was strategic about the people he surrounded himself with. He intentionally selected men of strong character who were going in the same direction.

But David was also a great friend to others. He honored his word. He was a generous friend. He cared deeply for the men who fought on the front lines of his army. David was committed to his friends, and they responded with unbreakable loyalty and commitment to their warrior-king.

Samson ended up blind in a filthy prison. He was made a mockery. David ended up as the king of a mighty nation, driving out the enemy Philistines and many other nations. David's leadership led to prosperity and, ultimately, to peace for his nation.

Samson had these Philistine friends. David had these Israelite friends. Samson wasted his potential; but David, the Hebrew hillbilly and great underdog, rose to the throne of a mighty nation.

FRIENDS ARE A FORCE THAT CAUSES EITHER POSITIVE OR NEGATIVE ENERGY

Friendships are a powerful force for both good and bad. They can either build us up, taking us to higher highs, or they can tear us down, bringing us to lower lows. Friendships are never neutral. They can propel us forward or grind us to a halt.

Who are your friends? Are they causing positive or negative energy in your life? Are they taking you to new heights or grinding your life to a halt?

If Larry could do it all over again, I know he'd tell you, with tears in his eyes, that choosing great friends is essential. Don't make the mistakes that Larry made. And don't ignore the warnings of Samson's story, either. Don't pretend that you can go through this life without the influence of great people to build you up. David and Jonathan show us a great model of what can happen when two people come together in a committed and constructive friendship. It produced strength, courage, and conviction in the plans of God.

So ask God who you might need to cut from your life so you don't end up one day saying in dismay, "I had these friends . . ." And ask God for wisdom to select great friends that will keep you on track toward the amazing plans and incredible life of joy he has for you.

STOP AND THINK

FOLLOW THE SIGNS: Other people have a huge impact on our lives. The friends you choose will influence you positively or negatively.

CHECK THE MAP: "But it takes only one wrong person among you to infect all the others—a little yeast

spreads quickly through the whole batch of dough!"
(Galatians 5:9, NLT).

TAKE THE NEXT STEP: Are your closest friends building you up or tearing you down? What friends do you
need to remove from your inner circle? What would
your friends say about you? Are *you* a positive, godly influence on your friends?

12

RELATIONAL REVOLUTION

It will not do to leave a live dragon
out of your plans if you live near one.
—J. R. R. TOLKIEN, *THE HOBBIT*

There is a war going on. Bombs are being dropped, battle plans are being executed, and the casualties are piling up.

But it's not the war that has captured our attention for the past few years. It's not the war that has been debated on CNN and Fox News. It's not the one we've been reading about in the *New York Times* and every newsmagazine across the country.

This war has been going on for thousands of years. And to make matters more complicated, this war is multifaceted and is fought on two fronts: with God and with others.

But hope remains.

COSMIC REVOLUTION

The first facet of this war is cosmic. There is a war between our Creator and man. Each one of us is born an enemy of God (Romans 3:10–18). We were born into a war that we didn't start. The Bible tells us that not only were we born on the wrong side of the battle, but we each make it worse. We escalate this war by our own attitudes and actions.

You may not have realized that you were in a fight with the God of the universe, but that's the reality. And it's not hard to see the fruits of our collective rebellion. The sickness of sin produces oppression, murder, rape, greed, and a host of other problems. These are global issues that infect and affect all of us.

The war started with the perfect couple. Adam and Eve picked a fight with their holy God by rejecting his law. When they turned aside from his ways, all hell broke loose—literally. This rebellion created a giant chasm between this holy God and his creation. The Bible says that because of Adam and Eve's sin, we are no longer on God's side. We are born alienated from God and can't do anything in our own power to fight this pervasive problem.

But don't point the finger too quickly at the first couple. You've messed up, too. You've done some spectacular sinning of your own. We're as much to blame as Adam and Eve. We're in this war, and we have every right to experience the consequences of picking a cosmic fight with an all-powerful, all-knowing, and holy God. We deserve to be blown off the map. Our ungrateful and selfish response to this loving Creator warrants extermination. But as I said earlier, there is hope.

And it's found in one man. His name is Jesus.

Christmas is the special time of year when the world celebrates the birth of Jesus Christ. The significance of this event is that Jesus, the Son of God, became a baby. That day, God unfolded his master plan to win this cosmic fight. He bounded down the staircase of heaven with a baby in his arms. And he gave this baby, his only Son, to all of us. God sent Jesus to identify with our human condition. But here's the catch: Jesus was not infected by sin, being immaculately conceived. Jesus was born sinless and remained sinless.

Easter is another Christian holiday that celebrates a second significant event in this war's history. During this season, we celebrate the fact that Jesus, the holy Son of God, died on a Roman cross as a substitute for our sins. He took your junk and my junk and hung on the cross for our due punishment. We picked the fight with God and deserved extermination, but Jesus was the one who paid the ultimate penalty. Fortunately, death wasn't the end of the story.

Easter is primarily about the resurrection of Jesus. We celebrate the fact that Jesus did not stay in the tomb. The Bible says that he rose three days later and then appeared to over five hundred of his followers before departing back to heaven. His resurrection proves that he is God, and affords each one of us the opportunity to have a relationship with a living God, and provides Christians with hope that they too will have their bodies resurrected.

The best part of this amazing cure for our cosmic rebellion is that we are invited to join God's side as a friend and even an heir to all of his blessings (Romans 8:17, Galatians 4:7). All we have to do is accept the free gift to end our war with God. We just need to receive his cure. The work has already been done. We can't do anything in and of ourselves to cure our problem.

Only a holy God can do that. And he did it through his Son, Jesus.

You may already consider yourself a "follower of Christ." You have already received the free gift of salvation. But think back for a second with me. Think back to the era in your life before you became his follower. Do you remember feeling a little bit uneasy? Do you remember feeling at odds with God? Do you remember during those semiannual moments of introspection the fear that paralyzed you knowing that, if you were to die, you would face a holy God and have to give an account of your life to him? Do you remember that? I'm sure that you, like me, were keenly aware of this cosmic conflict. And this awareness is what drove you to make this faith decision.

The moment that we come into a personal relationship with Jesus Christ, the moment we bow the knee to him, the moment we turn from our sinfulness and surrender ourselves to the Lord, the Bible says something spectacular happens. We are reconciled to God through Christ (Romans 5:10). The Bible also says that we have the peace of God, and that peace permeates every part of our inward being (Romans 5:1).

Once again, we are in an unwinnable conflict with God. There's nothing we alone can do to bridge the gap. God, though, did the work when he commissioned Jesus to spill his blood on that rugged cross for our sins. If we accept that and embrace this truth, we are reconciled to God. And then your war is over. No more fighting or hostility with your Creator.

By now you might be saying, "I thought we were talking about relationships here, Ed." We are. And the first thing that we need to address is our cosmic conflict with God. Our relational conflicts will never experience healing and peace without addressing our cosmic conflict. You cannot be at peace

"*God Has Blessed Us with a Marriage We Neither Expected Nor Deserved.*"

STEVE AND KIM'S STORY

"Like millions of couples, our marriage has had its ups and downs. More than anything else, we were clueless about how to handle the conflict we experienced as a young couple.

"Looking back, I wish we had sought counseling. Eventually, the name calling, criticism, and avoidance did nothing but drive us apart.

"Then in the summer of 2000, something happened that drove the ultimate wedge between Kim and me. I had an affair.

"The night I told Kim about the affair, she simply said, 'Go kiss your son (who was three months old at the time) and leave the house. Do not come back.'

"That was the most difficult time of my life. But by God's grace, and through the faithful prayers of our friends, family, and church, we gained a strong desire to save our marriage. And over that time, we both began to take ownership of our mistakes and began to recognize the truth—marriage takes a lot of hard work, especially when there's conflict.

"Kim and I finally got the counseling we needed, and we began the long and difficult healing process. Eventually I regained the trust of my wife, and we got back together.

"The process was anything but easy. But over time,

God has blessed us with a marriage that we neither expected nor deserved. And he has shown us that when we deal with conflict his way, he will bless our lives in ways that we could never dream possible."

---

with others until you, yourself, are at peace. And you can't be at peace with yourself until you're at peace with God.

The good news is that God has offered to address our cosmic conflict and our relational conflicts. Once we accept the fact that God took the initiative to reconcile us to himself through his Son, and receive his help, we'll be given the power to reconcile relational conflict with other people. And this ability will grow as we learn to do this with more wisdom and consistency (2 Corinthians 5:17–18).

Essentially, we are given a new weapon in our relational arsenal. The Bible calls it the "ministry of reconciliation." When we accept the work of Christ in our lives, he will begin to transform us from the inside out. He will make our lives more in line with his principles. And he will also help us make peace with people. This means that we have a responsibility to depend on God when we face relational conflict. And we have a responsibility to mimic the character of God by being proactive with the conflict in our lives. We can't just shrug our shoulders and ignore it. Because God initiated peace to us, we are given the responsibility of initiating peace with the people in our lives. That is what gives God's people the octane to have great relationships—it's handling conflict God's way.

CONFLICT REVOLUTION

I don't care how much money you have, how effective you are at communication, or how satisfied you are with your sex life. A true measure of success in any relationship is how you process conflict. Conflict is going to happen; but how you handle it will separate the constructive relationships from the destructive, and the strong marriages from the weak.

Most of us have never had a crash course in conflict resolution. But all of us need it desperately. You know what we do when we haven't been trained to handle conflict properly? We revert back to our natural tendencies. And guess where we get our conflict-resolution tendencies? You got it: Mom and Dad.

You've probably said at some point in your life, "No, I'll never act like my mom," or, "I'll never become like my dad. No way!" But you do. And you'll find yourself saying the same things you heard around your home while growing up because that's the only model you've ever known.

Maybe you grew up in a home where conflict was handled "missile style." You saw your parents employ the shock and awe strategy that tries to destroy the combatant with an onslaught of aggression. One missile. Then another. And another. Kaboom! It was most likely ugly and chaotic at home.

Maybe you grew up in a home where conflict was handled "land-mine style." You saw your parents fight and then you saw them take out little shovels, dig holes in the sand, and bury land mines. You would think the argument was over, that everything was okay. But one day you would be walking through the den and bang! World War III would begin.

Maybe in your home your parents handled conflict "foxhole style." They had a bunch of conflict going on, but they wouldn't really deal with the issue. Instead, they would just jump in foxholes and hide. The thinking here is that the other person will forget about the issue, or that it will magically disappear after a good nap in the bunker.

Maybe you find yourself handling relational and marital conflict the same way. You said you wouldn't, but you're acting just like your dad, and your partner is acting just like her mother. That's okay because that's the only model you've ever had. But it's not the most effective strategy.

If these aren't the proper ways to handle conflict, then what's the solution? What should we do when we have a conflict? Our first reaction, oftentimes, is to think, "I'm just going to straighten her out." Or "I'm going to *get* him . . ." That's the natural thing we want to do. But what we should do is totally unnatural. What God wants us to do goes against our natural, selfish tendencies.

Take It to God

The first thing you should do is to take the conflict to God. After all, you've been reconciled to God through Christ, so you should take it to God. You should pray about the problem. Many times I have dropped the ball when an issue was on the table, and I blew it because I refused to talk to God about the issue. Instead of diffusing tension, I made it worse by trying to handle it without God's intervention. That just doesn't work. In Texas we say, "That dog won't hunt!"

When I have prayed about the problem and taken the conflict to God, here's what I've done. I've taken my journal out, gotten alone somewhere, and just said, "God, speak to me about the conflict I'm having in my marriage. I know, God, that I should love Lisa like Christ loved the Church. Please show me how to resolve this."

And God will begin to speak. I've never heard an audible voice, but I feel him speaking to my spirit. About 95 percent of the time, guess who is the one who ends up being convicted of the need to change? Me! When each person deals with his or her own junk first, it makes solving the relational conflict so much easier. It'll clear away the smoke and mirrors and reveal the real issue. And that's when you'll solve your problem.

So take your conflict to God in prayer. Before you react in anger, just chill, press the pause button, and take it to God.

Take It to the Other Person

The second thing you need to do is to take it to the other person. That seems obvious, doesn't it? But out of pride or anger or bitterness, we often neglect this important, yet obvious, step. You can't solve a two-party problem with just one person involved. Take it to your spouse. Take it to your friend. Take it to your girlfriend or boyfriend. Negotiate the issue in a neutral setting and have what I call a solution-driven conversation. When you deal with an issue—maybe about priorities, budgeting, gossip, or parenting—have a *solution*-driven conversation, not an *accusation*-driven conversation.

Remember, God wants the very best for us relationally. He wants us to have thriving marriages and dynamic friendships. When we do things his way, every relationship in our life will be better. When we don't, that's when the wheels start to come off.

TLC

Ephesians chapter 4 in the New Testament is basically a treatise on conflict resolution. So, if you have a problem with that jerk at work, read Ephesians 4. If you have a problem with a family member, read Ephesians 4. If you have a problem with a teacher, coach, or friend, read Ephesians 4. In it you'll find the TLC principle that we need to end our relational battles. Most of us know *TLC* as meaning "tender loving care." That's a great acronym to help us express ourselves in our interpersonal relationships. But I'd like to amend this popular short form so that we can experience true conflict revolution in our lives. This TLC principle is straight from the apostle Paul in Ephesians 4.

Now, before I unpack TLC for you, I want you to think about your most recent relational conflict. How did you process this battle? How did you react? How did the other person react? Did the issue get resolved?

The TLC principle means I should resolve conflict truthfully, lovingly, and compassionately.

Truthfully

As a husband, I need to communicate truthfully to Lisa. The Bible tells us to speak truthfully, putting away falsehood (Ephesians 4:25). As a husband, I am to speak truthfully. As a friend, I am to speak truthfully. As a neighbor, pastor, and community member, I am to speak truthfully. I am to put off falsehood, strip it away, and speak truthfully.

Every time I speak truthfully, God shows up, God blesses, and God convicts. Every time I twist the truth, the evil one rears his ugly head and stirs up trouble. So, we have a choice. We can defer to God, allowing him to work on us from the inside out;

or we can defer to the evil one, allowing him to blow up the whole deal. We need to speak truthfully. Truth is the very fabric and framework of who God is.

Lovingly

Also, speak lovingly. The Bible tells us to speak the truth *"in love"* (Ephesians 4:15). Truth is great, but it can also be painful. Truth without love can be brutal. And love without truth is hypocrisy.

We need to wed truth and love together. You have to speak the truth *in love*, considering the well-being of the other person. A great proverb says that "a gentle answer turns away wrath, but a harsh word stirs up anger" (Proverbs 15:1).

I have a loud voice. My entire life people have said, "Ed, volume down." A couple of months ago, Lisa and I were in a little "marital discussion," and Lisa was keeping her voice even and steady as usual. She has this amazing ability to remain calm in the storm. But I was a little bit more animated, and I was talking a bit too loudly. All of a sudden, the phone rang, and I went from speaking loudly to my wife to a soothing and calm telephone voice. "Hello? Yes, how are you doing tonight? Yes, I'll pray about that. . . ."

I was amazed at how quickly my tone and voice changed! Here I was talking harshly to the woman that I love and to whom I pledged my life. Then some friend called, and I was much nicer to him than I was to my wife. Isn't that something? When we speak kind words to our spouse, our girlfriend or boyfriend, our fiancé, or our friend, we diffuse anger and make the move toward reconciliation. Even in conflict, words of truth—and words of love—change things. Conflict gets resolved.

Conflict can be like a leech or a ladder. It can suck the life out of a relationship or it can take you higher and higher. It can take any relationship to a higher plane than you ever thought possible.

Compassionately

Speak lovingly, truthfully, and compassionately. Put yourself in the other person's shoes. The Bible tells us to be kind and compassionate, forgiving one another like Christ forgave us (Ephesians 4:32). Forgive each other when you feel like it *and* when you don't.

Remember, any good relationship is built upon compassion that grows out of a mutual commitment. When you commit and give yourself to the other person, the feelings of love and forgiveness will follow. But you can't live by feelings alone. You cannot say, "Well, I just won't forgive you until I feel like it," because you might not ever *feel* like it. God commands us all to forgive each other. I'm commanded to forgive whether I feel like it or not. God asks us to speak words that will build each other up, not tear others down (Ephesians 4:29).

So, no matter what relationship I have committed myself to, I need to ask myself, "Am I being constructive? Am I communicating compassionately? Am I building this other person up?" These are tough but excellent questions for all of us.

The 20:1 Principle

I have a weakness for Krispy Kreme donuts. I truly believe that they are the greatest donuts in the entire universe. They come in a little box of temptation. I grew up on these things. They're so light and innocent looking, yet so bad for the waistline. Whenever I drive by Krispy Kreme and see the "Hot Dough-nuts Now" light on, I have to look the other way to avoid the urge to stop. Through years of personal "research," I've found that it takes me about twenty-one seconds to eat one of these hot donuts. That's got to be some kind of record, but remember, I also have an unfair advantage: a big mouth. I've also found out through more painful scientific research that it takes me twenty minutes of intense aerobic activity just to burn off the calories found in one little donut.

Psychological researchers have also determined that there is a twenty-to-one ratio when it comes to relational conflict. It takes twenty encouraging, positive, uplifting words just to negate one negative look or harsh word. It's the 20:1 principle. A lot of us ignore the impact of our words and body language on others. It's just like eating one harmless little Krispy Kreme donut. It's harmless until you eat it. Then, you'd better get ready to work it off.

Speaking of harsh words, the Bible says, "In your anger do not sin: Do not let the sun go down while you are still angry, and do not give the devil a foothold" (Ephesians 4:26–27).

It's those little shovelfuls of negativity that dig a relational grave. Every little angry word reaps enormous consequences. This is one of the main reasons why I challenge married couples to pray every night before they go to bed. It could be a five-second prayer or it could be a five-minute prayer. Just pray. You cannot pray if you have a problem in your marriage. You cannot pray unless you have been reconciled. So, do the work of recon-ciliation and keep short accounts between you and God, between you and your spouse, and between you and your friends. Settle your issues as quickly and as thoroughly as possible.

We have a beautiful oak tree in our backyard. Well, we *had* a beautiful oak tree. One day I noticed that this oak tree was turning dark and had several black splotches on it. A few weeks later, it was covered in black, the leaves fell off, and some limbs started falling off. It was so bad that half of the trunk split off. I'd never seen anything like that before. It was horrible. Obviously, some kind of disease had attacked the tree silently, methodically, little by little in the core, and eventually destroyed our magnificent oak tree. I don't know much about horticulture, but it doesn't take an expert to know that disease had totally torn the tree up from the inside out.

Relationships are the same way. We have these little problems and we think they're no big deal. But they tear our relationships apart from the inside. If the problems are unresolved, if you go to bed angry and don't resolve conflict, your relationships will collapse. So practice TLC and the 20:1 principle, and check out Ephesians 4—the best material you can read about learning what the ministry of reconciliation is all about.

When we defer to God and ask him to work on us from the inside out, we will understand how to fight the good fight, how to engage in relational battles in a godly manner. Poor relationships and powerhouse relationships all have the same issues. The difference comes from how the storms of conflict are processed. Great relationships handle conflict biblically, honestly, openly, truthfully, lovingly, and compassionately.

The sounds of war are all around us. When you have a couple of egocentric people together, there'll be explosions and eruptions of emotion. But if you handle conflict God's way, your conflict resolution can become a conflict *revolution*.

STOP AND THINK

FOLLOW THE SIGNS: All of us face conflict in our relationships. And each one of us has to settle our conflict with our Creator. With God's help, you can learn to better respond to the conflicts in your life.

CHECK THE MAP: "Be kind and compassionate to one another, forgiving each other, just as in Christ God forgave you" (Ephesians 4:32).

TAKE THE NEXT STEP: Which of the conflict-resolution styles described in this chapter best reflects how you handle conflict? What will it take to help improve the way you handle relational conflict so it is more constructive?

13

THE LOVE CONNECTION

I figure that the degree of difficulty in combining two lives ranks somewhere between rerouting a hurricane and finding a parking place in downtown Manhattan.

—CLAIRE CLONINGER

We live in a contract-crazy culture. We sign contracts with a credit card company and our local bank. We sign contracts when the cable guy comes to our door. We sign gym contracts every January to burn off the pounds we added during our holiday binges. We can't even replace our cell phone without a twenty-page contract. Everywhere you look you run into affidavits, stipulations, fine print, and the obligatory escape clauses. Some contracts are so complicated that we need to retain the services of a lawyer. Even that romantic, fairy-tale wedding requires a verbal and written contract. Talk about taking the romance away! Our culture is contract crazy.

A contract is an agreement between two parties. If you keep your end of the deal, I'll keep my end of the deal, and everything is cool. As long as my needs are met, as long as I'm happy, everything is fine. But the moment you mess me around, I have a contract to hold you accountable and keep you in line.

But how binding are these contracts? Business contracts are enforceable by law. Once you sign on the dotted line, you are responsible for fulfilling your obligation. If you don't, there may be a financial penalty, or you may even have to go to court.

But why are there so many contracts these days? You see, we live in a culture that fears commitment. We hate to be tied down. The last thing we want to do is join something. When we do make a commitment, it is often based on our feelings, and feelings change. When the wind blows, we want to be able to go somewhere else. Not long ago, a handshake was like a blood bond. Verbal contracts were all you needed. But that's not our world. These days, commitments must be enforced. That's why so many contracts have become a cultural necessity.

But what about relationships? Commitment is the foundation of any relationship. How do we enforce those commitments? How solid is the contract you signed on your wedding day? What about the commitment you made to your best friend?

Over the last twenty-four hours, three thousand couples have divorced. That's just one day! Imagine the carnage over a whole year. It seems that while marriage is still respected, it does not hold the same value as it once did. Many people seem to treat their marriage like a disposable camera; some studies suggest that as many as five out of ten couples will end up in divorce. Of the marriages that do survive, many of them report that they are miserable. If you put all the stats together, somewhere between 60 to 75 percent of first-time marriages effectively end up in the deep weeds.

How would you like to sign a lease contract on a new car knowing that the car would have trouble 75 percent of the time? How would you like to sign up for a two-year cell-phone contract knowing that 75 percent of your calls would be dropped? How would you like to purchase an airline ticket knowing that the airplane has a 75 percent chance of crashing and burning? I don't think too many of us would jump at the chance to sign our name to these contracts.

Let's go ahead and put the cards on the table. Seventy-five percent of all new marriages end up a mess. Should we just plan on divorce? Is that how our culture values the marriage contract we sign?

The thing is, if we view marriage as a contract, then we're in for some trouble. If it's only a piece of paper that can be manipulated, if it's like other contracts that can be voided by paying a penalty fee, then it's no wonder the stats are as depressing as they are.

But what if marriage wasn't built on a contract? What if marriage was built on something more solid?

God didn't create marriage as a contract between two emotionally charged people. God has something else in mind upon which we can all build our relationships.

As I listen to the popular talk-show gurus of mainstream media discuss marriage, I realize pretty quickly that something fundamental is missing in the way most of us view marriage. With all the information, books, periodicals, and shows about marriage, these media outlets rarely touch on the most important aspect of marriage. Rarely do they talk about the foundation of what it means to be a husband and a wife.

THE COVENANT

God says that marriage is not merely a human contract. God says throughout his Word that marriage is a covenant.

What's a covenant? The biblical meaning is a *blood bond of life and death*. It's an all-or-nothing commitment that was illustrated through the slaughtering of a sacrificial animal. If you described a covenant in our modern-day vernacular, you might say that a covenant is a contract on steroids, which is why I often refer to marriage as a commitment on steroids.

God has a great plan for every marriage. And he has a great plan for every relationship. If your marriage is unhappy, if you're miserable, if you're hanging on by a thread and thinking about divorce, embrace this concept called "covenant" and allow God to morph your marriage relationship from tired and hopeless into something that is full of vitality, creativity, and pleasure.

Making the Cut

There are many, many covenants throughout the Bible. Let's take a closer look at what is specifically involved in a covenant. Let me warn you, though—this is tough stuff. It isn't sweet and happy; it's messy. In a way, it's a lot like our relationships. They're not always pretty.

In biblical times, a covenant ceremony began when animals were cut in two, and the two halves were arranged opposite each other, leaving a gap. The Spirit of God would walk through the gap between the bloody halves of these animals, signifying that he was the initiator of this covenant (Genesis

15:9–21). God did this to symbolize the fact that he was completely trustworthy and that his love was unconditional. By initiating this covenant, God was illustrating that he would never break his word or let the other participant down. God initiated a covenant with Noah when he created the rainbow that continues to serve as a reminder of his promise. He initiated covenants with Abraham, Moses, David, and many others. And there are several examples of interpersonal covenants throughout the pages of Scripture. Ruth made a covenant with Naomi. David and Jonathan made a similar agreement.

In a covenant between two people, after cutting the animals and arranging the halves opposite to each other, the two parties would then put their backs against each another and solemnly walk through the path of the slain animals. The two parties would walk a figure-eight pattern through the blood-soaked path, signifying the eternal aspect of the covenant and the fact that they were dying to themselves, dying to their egos, and dying to their rights so they could be united together. As they walked this bloody path, it also symbolized the seriousness of their agreement. It illustrated the fact that if one of them turned their back on the covenant, they were essentially saying, "God, may you do to me what we have done to these animals if I fail to uphold this covenant. If we fail to come through, strike us dead as we have slain these animals." As a result, initiating a covenant was never entered into lightly.

After walking the path, they would make a public pronouncement detailing the terms of the covenant. By involving others in this ceremony, they added more accountability to their covenant. Many times, the covenant that was made between individuals extended to the families. In the biblical covenant between David and Jonathan, their covenant extended to their families (1 Samuel 18:3, 20:15; 2 Samuel 9:3,7; 21:7). Finally, the ceremony would conclude with a covenant meal together. They would eat each other's bread, symbolizing their unity and agreement.

A covenant had absolutely nothing to do with feelings, it was not an emotional decision, and it did not include escape clauses. It was about unbridled commitment—a blood bond for life.

Abraham's Covenant

Think about the two most intimate relationships known to man: our relationship with our Creator and our relationship with our spouse. Both are founded on covenants. Early in Genesis, God initiated a covenant with a very significant biblical character—Abraham (see Genesis 12:1–3).

Abraham was successful and was beginning to accumulate some serious wealth. (He was called *Abram* at this point in his life, but I am using Abraham throughout the illustration because this is the name God later gave him.) Then, out of the blue, God told Abraham to leave his country, his people, and the security of his family's household. That's it. He didn't tell him where to go; he just said, "Leave." The land God had in mind was a place that became known as the Promised Land. It was a land "flowing with milk and honey," a land called Canaan (Exodus 3:8).

For Abraham to leave home was not a minor operation. By our standards, he was seriously wealthy with a huge family, servants, and more than a few wagonloads of possessions. We're talking about a heavy hitter. If he were alive today, he would have a massive multimillion-dollar portfolio. Maybe he could be compared to someone like Bill Gates. For Abraham to move was more like a Fortune 500 company relocating than a family driving one moving van across state lines.

God told Abraham to leave for a land that he was going to show him. God promised to make Abraham into a great nation. He also promised to bless him. He promised to make Abraham's name great and that he would be a blessing to many. God also promised that those who brought harm to Abraham would be harmed by God. To top it off, God said that all the peoples of the earth would be blessed through him. Those are some serious promises!

A little while later, God made a covenant with Abraham (Genesis 15:18). Remember, a covenant is a blood bond of life and death. The blood of animals was spilled. The Spirit of God walked the walk of death on behalf of both parties. God initiated the covenant and then they began a new relationship together. They were united together through the terms of this covenant. Not long after this ceremony, Abraham's descendants actually inherited this land. In fact, many of the terms of this covenant are still in effect today.

David's Covenant

Let's press the fast-forward button and move to an example of two men initiating a covenant (see 1 Samuel 18:1–4). This example will show you what real friendship is all about, the friendship between Jonathan and David that we addressed in a previous chapter. David was the guy who killed that big behemoth, Goliath. Jonathan was the son of the unstable, troubled, schizophrenic King Saul. But David and Jonathan had an amazing bond of friendship.

David was in serious trouble. After his victory over Goliath,

Saul became very jealous of him. And Saul was more than a little bit disturbed mentally. After inviting David over for dinner one evening, Saul threw a javelin at his head. David's life was being threatened repeatedly by King Saul.

All the while, the king-in-waiting, Jonathan, formed a friendship with David. Though Jonathan was the family heir to the throne, he saw right through the antics of his father. Jonathan loved David as he loved himself. And he knew the desperate situation that David was in. It was at this time that Jonathan and David entered into a covenant together.

Jonathan took off his priestly robe and gave it to David. He also gave him his belt and his weapons. That sounds kind of strange, but let me unpack what this meant. When these two guys began a covenant relationship with each other, they exchanged robes. That was an illustration of the fact that they were giving 100 percent of themselves to each other. It's similar to the meaning behind giving someone "the shirt off your back." They also wore these big belts that held their weapons. I'm talking about Texas-sized belts! When they traded belts and traded their weapons, it showed that they were going to fight each other's enemies. David's problems were now Jonathan's problems and vice versa. It showed that they were committed to each other, no matter what happened. In effect, they were saying to each other, "I've got your back." That's what a covenant relationship is all about. How many friends do you have like this?

As I said earlier, there are different kinds of covenants. There are covenants between God and man. There are also interpersonal, friendship covenants. And there are marital covenants. Let's take a look at some of the symbols and meanings of the marriage ceremony and that covenant.

THE WEDDING CEREMONY

Throughout my ministry, I've officiated hundreds and hundreds of weddings. And I'm not sure if you realize this, but the tradition of a modern-day wedding reflects and illustrates God's covenant relationship with us. God takes marriage seriously.

In most wedding chapels, there is an aisle that divides the sanctuary in two. On one side you have the family and the friends of the bride. On the other side you have the family and the friends of the groom. The groom waits at the end of the wedding runner for his bride. The bride and groom make a public pronouncement of their intention to marry before God and witnesses. At the end of the ceremony, they walk back down the aisle as they are pronounced husband and wife. This walk symbolizes the walk of death, just like the participants of a covenant walked through the bloody halves of the animals in biblical times. In effect, they are telling everyone that they are dying to their selfish nature; they are dying to their autonomy and to their existing family structure. They are telling everyone that they are prepared to merge their two separate lives into one. It's an amazing visual picture of two independent people becoming one.

Usually there is a *white wedding runner*. This symbolizes that the wedding is a holy ceremony performed in the sight of God. It reflects an example in the Bible wherein God told Moses to take his sandals off because the ground he was standing on was holy (Exodus 3:5). Since God invented marriage, any wedding is a holy ceremony.

Have you ever wondered why the *parents* have a prominent

place in the wedding ceremony? It's because parents are an integral part of the covenant. They are blessing the marriage. They are acknowledging they have prepared their son or daughter for this time. Parents have the job of teaching and training their children to leave home and start a family of their own. They have the job of preparing their son or daughter to be independent. Children have the job of obeying and honoring their parents. It's a special relationship that is only for a short time, but with lifelong implications. Parents have been put in your life by God himself, and they are there for a reason—to help shape you and mold you into someone special. So honor them. They are a major part of this covenant commitment.

Why does the *groom wait for the bride* at the end of the wedding runner? It's because the groom is the initiator of the relationship. He has romanced her, he has dated her, he has most likely purchased a very expensive symbol of his love, and he has "popped the question" to her.

This is a picture of what Jesus Christ has done for us. Jesus took the initiative to enter into a relationship with us. We didn't deserve it, but he initiated the covenant. He voluntarily gave his life and spilled his blood on a rugged cross. He initiated the New Covenant just so you and I can respond to his unending love, just so we will say, "I do," to him. That's what Jesus did.

The groom waits for the bride, reflecting the leadership of Jesus. The Bible tells husbands to "love your wives, just as Christ loved the church . . ." (Ephesians 5:25). And the Bible tells us that Jesus loves each one of us unconditionally, no strings attached.

Next, we have the *bride walking down the aisle*. She takes that "walk of death" (I'm not joking; this covenant can only be broken by death itself), and this symbolizes the biblical idea of the covenant. Remember that the two halves of the animals were separated to create a path for the parties to walk through. As the bride walks toward the groom, she is representing the idea that she is dying to herself and becoming one flesh with her husband. She is dying to her past relationships (forsaking all others), and dying to ego (promising to love, honor, and cherish him). The groom is committing to the same things as he receives his bride at the end of the wedding runner.

Next, the *father gives his daughter away*. God gave Eve, the very first bride, as a gift to Adam (Genesis 2:22). This is the same picture that is presented when the father gives his daughter to the groom. Then the father brings the bride's and groom's hands together. As they bring their hands together, it signifies two independent people becoming one flesh.

A sermonette is followed by the vows. Please don't cheapen or enter into your vows flippantly. I read about one Hollywood couple who wrote their own vows and one of the things the bride promised was, "I'll make your favorite banana milkshake every day." That's not the kind of covenant God had in mind. And we all know how long most of those great Hollywood romances last. Unless you have a solid, theological background, I wouldn't recommend writing your own vows. You can have creativity and fun during the wedding ceremony, but remember that this time is a sacred covenant before God. The vows are a crucial part of the covenant, and as such, they should be straight from the Word of God.

"Until Death Do Us Part"
DAVE AND ELLEN'S STORY

I got to know Dave and Ellen many years ago. They were an extremely active couple who lived a very busy life with their two children, Daniel and Sara.

During a family vacation one spring, Ellen felt some discomfort in one of her legs. That next summer, she was diagnosed with a debilitating disease that slowly cuts the oxygen flow to the brain, sentencing the victim to a life completely dependent on others. The inevitable progression of this disease leads to death.

Three years after Ellen was diagnosed, she was confined to her bed and totally dependent upon others for everything from hygiene to health care. It was a huge shock to see this young, active woman become a prisoner in her own body.

To make matters worse, Dave's income was 100 percent commission. The amount of money he made to support his family was directly tied to the amount of time he spent in the field. Yet despite the sacrifices Dave and Ellen made, the Lord really blessed this family by providing for them in this crucial time.

Ellen has now gone to be with the Lord. But talking to Dave back then, I knew there were days when he wished he didn't have to do what he did. I knew there were days when he didn't want to get Ellen up. There were days when he didn't feel like bathing her. There were days when he didn't want to be the one who fed her and dressed her. I can imagine there were days when he wanted to go fishing with his buddies or play some golf.

Dave, though, never forgot the vows he made before God to his wife, Ellen, many years ago: "until death do us part." They weren't able to share physical intimacy in those later years, but they shared a depth of commitment that few of us will ever experience. And I know one thing for certain: God will honor that commitment in this life and the next.

The vows should reflect this covenant, this unconditional love, this picture that I've been painting. Remember, when people went into covenant relationship with one another in the Bible, it was a public event. Marriage should not be a little private thing. It should be public because you are entering into a covenant with God, with one another, with your parents, with your family, and with your friends. If you break the marital covenant, then you break a covenant with God, with each other, with your family, and with your friends. We're talking about collateral damage. That's why God hates divorce.

Maybe you didn't know how seriously God views marriage. Maybe you've been divorced and you're hurting from the breakup. If that's the case, there is good news. God loves you unconditionally. And he can heal you from the inside out. But don't internalize the emotions and pain you are feeling. Take them to Jesus and allow him to give you what you need to move on. You can start today, fresh and new. You can make a vow before God and say, "From this day forward, I'm going to do it God's way." Divorce is very serious, but it is not the unpardonable sin.

With this ring, I thee wed. I know rings are beautiful pieces of jewelry with maybe a nice diamond. But they represent the covenant commitment, this blood bond that is made. First, the ring is a precious piece of jewelry that symbolizes the special significance of the relationship. Second, the ring's circle is eternal, just like your unconditional love is eternal for each other. It showcases your covenant with your spouse. The groom loves the bride even when she's tough to love. The bride loves the groom even when he's stubborn and wrong at the same time. Happiness and all those touchy-feely emotions are not mentioned in biblical vows.

Too many people see it as just a contract based on feelings. That's precisely why so many marriages are messing up today. We think in terms of conditions. If our spouse does everything we want, then we'll hold up our end of the agreement. Unfortunately, there are many times that you'll need to come through even when your own needs aren't being met. That's just the way it is. People that bolt when they hit a tough spot tend to have a weak and shallow view of marriage. Marriage is about a covenant and a commitment, and the ring represents that reality. It's an outward symbol of the inward covenant we made before God. And when you wear your wedding ring, you are communicating to the world that you are spoken for, committed to someone else. It's a powerful symbol that communicates a powerful message.

Now, sometimes you'll have a *unity candle* in a wedding covenant. At most weddings, the bride takes her candle out of the candelabra and the groom takes his candle out so they can be used to light the unity candle. It represents two independent people becoming one. And then they extinguish the two separate candles.

One time I did the wedding of two bodybuilders. And when it came time for the unity candle, the candles got stuck in the candelabra. So, this big bodybuilder groom took the candles in his massive hands and bent them inward until they lit the middle unity candle. I thought that was both hilarious and highly creative!

Marriage takes some bending from time to time. Marriage is hard, but it really is worth it. Marriage is not the easiest thing—it's the hardest thing. But when it is done God's way in covenant, it will be the most joyful relationship that you will ever experience on this earth.

At the end of the wedding, the bride and groom will walk back down the aisle, signifying the fact that this covenant has been made, that they have a blood bond of life and death—a commitment on steroids.

Do you see the genius of God in the marriage ceremony? Do you see how important marriage is to him? If you are not experiencing the joy you want in your marriage relationship, maybe you aren't taking the commitment seriously enough. Are you viewing it as a holy covenant that mirrors the covenant God has made with us through Christ? It is only when you see marriage as an unshakable and sacred covenant—even when your feelings tell you otherwise—that you will be able to experience the kind of joy that God intended for this unique union between man and wife.

STOP AND THINK

FOLLOW THE SIGNS: Marriage is a contract on steroids. It is rooted in the practices of a sacrificial covenant, not on our feelings.

CHECK THE MAP: "Come now, let's make a covenant, you and I, and let it serve as a witness between us" (Genesis 31:44).

TAKE THE NEXT STEP: If you are married, spend time reflecting on the different covenants mentioned in this chapter. Now apply them to your marriage. What can you and your spouse do to recommit yourselves to one another?

If you are single, look for a good marriage in your church, in your family, or among your friends that can serve as a model for you as you wait for Mr. or Ms. Right to come along.

PART 4

WHY ARE YOU HERE?

All that we call human history—money, poverty, ambition, war, prostitution, classes, empires, slavery—[is] the long terrible story of man trying to find something other than God which will make him happy.

—C. S. Lewis

Until you have given up your self to Him you will not have a real self.

—C. S. Lewis

14

MIRROR IMAGE

*So long as man remains free he strives for nothing so
incessantly and painfully as to find someone to worship.*
—FYODOR DOSTOYEVSKY

We love mirrors. You might even say that we are mirror maniacs. It's hard to walk by one without taking at least a quick glance. Some do it in a clandestine fashion, giving a brief sideways look as they walk by. Others are more overt, walking right up and checking themselves out—their hair, teeth, clothes. You can't escape mirrors in our world today; they're everywhere. We use them to help us apply makeup, style our hair, insert contacts, straighten our tie, and any number of other personal chores. I've heard rumors that sometimes guys flex in front of mirrors. That's just a rumor, though.

Not only are mirrors a big part of the physical world, but they are huge in the spiritual world as well. God's original design was for us to reflect his image perfectly. We're made to be a mirror of God's glory, the crown of his creation. Humankind, though, missed its purpose in the creative order. When sin entered the world, it marred the mirror. It warped our reflection. And since that day, we've been struggling for significance, trying desperately to discover our purpose for living.

So many people make their way through this one and only life without ever understanding the true significance of mirrors. They don't know what life is all about. And because of that, their lives are a mere shadow of the crystal clear reflection God intended when we give our lives in worship to him.

The critical question we must ask ourselves is, Why am I here? Why do I exist? Am I just taking up space on a planet spinning into nowhere? Am I just here to perpetuate the species? To dream, scheme, and collect a pile of stuff? To do deals and die? Or is there a higher purpose for my life?

When God looked at humanity's marred mirror, he could have said, "Well, this is the end. Mankind has messed up; it's all over."

But God still wanted us to be his mirror, to reflect his glory and give our worship to him. So God commissioned Christ to live a perfect life on our behalf. As God in the flesh, Christ reflected the perfect image of God the Father, something we could not do.

During his ministry, Christ made this bold statement, "Anyone who has seen me has seen the Father" (John 14:9).

He was saying, "When you've seen me, you've seen God reflected perfectly in the mirror of my life." This was something no mere mortal could say. In other words, he was declaring himself to be God. This was a statement of his deity—a declaration that got him into trouble with the religious leaders of the day.

He was falsely accused of crimes he did not commit and was arrested, then tried before Pontius Pilate and nailed to a cross. Jesus suffered for six hours. And right before he died, he said, "It is finished" (John 19:30). The work had been done to restore us and redeem us.

And if we apply his finished work, he refinishes our mirrors to their original purpose—a vivid reflector of God's glory. Through our association with Jesus, the perfect God-man, our image can be restored to its former glory.

You might be asking, "What does it mean to reflect God's glory? What does it mean to glorify God?"

Glorifying God is all about reflecting his image. Creation reflects the glory of God. We do, too, when we're humble, when we exhibit the love of God in our relationships, when we manage our time and priorities well, when we're generous, when we take care of the bodies God has given us by eating right and exercising, and when we treat each other the way we would like to be treated. That's when we are the mirror image of God. We glorify God when we take the design he's given us and display it for the world to see. In one word it means what we have been talking about all along . . . worship.

WIRED FOR WORSHIP

Several years ago, I had the opportunity to attend a U2 concert with my brother. We had seats in the fourth row, and when we sat down, we were close enough to practically touch Bono, the lead singer. The sold-out concert was at the Astrodome in Houston. As we made our way through the thousands of people, I actually bumped into a group of people from my church. When they saw me, they all had the same "Is that our pastor at a rock concert?!" look on their faces. I wanted to say, "Yes, pastors listen to music, too."

During the concert, I looked around the stadium. I noticed that everyone was standing and singing, and some people were raising their hands and swaying back and forth. I think a few tears were even flowing. As I watched the audience enjoying the concert together, I looked at my brother and said, "Check this out! Look at all these people. What they're doing is worshipping!"

But at the same time, another thought occurred to me: these people were worshipping but they were focusing on the wrong object of worship. Great worship. Wrong object. These people who were giving it up for Bono and the band had great enthusiasm, great expressions of worship, but their focus was all messed up.

We all do that, don't we? We often have great worship going on, but for the wrong object. Whether it is our jobs, our cars, our houses, or even ourselves, we all worship something. And we do that because God has wired us that way. We're wired for worship. That desire to give our lives to something bigger and greater than ourselves is sewn into the very fabric and framework of who God created us to be.

Worship is an intense passion or esteem for the person, place, or thing we value most. It's an outward reflection of an inward connection—that thing that is nearest and dearest to our heart. And if we call ourselves children of God, he, more than anyone else, should be closest to our hearts and the one whom we should be worshipping.

We live in a world of worship. What you worship is what you serve. People will say they don't worship cars, homes, etc. But if that's the most important thing in your life, that's what you worship. God has instilled the desire for worship into us, so we will worship something—if not God, we'll transfer our worship to something else.

In the throne room of heaven before the creation of the world, Satan said, "Mirror, mirror, on the wall, who's the fairest of them all?" And he tempts us to do the same. We think we're here to worship ourselves. We think we're here to stare at and admire our own reflection. But we're wrong.

Our lives are tied to God—he's woven himself into our very being—so we don't have to be insecure about what's happening here and now. We don't have to live life under the circumstances; we can rise above them. Appreciative people, people who reflect the image and character of God, understand that God gave us everything and that our purpose is to glorify him. It's not a fake or showy thing about sounding holy on Sunday morning. It's an authentic lifestyle of worship—reflecting in every area of our lives that which is most important to us.

Don't misunderstand me. I'm not talking about a constant "Hallelujah Chorus" twenty-four hours a day, seven days a week. I am saying that everything we do should glorify God.

Our work should glorify God: "So whether you eat or drink or whatever you do, do it all for the glory of God" (1 Corinthians 10:31).

Our sexuality is for the glory of God: "Flee from sexual immorality. . . . You are not your own; you were bought at a price. Therefore honor God with your body" (1 Corinthians 6:18–20).

Our prayers glorify God: "And I will do whatever you ask in my name, so that the Son may bring glory to the Father" (John 14:13).

Our good deeds glorify God: "Let your light shine before

men, that they may see your good deeds and praise your Father in heaven" (Matthew 5:16).

We exist to reflect the glory of God, and when we fulfill this reason for living we will have the abundant life Jesus promised us. Conversely, when we don't reflect our Creator, we live a vacuous life.

At this point, I want to introduce several statements to bring some clarity to this whole idea of worship. If we're going to take the worship of God seriously, if we're going to make it a real part of our everyday lives, we need to understand what it is and isn't.

Worship Is Comprehensive

Worship is wrapped around everything we do, say, think, touch, and feel in this life. Some people erroneously think that worship is reserved for religious people, for those who bow their heads in a stained-glass cathedral or who sit in a lotus position and hum a mantra. That's not true.

Worship is all-encompassing; it's about lifestyle, not liturgy. It envelops our lives. It is intrinsic. Remember, we're wired for worship. We're made for the glory of God, and to glorify God simply means to worship the right object, to be passionate about him because he matters most.

All someone has to do is look at your calendar or checkbook, or maybe talk to your friends, and they can tell very quickly what you're passionate about. You might not call it worship, but let's scroll through some things that we are passionate about—a car, a house, a sport, money, position, a relationship, clothing, or looks. Maybe you worship the most popular god in our culture—you.

Even those who say they do not believe in God at all have put their faith in someone or something. The rationalist worships intellect or reason, believing only in the power of the mind to solve all of life's problems. The evolutionist worships the random nature of the universe, believing we are all here by chance. The materialist worships matter, believing in things he can touch, taste, feel, buy, or sell. The atheist worships himself as a god (with a small *g*), believing in the power of self and that God (with a capital G) is the figment of a weak-minded imagination.

The point is, we all worship. So what are you worshipping? What person, place, or thing has become a comprehensive part of your life? Is it God? If you aren't strategically and intentionally putting God at the center of your life, someone or something else will take his place.

Worship Is Competitive

When the apostle Paul was teaching in Athens, some of the Epicureans and Stoic philosophers took him to the Areopagus, which means a place of war or competition. They brought him to this place because they were compelled by his words. This area, though, was littered with idols. One in particular caught Paul's eye. The inscription on the bottom of the idol said, "To an Unknown God."

These Athenian men wanted to cover all their bases. They didn't want to omit a god, so they constructed an idol to make sure they didn't leave any deity out. Paul, prompted by the Spirit, had something to say to these polytheists, these worshippers of many gods. Let's look over the apostle's shoulder and listen to his words.

Now, picture him against the backdrop of all these idols saying these words, "The God who made the world and everything in it is the Lord of heaven and earth and does not live in temples built by hands. And he is not served by human hands, as if he needed anything" (Acts 17:24–25).

These people were duped into thinking that there was a god here and a god there and that God was part of some hallowed statue or maybe living in a holy temple.

Paul continues, ". . . because he himself gives all men life and breath and everything else. From one man he made every nation of men, that they should inhabit the whole earth; and he determined the times set for them and the exact places where they should live. God did this so that men would seek him and perhaps reach out for him and find him, though he is not far from each one of us" (Acts 17:25–27).

In other words, there is a search engine in our spirit, and we're going to grope and seek and try to find that person, place, or thing to worship. We're trying to find the ultimate object of worship. We're trying to get this desire quenched, and we move from one person, place, or thing to another trying to find the ultimate. What happens, though, is that we spend so much of our lives wasting our worship.

God pursues us, loves us, and wants to have a relationship with us because he knows if we chase after anything else other than him, if we're intensely passionate about anything else, we're going to waste our life. We're not going to fulfill the purpose for which he created us.

We have to understand that our world today is just like the Areopagus, a place where so many gods are vying for our devotion and attention. Yes, worship is comprehensive, but it's also played out on a very competitive court.

I ask you, Where is your Areopagus? Where is your competitive court? Is it around the neighborhood, the office complex? The sports arena?

So many of us have so many idols vying for our worship, and the enemy wants us to burn up our energy and time. He wants us to waste our worship and our lives because he knows when we bow the knee to the true God, when we become intensely passionate about him, we discover our reason for existence. And incredible things begin to happen.

Worship Is Continuous

God's plan for man is that every human being from every culture will worship him. We were made, bought, and brought into a relationship with Christ because of worship. We grow and develop into true worshippers here and then we become ultimate worshippers in heaven after we die. I'm not talking about some extended eternal church service. It's much more than that. It's a place of perpetual, perfect activity as we reflect the glory of God.

Worship starts with Christ's finished work on the cross and culminates in eternity when our mirrors are finally and eternally perfected into pristine reflectors of God's glory. Even now, though, we are being changed and perfected. In this life, we are continually being transformed into the person we will eventually become in eternity. In other words, Christ is repairing our cracked and dirty mirrors so that we will one day reflect him perfectly.

How is that transformation going in your life? Think back to the last week, all the things you said, the thoughts you processed, the places you went, the relationships you negotiated, the images you put before your eyes. If you could freeze-frame each one, what would God say? Would God look on that and say, "That's worship. That's a reflection of me," or not?

What kind of mirror are others seeing? Maybe a mirror that's cracked because of anger, that's foggy because of lust, that's marred because of bitterness, that's gaudy because of materialism?

Worship is not confined to a church campus. It's defined and refined by our lifestyle as well. It's a continuous, twenty-four/seven reality. If you wait until the weekend to worship, you're wasting most of your worship during the week.

AN AUDIENCE OF ONE

As a kid, I fell in love with the game of basketball, probably because my father loved it so much. Not only was he a pastor at the time, but he was also coaching a high school team. I have fond memories of shooting baskets with Dad in the backyard, as he worked on my shot, passing, and dribbling.

When I was about twelve years of age, I made an announcement to him. I said, "Dad, I want to play college basketball."

He said, "Good. You have to practice and be disciplined, but go for it, Ed."

So I went to basketball camps in the summer and practiced every day of the year to reach my goal. I think my dad saw just about every game I played from the time I was in third grade until I was a senior in high school. After my senior year, I received a full basketball scholarship to Florida State University and moved a thousand miles away from home. I found myself surrounded by a lot of incredible athletes, guys that were much better players than me. So I didn't get to play much my freshman year. I think that first year I played a total of seventeen minutes and thirty seconds the entire season. We made it to the mid-east regional, and I had the best seat in the house—the bench. I did, though, lead the nation in warm-up scoring. I counted my points every time I warmed up and averaged 72.5 points a game in warm-up. I'm pretty sure that record still stands.

During my sophomore year, my time finally came. We were preparing for a big game against Auburn, and one of the coaches told me that I would start. I thought, *This is it, from a benchwarmer to a starting position.* I picked up the phone and called my parents. Dad hopped a plane and flew to Birmingham, Alabama. He was one of the seventeen thousand people in that arena watching the Florida State Seminoles take on the Auburn Tigers. I remember scanning the crowd before the game trying to find Dad in the crowd. And when I saw him, we locked eyes for just a second. I got a little emotional because I thought of all the practicing, the time, the energy, the effort, and the money he had paid to put me into camp and other training situations.

There is no one else I would have wanted in that arena to watch me play more than my dad. In fact, as far as I was concerned, Dad was the only person in the audience that night. When I played in that game, I didn't care about the 16,999 people who were there. I only cared about pleasing and playing and performing for an audience of one.

That is worship. It is performing for an audience of one . . . our Father in heaven smiling over us.

As we conclude this chapter, I want you to declare war over your worship. I want you to ruthlessly remove those idols that reside in your Areopagus, those things that compete for your passion and make you waste your worship. And I want you to pray, "God, I want to serve you and worship you only." When you do that, you will discover the full life that results from being a mirror image.

STOP AND THINK

FOLLOW THE SIGNS: Why are we here? We're here to worship our Creator. And we do this through a lifestyle of commitment to his principles.

CHECK THE MAP: "Come, let us worship and bow down. Let us kneel before the Lord our maker, for he is our God. We are the people he watches over, the sheep under his care" (Psalm 95:6–7, NLT).

TAKE THE NEXT STEP: Devote thirty minutes for a time of personal worship. You can read the Bible and meditate on its truth. You can spend some time worshipping God through prayer. You can go for a walk and enjoy his creation. Journal about your experience.

15

A PLACE TO BELONG

The local church is the hope of the world.

—Bill Hybels

What is our reason for living? Why do we exist? We've already discovered the answer to that question: *We exist to worship God.* And we've seen throughout this book that worship is something that should transcend everything we do. When we understand that we are made in God's image for the purpose of worshipping him, it frees us up to live the way we were designed. But there are some looming questions that need to be addressed before we close this book. What is worship? Where do we worship? And how do we worship?

I like how the *New Bible Dictionary* defines the term *worship*. "Worship ('worth-ship') originally referred to the action of human beings in expressing homage to God because he is worthy of it. It covers such activities as adoration, thanksgiving, prayers of all kinds, the offering of sacrifice and the making of vows."[1] . . . Worship is human response to a gracious God, and it needs to be placed in this context if it is to be properly understood.

Worship is not a stained-glass building. It is not about empty rituals. Worship is a twenty-four-hour-a-day kind of commitment that results from a response to our understanding of God's character. We worship when we sync our lives by aligning our priorities with God's principles. We worship when we work and when we rest. We worship when we care for our physical and financial bottom line. When we read God's Word, his love letter to all of us, we worship him. When we pray, thanking him for his goodness and asking for his guidance, we are worshipping. But these are all individual responses of worship. So what's the big deal about church?

There is a corporate dimension to worship that we cannot ignore. It's great to do all that stuff on your own, but worship has a strong community aspect to it. One of the New Testament writers encouraged us to support and love other believers through an active participation in a local church (Hebrews 10:25). He was facing a challenge that still plagues us today: we tend to shut out other people and do the "Lone Ranger thing." Church participation was a problem two thousand years ago, and it's a problem today.

We've all been there before. It's not always easy belonging to a group. You'll have personality conflicts with certain people. You'll disagree with others. And sometimes, you'll just want to be on your own. Think about all the things you could be doing instead of going to church. There are outings to the

---

[1] D. R. W. Wood and I. H. Marshall, *New Bible Dictionary, 3rd ed.* (Downers Grove, IL: InterVarsity Press, 1996), 1250.

lake, golf games, and just spending the morning sleeping in. But God, our Creator, wants us to make that time on the weekend a priority because the local church is vital in God's economy. It's vital for us, and it's vital for God's plan for the world.

Before we talk about three unique characteristics of the local church, let me share a few things from the Bible concerning how Christians are related to the church. First, Christ is called the head of the body, which is another name for the church (1 Corinthians 12:12). Pastors, bishops, and various denominational leaders take a backseat to the Lord Jesus Christ. He is the one who created the church, and the one who leads the church. Second, in a related Scripture, Jesus is called the cornerstone of the church (Ephesians 2:20). In other words, he is also the foundation of the church. Third, Jesus is called the vine, and we are called his branches (John 15:1–11). Jesus is the divine source of strength, and he empowers his followers to bear fruit for God.

And what does the Bible say about his followers? First, those that want to follow Jesus Christ are asked to be baptized. The symbol of baptism is the manner in which the early Christians identified with the death, burial, and resurrection of Jesus. This is how they gained entrance into the church body (Romans 6:3–4). In other passages, believers are called the temple of God (Ephesians 2:21–22). Those who have received God's free gift of salvation have also been given the gift of his divine presence. Christians don't have to sacrifice animals in a temple as the Old Testament saints did. Christians are now the temple where God resides.

There is a lot of baggage when it comes to the word *church*. Some churches have let us down. Others have burned us or close friends of ours along the way. But the church is the place where the "manifold wisdom of God" resides (Ephesians

3:10). We cannot turn our backs on the church because it is through the church that Jesus, the head of the church, accomplishes his work in the world. Let's finish this chapter by looking at three unique characteristics of the local church.

The Local Church Is the Place Where Issues of the Heart Are Championed

Think about the marriage relationship with me for a moment. It is a relationship built on intimacy, trust, and love. A big component of a thriving marriage is time together. Time is needed to develop emotional intimacy and the resulting physical intimacy. The Bible commands us as husbands and wives to connect together strategically, intimately, and regularly. And God—the inventor of sex—tells husbands and wives not to deprive each other in this area (1 Corinthians 7:5). That may be the favorite verse of most men I know!

Marriage should be (and can be) satisfying, pleasurable, and downright fun. And when there is time invested to develop the relationship, it will blossom. Intimacy is a big part of being married. It is the manner in which a man and his bride can be one in spirit and body.

Imagine one of the partners telling the other, "You know, honey, we are just going to make love together once a month from now on. We'll reserve those intimate conversations and our deepest emotional moments for that one day each month." Do you think that would go over well? Do you think the other partner would really be into that? I think I can predict what the spouse would say. "Are you kidding me? No way; we're married. Come on!"

Intimacy in marriage is huge. It is where the deepest needs

are met. Intimate communication, romance, and an emotional and physical connection are needed to sustain a healthy marriage. That is where the deep issues of the heart are championed. The institution of marriage was created by God himself.

There is another institution where the issues of the heart should be championed and dissected and discussed and lived out: the church—the bride of Christ.

Have you ever wondered why God chose the church? I think right up front that God chose the church because it is a place where we can talk about and deal with those deep questions that affect us all.

Jesus has a very special connection with the church. He protects it, sustains it, and blesses the church. And the church is the manner in which God has chosen to carry out his plans for the world. He does work through individuals, but the church is set apart. This bride is one of unity and diversity. The church describes one entity that contains every believer in Jesus Christ across the world. So there is unity in what he is doing through this one, global church. But there is also diversity. The vast majority of references to *church* in the New Testament describe a specific, local community. The Church (universal) is made up of all local churches all over the world. It could be a large collection of believers in a city church or a smaller collection that meets in a house church. And in these local houses of worship, the issues of the heart are championed. The really weighty questions of life are answered from God's Word. Christ-followers are given support with their difficulties. And a world-view that is based on God's principles is presented to counter the vacuous worldviews that we find in the media.

Every time you drive past a church, you should hear wedding bells. I want you to think about the local church as you think about marriage. This is the beautiful relationship that Christ has initiated with his followers. Too many of us think we can get by with just showing up on Easter and Christmas. Some will get to church once a month—you'd never think of relating to your spouse in this manner. You can't have a good marriage this way, nor can you have a good connection to the bride of Christ this way. The church is to have an integral part in your life and mine.

You're not going to find a mature, growing believer who is disconnected from a local church. It is the place to be for anyone who wants to follow Jesus. It is one of the major priorities that we must revolve our week around. The church is a place for us to connect with people who have the same values, where we hear the profound issues of life discussed, dissected, and lived out. It is where we get into the real deal of life. God invented and sustains the church with his presence and power.

The Local Church Is the Place Where We Have a Common Source for Community

At church we receive a community base with like-minded people pursuing similar goals. But we also have a common source to this community. Our common source, our common denominator, is Jesus Christ. God (the Father, Son, and Holy Spirit) invented and encouraged interpersonal relationships. He also invented the church. If I am single, my base should be the church. If I am married, my base should be the church. If I am a student, it should be the church. If I am a child, it should be the church. If we don't place a huge priority on this community of believers, we'll set ourselves up for failure. It'll be only a matter of time before we head for a serious nosedive.

People today are looking for community. We are all looking for a deep and a real connection with other people.

Lisa and I were at a coffee shop two weeks ago. A woman with three children walked up to us and began to talk to us. I had never seen her before, nor had Lisa. She introduced us to her children and told us that they had just moved down to Texas from up north. She said she was lonely. Lisa and I heard her tell us about the struggles they'd had since the move. She said that she needed to connect with some people, that she needed some adult dialogue, and that her children needed friends.

I could sympathize with her situation. It's not easy to find good relationships in a new city. So we suggested that she check out our church because of the great relationships we've built through Fellowship Church. After a couple of minutes, she walked off, and I knew that our suggestion didn't take heart.

I turned to Lisa and said, "How sad. She will never understand true community unless she gets connected into a local church." If your community base is not the local church, it is just a matter of time before you do a nosedive relationally speaking. We're not wired to do life alone. Even if you have Hollywood looks and a stainless steel vault with millions of dollars, until you orient your life and deepest relationships around a local church, you will miss out.

God has set up two big pillars for all of us: the family and the church. Our families and our churches form the foundation for our society. As they go, so our way of life goes. If you want to live with purpose, orient your life around your local church. If you want to experience amazing relationships, get involved in the church. If you want to find a place where you can invest your time and money for maximum impact, the church is your

"It's Given Me a Home"
SAM'S STORY

"I accepted Christ while I was in college, but I never really found the place I was looking for. I never found a place to belong. And as a result, my faith began to waver. Without realizing it, I began to drift away from God. The people I hung out with, the things I did, and the places I went all told the world that I was not a follower of Jesus Christ. And ultimately I hit rock bottom.

"Despite the successful outside appearance of a great job and lots of 'friends,' I felt utterly and completely alone. Deep down I knew what the problem was. I was looking to other people and things to provide the comfort, hope, and security that can only come from God. I turned to alcohol and partying—anything to try to fill the void that I felt. But nothing worked. Nothing, that is, until I entered the church I currently attend.

"When I stepped through the doors of the church for the first time, I found what I had been searching for. I felt God's presence from the very first moment.

"I was so excited that I got involved in any area of the church I could—serving, small groups, the weekend service. I no longer felt like I had to hide my faith, and I wanted to run full on into a new life—a life full of purpose and direction.

"Getting involved in church has given me a new outlook on life. I don't have to hide anymore. I don't have to be afraid of my shortcomings. I am surrounded

> by people who want to help me succeed in every area of life and who want to help me grow. I've found a group of people who are committed to me. And I'm committed to them. What has church done for me? It's given me a home."

answer. The local church is the greatest thing going and growing. I really believe that.

The Local Church Is the Place Where True Life Change Takes Place

People always tell me that they want to do something that really matters. They tell me they want to leave a great legacy behind. I know I'm biased, but I truly believe that the local church is the place to be if you're looking for maximum impact. I cannot begin to tell you of all the lasting life change that I've seen over the last sixteen years in the church for which I've served as pastor. I've seen marriages rebuilt. I have seen healthy dating relationships full of purpose and direction. There have been thousands who have overcome addiction, emotional problems, and serious financial issues. I have watched thousands begin a new life as Christ-followers, and many more choose to live with more authenticity and maturity. The cycle of life change is all around me, and I can't explain any of it on a rational level. It all relates to God's supernatural work in and through his church.

Not too long ago, I was having lunch with a man who was telling me that he would soon be forty years old. He looked at me and said, "I have been successful during the first half of my life. I have the toys and the trinkets and have been successfully doing deals. I have made money. But recently God has been dealing with me over some issues, issues regarding the church and the second half of my life. I am beginning to wonder what will happen over the next twenty to thirty years. Am I just going to collect more toys and more trinkets, join more country clubs, stockpile more wealth, do more deals, and then die? Or am I going to be able to taste significance?" And then he began to tell me how he was in the process of leveraging his time, his resources, and his family to get more involved in the life of our church. What was going on? This man understood that the church is the true agent of lasting life change.

The local church is huge in God's economy. Not only does God command his followers to assemble together for corporate worship, but the church is also the place where the issues of the heart are championed; where true community takes place; and, finally, where true life change happens. Getting involved in a local church isn't always easy, but you can guarantee that church is the place to be if you want to follow God's Word and if you want to experience the incredible blessings that come from an active connection with the bride of Christ.

STOP AND THINK

FOLLOW THE SIGNS: The local church is also called the bride of Christ. It is the place where God asks his followers to join together to find answers for life, true community, and transformational life change.

CHECK THE MAP: "And let us consider how we may spur one another on toward love and good deeds. Let us not give up meeting together, as some are in the habit of doing, but let us encourage one another—and all the more as you see the Day approaching" (Hebrews 10:24–25).

TAKE THE NEXT STEP: What are your thoughts about the local church and its place in your life? Journal your thoughts and feelings and ask God to provide you with a local church where you can participate and be involved in his plans for the world.

16

AT YOUR SERVICE

You find the meaning in life by giving yourself away not by satisfying yourself. The most gratifying thing, at seventy-three years old, is to be able to think that your life was used to help others.

—CHUCK COLSON

Sixteen years ago we started Fellowship Church, and I was the first full-time staff member ever hired. I was flying solo. I remember when we bought our first typewriter, a used one. I remember when we hooked up our first phone. I remember when I knew the name of every person who attended, the names of their pets, and everything else about them. One night I was in a restaurant with some people from the church, and someone asked me a very profound question: "Ed, what are you going to do about a staff? You're all alone. What are you going to do?"

I thought for a second about what the Bible says about the church, and I answered, "You are going to be the staff. We can't pay you right now, but I need you to step up and help run this church." And because that dedicated and hardworking group of individuals gave of themselves through sacrificial service, Fellowship Church became what it is today. If it had not been for them, I probably wouldn't be writing this book right now. Their work and ministry paved the way for the church to grow and expand its influence across the world these past sixteen years.

If you're hooked into a local Body of Christ, it means that you should use your God-given skill set within that church. It means you are a player on the field of faith. It means you should leave the stands, hit the field, score touchdowns, make tackles, and make some great plays for God. Service and joy are intertwined in the Christian life. I don't believe we can ever experience the kind of joy we've been talking about in this book until we step outside of ourselves and serve others. That is the essence of the Christian life.

Jesus said, "Whoever wants to become great among you must be your servant." Then he added that "For even the Son of Man did not come to be served, but to serve, and to give his life as a ransom for many" (Mark 10:43–45). See those two words *serve* and *give*? When you net those words out, they form one all-encompassing term: *ministry*. And ministry simply means to use your God-given skill set on the field of faith.

Now, when I just recited the definition of *ministry*, you might have had this idea bounce into your brain: *Ministry, using your God-given skill set on the field of faith, is reserved for those ringers, those power players, those Billy Grahams and Mother Teresas and Rick Warrens of the world. Surely, ministry is not about ordinary, simple me.* If you're thinking that, you've got it all wrong. That doesn't hold water. The Bible says, from cover to cover, that when we're hooked into a fellowship, we should be exercising our gifts through ministry.

You might buy into this idea that ministry is for everyone. The notion that we're all to use our God-given skill set on the field of faith sounds good in theory. But why is it so important? Why should we do this if we want to live a life of outrageous, contagious joy? Well, over the next several pages, I'm going to list several reasons why all of us should involve ourselves in ministry.

WHY SERVE?

You're Drafted

First, you should get involved in ministry because you've been drafted. Just think about it. You are God's man. You are God's woman. He's watched you. He's had his eye on you. You're one of a kind. You're unique. God has made you a special way so you can make a unique impact in this world. Think about it this way: you are the greatest "you" there'll ever be in the universe. When you get to heaven, God's not going to ask why you weren't more like this person or that person. He's going to ask, "Why weren't you more like you?"

When I first started Fellowship Church, I was overwhelmed with the responsibility and the pressures of getting a young church off the ground. And I was really young for a senior pastor. Although God had gifted me as a speaker, I was bombarded with the pressures of delivering a biblical and relevant sermon week after week. So you know what I did? I listened to other speakers and learned from them. During the first few years, I listened to the sermon tapes of the pastors that I most admired. And that's not a bad thing; I think we can learn from others and then put our own creative spin on it.

One week I heard one of my favorite speakers say, "God is tired of your coldhearted servility!" (Yes, *servility* is actually a word!) And I tried to use that phrase in my sermon that weekend. The response I got from my audience was—you guessed it—just like coldhearted servility. What was the problem? I tried to be someone I was not. I was trying to be this other pastor even though he and I are very different. Let's just say his vocabulary is a little better than mine. And it would be just as ridiculous if this speaker tried to imitate some of the crazy things I like to do when I talk.

The point of that story is to encourage you to be the person God has made you, and only you, to advance his purposes in the world. If you aren't you, there's going to be a hole in history, a gap in creativity, a missing link within the church, the Body of Christ. In the Body of Christ, everybody is crucial. When even just one person is sitting on the sidelines, the whole church suffers.

The Bible says it this way, "For we are God's workmanship"—or you could say masterpiece—"created in Christ Jesus to do good works, which God prepared in advance for us to do" (Ephesians 2:10). I hope you noticed that phrase "to do." The Christian life is about A-C-T-I-O-N. God wants ACTION. What kind of action are you giving God? I've been drafted and you've been drafted to serve others in the name of Christ.

You're Gifted

Also, you are gifted in incredible ways. You've got some special talent given to you by God himself. The Bible tells us that God has given gifts to each of us from his great variety of spiritual gifts. And then it says this: "Manage them well, so that God's generosity can flow through you" (1 Peter 4:10, NLT). Manage your gifts, talents, and skill set well.

No one owns a thing. You don't own a thing, nor do I. No clothes, no cars, no houses—zilch, zero. It all belongs to God. We are just managers of what he's entrusted to us. The same is true of the talents and skill set he's given to us. I don't own my skills. I don't own my creativity. I don't own my innovation. God does.

So, if you try to be an owner, you are going to mess up your life. We're just managers. And God tells us to manage his stuff well. We have unique talents and unique skills, and we're to develop those skills to the best of our ability. While we develop them in the context of the local church, on God's playing field, it will be an act of worship to give back to God what he's given us. A nonparticipating, nonministering Christian is an oxymoron. If we're not using our gifts in ministry, we're taking up space; and we're taking up God's grace.

You're Coached

Not only are you drafted and gifted, you are also coached. You are playing the game of life for the ultimate coach, Christ himself. "Whatever you do, work at it with all your heart, as working for the Lord" (Colossians 3:23). Every time I say, "God, I want to please you. I'm working for you. I'm serving for you. You're the coach," then my life soars. But as soon as I begin to wonder what everyone else is thinking, what this group or that group says about me, that's when I mess up my purpose in life and rob myself of joy. It's about God. Remember, we're playing for an audience of one. = God

If we start looking for the applause of others every time we serve, we've missed the point. The real joy comes when we give our time, talent, and treasure solely to please God and show our love for him. As we keep our eyes on the coach, we'll be getting our cues and our kudos from the right place.

You're Graded

The final reason you should be involved in ministry is that you will be graded. Talk to NFL football players, and they'll tell you that they spend hour after hour watching films, evaluating their performance. They're grading, watching, holding each other accountable. "Hey, man, you missed that block. You missed that tackle." It's accountability time. It's time to be graded.

Those of us who know Christ personally will one day face God in eternity and be graded. I believe he's going to review the film of our lives, so to speak, and hold us accountable. "What did you do with what I gave you? What did you do with your stuff, with your resources, with your gifts and abilities? What did you do with your life?"

There will be greater rewards for those believers who develop their gifts compared to those who just sit back and do nothing. For those who really used their skill set on the playing field of life, God will say, "Well done, good and faithful servant; you were faithful over a few things, I will make you ruler over many things. Enter into the joy of your lord" (Matthew 25:21, NKJV).

For others it will be more like this: "I gifted you. I loved you. I tried to communicate to you. I tried to get to you. I led you to a great church in which to serve and minister, but you didn't do it." And you'll miss out. You'll miss out now on the joy you can receive through service, and you'll miss the rewards that God wants to give you in eternity. A mature Christian serves others as if serving Christ himself. "How can I help you? How can I serve you? How can I get outside of myself and do something for you? How can I work in the most important thing around: the local church?"

If you were to ask me how I've grown the most in my life, I would say without a doubt that it has been through service. That's how I have received the greatest blessings and joy in life. The joy of our salvation is made complete as we serve. As we minister, then we receive the rewards that accrue in our account for eternity.

THE BENEFITS OF SERVICE

Service sounds like such a daunting word. When we hear it, other words like *sacrifice* and *work* come to mind. We think in terms of giving up our wants and desires to help others. But while serving others does mean that we have to give up some things, we gain so much more in return. There is a lot of good stuff that will happen when you commit yourself to ministry. When you decide to get it in gear on the playing field of ministry, here are just a few of the awesome benefits you'll enjoy.

You Can Touch Eternity

As you walk the streets of heaven someday, using your skill set in an even greater way, you are likely to bump into someone who will say to you, "Hey, thank you for serving in the church. Because you loved me, because you spoke to me, because you

"I Can Continue to Help Shape the Future"
JACKIE'S STORY

"After Jesus rescued me from a very difficult situation, I knew that it was time for me to give back to him. Even though it had been several years since I had been involved in church, I was excited to dive back in and get involved in the student ministry at my church. I love working with junior and senior high school students because they are not children anymore, and yet they are far from becoming adults.

"These kids need the guidance of an outsider for the difficult things they don't want to talk about with their parents. It is a critical stage of life for each student. Not only are their bodies changing, but their entire world is shifting in their eyes. And being involved gives me the opportunity to help guide them and help them prevent mistakes, or I can hold their hands while they are going through the consequences of their mistakes.

"I know that my own kids will grow up, move out, and move on with their lives one day. But I also know that I can continue to help shape the future and impact hundreds of young lives each time I serve this age group. I never know how God may use one hug, prayer, or word of advice to impact a young person's life.

"My own son accepted Christ late in his teens, not through what I said or did, but through the Christian example of one of his school friends. I am so grateful for the teenager who helped lead my son to Christ that it motivates me to give back in the same way. I know that if I can equip 'my girls' to say and do the right things, they can be used to reach each one of their friends for Christ.

"From that standpoint, it's an amazing investment of my time. If I can impact just one girl to do the same thing, all the hours of prayer and counseling are well worth it.

"And more often than not, it's me that grows when I serve. Week by week, these kids make me a better person, a better mother, and a more devoted follower of Christ."

---

said, 'I will help you,' you paved the way for God's truth to be delivered into my life. And I became a Christ-follower because of you."

The stakes are sky high. We're not playing Monopoly, Trivial Pursuit, or tiddlywinks. We're talking heaven or hell. What we do, or don't do, has eternal ramifications. As you touch the lives of people through service, you are touching them for eternity.

I have the privilege of leading, without a doubt, one of the most unselfish and positive churches I've ever seen in my life. I'm amazed by the unselfish and positive attitudes that I see week after week at Fellowship Church. I relate it back to the word *fellowship*. The word refers to a bunch of fellows, men and women, rowing the ship. That's fellowship. The members of the church are so busy rowing, they're so busy in ministry, that they don't have enough time to rock the boat or whine or complain.

Find a place like that where you can be a part of the rowing team, where you can exercise your gifts within the ministry of a growing body of believers. There are hundreds of dynamic churches like that all over the country. Get connected and watch your life soar as you serve.

You Can Live Out True and Lasting Joy

As we serve, we can live out the joy of our salvation. As we get involved, as we bless others with what God has blessed us with, we will experience the greatest times of joy and growth in life. If you want to grow in your faith, you can study the Bible and pray. And you can attend church week after week. Those are definitely critical components to spiritual maturity. But those great things are simply meant to be fuel for ministry. If you only did these things, you'd become fat with knowledge and become useless as a minister of Jesus Christ. If you don't marry knowledge with service, you'll never experience the deep and lasting joy that Christ promises. When you begin to apply what you know through service, that's when your spiritual life will really soar.

That's why Jesus said, "Therefore everyone who hears these words of mine and puts them into practice is like a wise man who built his house on the rock" (Matthew 7:24). Don't just hear the truth, do it. That's why James, the half brother of Jesus, said, "Do not merely listen to the word, and so deceive yourselves. Do what it says" (James 1:22). Again, we're talking about action. It is through action that you can live *out* the joy that God has put *in* your heart.

When I think about service, I can't help but think of an employee who recently passed away at our church. As we listened to his closest friends speak about this man's life at his funeral, we were moved to tears as person after person shared funny stories and, more importantly, his purpose in life.

This man wasn't especially charismatic or good looking. Truth be told, he was happiest when he was left alone to do his work. This man struggled with different problems throughout his life, but in his sixties, he committed his life to the ministry of the local church.

He wasn't an eloquent speaker. And he wasn't a minister in the way we commonly think of the word. This man was gifted with skilled hands, and he used them well. He was on the maintenance staff of our church, and during the eulogies, each of his teammates shared how he came in early and stayed late to serve the Lord by fixing broken lights, painting scuffed walls, or working on some special carpentry project for a specific ministry. Again, he wasn't outwardly impressive, but his legacy casts a long, eternal shadow.

As I listened to his life story, I couldn't help but think, "Man, he got it! He served the Lord faithfully and is now hearing, 'Well done, good and faithful servant!'" And I wondered how many lives were impacted for eternity because of his faithful service. Our church was seen as an attractive place that honored the Lord because it was clean, safe, and well maintained. And all that is due to this man's faithful service.

Look closely at the word *ministry*. At the end of it is the word *try*. That's all God is asking of you, that you try. Start somewhere. Do something. Begin now. And, when you try, you'll have joy. God will smile as you exercise your gifts for his purposes.

STOP AND THINK

FOLLOW THE SIGNS: Service is an important component of a maturing faith. Giving back is one of the best ways to mimic the actions of Jesus, and to continue on the journey to everlasting joy.

CHECK THE MAP: "For even the Son of Man did not come to be served, but to serve, and to give his life as a ransom for many" (Mark 10:45).

TAKE THE NEXT STEP: Are you currently serving in a local church? If not, identify your gifts and match them to one of the ministries in your church.

17

BODY FOR GOD

I see my body as an instrument, rather than an ornament.
—ALANIS MORISSETTE

At the ripe age of fifteen, I began my journey as a driver. No longer was I confined to a ten-speed bike. This was my gateway to freedom. Of course, this gateway required some patience.

My father was the brave man who attempted the impossible. He tried his very best. But my poor dad, after only a few hours in the car with me, was left throwing his hands up in the air in surrender.

A couple of days later, I was in my backyard shooting the basketball around when I saw a long white car pull up in our driveway. I looked closer and noticed a sign that said, "Tony Sellers Easy Method Driving Training School." A guy hopped out with a starched jumpsuit and little horn-rimmed glasses. I thought he was Elton John. His hair was slicked back. He had "Tony" embroidered on his jumpsuit, a big clipboard in his hand, and he said, "Ed? Edwin Barry Young?"

Nervously I said, "Yes, I'm Ed."

He said, "Very nice to meet you. I am Tony Sellers with the Easy Driving Method and your dad told me to take care of you. So, please, get in the car."

I still remember the anxiety of climbing into this white car with this weird little guy named Tony Sellers. After the obligatory instructions to buckle my seat belt and take the "10 and 2" position on the steering wheel, Tony and I were off. As we navigated through my neighborhood without incident, he asked me if I was ready to tackle the freeway. Do you know any teenager who would say no?

And so Tony and I prepared to merge onto the freeway. He was pretty calm, cool, and collected, at least for the most part. After all, you can only be so calm when you're in the passenger seat of a car driven by a fifteen-year-old going sixty miles an hour!

He said to me, "Accelerate, accelerate, accelerate."

Not wanting to disappoint Mr. Sellers, I accelerated my way into the traffic. This was no problem whatsoever; my confidence was at an all-time high.

He said, "Now, Ed, we are going to change lanes. You need to put your blinker on, look in your rearview mirror and your side mirror, and then just ease over."

Check, check, and check. No problem. While I was easing over, I didn't realize that there was a car in my blind spot. In my defense, I didn't even know there was a "blind spot." I almost ran this guy off the road (at least that's what Tony told me). This other driver was giving me all kinds of enthusiastic gestures when he recovered from the assault of our white driver's training car.

Tony said, "Ed, what are you thinking? The blind spot, the blind spot. Why didn't you check your blind spot?"

I said, "Ummm . . . what blind spot, sir?"

"There is a blind spot in the car. There is a blind spot in every car, no matter what kind it is. You always have a blind spot. Look in the rearview mirror. Check your side mirrors. But Ed, never forget to turn your head and look back to check your blind spot."

EXPOSING THE BLIND SPOT

For too long, people have had a major blind spot when it comes to their view of the way God made us. Many of us have emphasized a person's soul over the body. We have been taught that the soul is spiritual and the body is merely physical. When there is talk about sin, it is the body that is seen as the culprit, not the soul. Christians have been guilty of this for hundreds of years. And this messed-up view of the body has caused us to miss out and misrepresent the way our bodies were made by our Creator.

"Why worry about the body," you may wonder. "Isn't talking about the body a little vain for a book like this? I mean, does God really care about buff bodies? You've already messed with my priorities and my schedule, now you're getting *really* personal. Now you're invading my refrigerator! Leave me alone already. Don't go there!"

I get that, and don't worry—I'm not going to raid your fridge. At the risk of pushing you over the edge, though, I am going to suggest that a proper view of your body is essential to accomplishing God's best for your life.

I wouldn't even attempt to talk about the importance of our bodies if I didn't see it working in my own life. Because of my commitment to health, my life at home with my wife and kids is on a higher trajectory. My life at work is more dynamic, as I have greater energy and clarity to tackle the many challenges of my workplace. Even my leisure is better.

I really believe this subject is vital for all of us. And that's why I decided to close this section by talking a little bit about our bodies. A complete picture of God's view for our bodies will give us the necessary octane to help us maximize our own health so we can carry out God's priorities for our lives through our daily commitments.

It's time to expose the blind spot and get real about our bodies.

OUR BODIES MATTER TO GOD

Blind spots cause a lot of damage, don't they? They cause serious injuries and will earn you more than a few obscene gestures. I believe the Christian community has a glaring, big, honking blind spot when it comes to physical authenticity. People talk about authentic spirituality, but we have neglected our physicality. We have done a great job emphasizing both the eternal quality of the soul and the spiritual nature of the soul. That's all fine and good, but we have some work to do to unite the body and soul together.

I grew up in the church, but would you believe I never heard a teaching series on the body? It wasn't until I did my own research a few years ago that all these thoughts came together to literally change my life. I was blown away by the amount of biblical references there are about our bodies. Scholars have talked about the body for quite some time, but the church has been strangely silent. Let's start by examining what God has to say about our bodies before we move on to discuss our response to God's amazing creation.

Created by God

So, what does God have to say about our bodies? For starters, our bodies are important because they are created by God. We see that in the first few chapters of the Bible, in the book of Genesis. Genesis chapter 2 is all about God's work in creation. It tells a story of God, the creative being who is responsible for everything we enjoy today. When he created the world, he didn't just wave a magic wand. The Bible says he spoke things into existence. He said, "Let there be light." And there was light.

Later on, God deviates from this pattern. He does his creative work with a more personal investment and "hands-on" approach (Genesis 2:7). The story relates that God rolled up his sleeves and literally got his hands dirty to create Adam and Eve.

God did more than just speak us into existence. He formed Adam with his own hands from the dust of the ground and breathed the divine breath of life into his nostrils. What about Eve? The Bible is equally clear that the first woman was made with that same kind of active participation in the creation process. I personally think that man was the rough draft and woman was the upgraded model!

When we compare our creation to the way animals and plants were created, we see that man is unique. We are created in the very image of God.

David, that famous Hebrew king in the Old Testament, wrote that our bodies are handcrafted by God: "For you created my inmost being; you knit me together in my mother's womb. I praise you because I am fearfully and wonderfully made; your works are wonderful, I know that full well" (Psalm 139:13–14). God knows us and forms us from inside the womb. He forms us right down to every last complex neuron in the brain and fiber that connects us together. The Bible says we are no fluke. We are actively created by God and known by God. The very best technology that exists in the world today cannot hold a candle to the complexity of the human body. Just ask an ophthalmologist about the complexity of the eye. Spend some time studying the anatomy and physiology of the body. You'll find pretty quickly that the body is a wonder.

The first reason why our bodies are so big in God's economy is that God himself fashioned the human body in his own likeness.

Worn by God

When I lived in Houston, I served for a while as chaplain of the Houston Astros baseball team. One particular game, I was approached by one of our perennial all-star players after the chapel service.

He said, "Ed, come here a second." I figured that my talk had upset him in some way, so I walked a little nervously over to him.

"Ed, I've got this pretty big shoe contract with Nike, and I've got a bunch of shoes. I want to give you a couple pairs of my game cleats."

He gave me two boxes of Nike game cleats. He had worn these cleats a little bit, but they were basically new, with his name embroidered on them with the team logo and everything. I was thinking to myself, "What am I going to do with these?" I didn't exactly see myself wearing these out to a nice dinner with Lisa. Nevertheless, I tried to show respect by saying, "Man, thank you very much. I really appreciate it."

I went home and thought some more about what I was going to do with those cleats. My wife Lisa suggested, "Ed, why don't you use them to mow the lawn?"

They were the best lawn shoes you have ever seen. I could turn on a dime. When it was a little bit wet, I had this insatiable urge to slide across the lawn like my all-star friend.

But I still had another pair sitting in my closet. So I decided to give that pair of cleats to a buddy of mine who was obsessed with baseball. I knew he would love them.

One day, when this friend was visiting, I said to him, "I want to give you something. These are the game cleats worn by (I named the all-star player), and I want you to have them."

This guy almost started crying. I've rarely ever seen someone so excited.

"Ed, are you sure you don't want them?"

"I'm sure. Enjoy."

"Ed, this is incredible! Thank you so much. These are real game cleats? Man, there is actual dirt from the Astros stadium on them! And look, it has his name and the Astros logo right there! You're not messing with me, right?"

"Nope, these are legit."

"I cannot thank you enough, Ed!"

Why was the guy so excited? Someone very valuable wore those cleats. It was one of his heroes. This relates to the second reason our bodies are so important. Not only did God fashion them with his own hands and breathe the breath of life into our nostrils, he also allowed his only Son to wear a body like ours. Our bodies matter to God because someone very valuable wore them. Someone special wore our cleats on the dusty streets of Judea, and his name is Jesus.

When Jesus became man, he put on human flesh, and that dignifies your body and mine (John 1:1–18). Churches around the world celebrate this event with services during the Christmas season each year. Lost in the shuffle of shopping lists and work parties is the reality that the God of creation became like us. Theologians call this the incarnation, the fact that God walked down the staircase of heaven with a baby in his arms. We celebrate the fact that Jesus was born in a humble farmhouse and was placed in a piece of ordinary farm furniture. Jesus cried and hungered like us. He walked and talked like us. He had a spinal cord and heart and lungs.

You and I share the same features that Jesus did. His body was made the same as the one that you and I enjoy today. The fact that he wore human skin gives great significance to your body and mine.

Indwelt by God

There is another reason our bodies matter. God not only created our bodies with his own hands. He not only sent Jesus to wear a body like ours. He also sent the third person of the Trinity, the Holy Spirit, to live within us (1 Corinthians 6:19–20). Believers are united to God through Jesus Christ. The Holy Spirit was sent to teach believers about truth and help them to become more like Christ. In fact, one of the key descriptions of the Holy Spirit is "the Helper" in the Bible (John 14:16, 14:26, 15:26, 16:7, NKJV).

A theme of Paul's writing is to honor God with your body

or "temple." In the Old Testament, the writers talked about God being in the tabernacle and the temple. These were the dwelling places where the Creator met with his creation. It's where followers of God hung out to worship him. In the New Testament, we have something a little different. The New Testament says that God does not live in the house anymore. He is not confined to a temple or tabernacle anymore. The place where God now dwells is in our bodies. Believers in Jesus are the housing for the Spirit of God. Our bodies matter because they are housing for the Holy Spirit. That's the third reason our bodies matter to God.

Let me summarize all this. I don't want you to miss this. In the Old Testament, God was in the house. In the New Testament, God was out of the house. Further in the New Testament, it says that *you are the house*. We are the dwelling place of the Holy Spirit of God. Let that sink in for a minute. Your body is the house of God.

Jesus is not just passing through your life or mine. He is not just spending two or three hours. Once we invite him into our lives, he takes up residence in the form of the Holy Spirit. He infiltrates our lives completely to clean out our junk and make us more like Jesus. Because of that, we should not trash our bodies. God calls our bodies "temples." We should use our bodies as a place of worship because God himself resides within us. Does that change the way you view your body? It should.

Some people play this dichotomization game where they separate the spirit, the soul, and the body. These same people have suggested that our bodies are evil, but our spirits and soul are holy. But when you look at the biblical evidence, there is a complex unity between spirit, soul, and body. God uses each of these elements to communicate his love to you and me. He expects us to use everything—spirit, soul, and body—to live the life we were created to live. This means that the way we treat our bodies has huge implications for our spirituality. All believers in Christ are given the righteousness of Christ. Christians are holy in spirit, soul, and body. Because the living God dwells in our "house," we should do everything in our power to make it a place where God can use us to our full potential.

Resurrected by God

The final reason our bodies matter to God concerns the afterlife. As a pastor, one of the most difficult questions that people ask me goes something like this, "Ed, what will our bodies look like when we get to heaven?"

People ask me that all the time, and here is my answer. You might want to get a pad of paper out and get ready to take notes. This is going to be deep. Are you ready? The answer is: I don't know.

Unfortunately the Bible isn't clear about this particular point. There just isn't much biblical evidence to make a clear case for what our bodies will look like in heaven.

I do know this, though, for certain. Our bodies will be resurrected in the afterlife. And that makes them valuable. Our flesh means something special in this life, but it also means something on the other side of the grave as well. A lot of things will be different in heaven, but we will still wear bodies of some kind. And so our physical bodies aren't just for this time and space; they will endure forever.

Yes, they will be different from what we have now. We will have new and improved bodies. The Bible is clear that we will all be living in new, glorified bodies in the afterlife. Jesus will be there in his resurrected body, and we will be there in ours. Our bodies identify us as God's special creation here on earth, and will identify us in heaven as well. It is clear that our bodies mean so much to God that Christ was sent to die and rise again to secure permanent and perfect new bodies for all of us.

God fashioned our bodies. Christ wore a body. The Holy Spirit lives in our bodies. And finally, our bodies will be resurrected. It's easy to see just how important our bodies are in God's economy. So, now the question for you becomes, "What role do I play to maximize this engineering marvel called the body?"

OUR BODIES ARE MADE FOR WORSHIP

Our bodies matter. The book of Romans says that our bodies can and should be an act and expression of our love to God. To put it another way, they should be an *act of worship* (Romans 12:1).

The way we treat our bodies is not just a physical commitment; it is a spiritual reality. A lot of us have these hang-ups or blind spots about our body. We've already seen what God has to say about our bodies. We now need to apply this knowledge by taking care of ourselves through nutrition and exercise. Some of us worship our body by standing in front of the mirror for hours on end. We get our cues from *GQ*, *Cosmopolitan*, or *Glamour*, and it's messing us up. Eating disorders, self-esteem issues, and vanity are the fruits of these wacky messages from pop culture. Some of us may hate the way we look and will try to change this image of ourselves through extreme measures. A lot of us struggle with a lack of discipline when it comes to our nutrition and exercise. Very few of us are actually living our lives with worship in mind as we go through our daily grind. Again, we need to go back to what God says to correct these dangerous misconceptions.

I want you to remember something that may change the way you think about God and your body. We don't use worship for our bodies. We use our bodies for worship. In other words, our bodies weren't made to be worshipped; they were made to be given in worship to the One who created them. That means that everything I put into my body has a spiritual reality to it. When I exercise, I am not only making my physical body better but also worshipping my Creator. As we correct the blind spots we have concerning the body, it is my prayer that we will begin to use our bodies to worship God and become the people that he has created us to be.

I want you to keep this short but powerful phrase from Scripture in mind: "Honor God with your body" (1 Corinthians 6:20). The question that begs to be answered is, how? God tells me that he created my body and that he wants it to be used for worship. How am I supposed to do that?

Worship Through Nutrition

What if, as you were exiting your office building or shopping center, someone was standing there and handed you the key to a brand-new Porsche 911 GT2, a $191,000 marvel of German engineering? Everything is paid for: insurance, tax, title, and license.

How many of you would accept this primo automobile? You'd be missing out on the opportunity of a lifetime if you

"I Am Now Able to Use My Body the Way God Designed It"

LISA'S STORY

"Food had always been a source of comfort for me, a stress reliever. I loved junk food. Lots of it. At twenty-one I found myself pregnant and facing a serious crisis in my marriage. I turned to fast food for therapy. And, because I was pregnant, I thought I could eat anything I wanted any time I wanted. I thought I'd lose the sixty pounds when I gave birth. When I went back to the doctor for my six-week checkup after delivering my girl, I found out that I was pregnant again. That meant more stress and more food.

"For the next several years, I tried everything to lose the weight. I joined different gyms and weight-loss programs, and even went to the doctor looking for a quick fix. None of it worked because I was still trying to fill a God-shaped hole with food.

"After the birth of my third daughter (and an additional forty pounds), I just decided that this was the person that God designed me to be, and I gave up trying to lose the weight. I became very bitter any time someone mentioned exercise or weight loss. And continuing my destructive path in the face of a failed marriage, I turned to the only thing I knew that could numb every emotion I had—more food.

"However, my relationship with Christ has changed everything. I now have the focus, strength, and hope to make the changes in my lifestyle I needed to make. He removed the anger, unforgiveness, resentment, and emptiness I had experienced for so long. And he filled me with his love.

"Through the encouragement of some strong Christian friends, I have now lost over ninety pounds and have a lot more energy than I ever remember having. I am now able to use my body the way God designed it. But more so than that, God has given me joy, healed me emotionally, and shown me how I can turn to him in the face of difficulties. He's also shown me that I need to take care of my body as an act of worship, not just for cosmetic reasons. To know that my lifestyle can be an act of worship for my Creator is an incredible motivator for me to stay with the program and continue to lose the weight."

didn't take it. What if, as this person gives you the keys, you are told: "You know, this Porsche is an engineering marvel. I ask you to do one thing for me: put super unleaded fuel in it. Don't ever put in regular unleaded, because if you do, it will burn up the engine eventually. Would you please do that?"

I think most of us would say, "Hey, that's the least I could do for this engineering marvel!"

What kind of fuel are you putting into the engineering marvel that God has given to you and me?

How do I honor God with my body? First, I put the right fuel in my body. I'm not going to bombard you with diets or a bunch of statistics because there are millions of them out there already. We don't struggle with a lack of nutritional knowledge; we struggle with nutrition. We know that we are supposed to limit our fats, salt, and sugars, but few of us are actually doing it. To check out more specific recommendations, go to the FDA website to see its new food pyramid.

My family and I often go out to lunch after church, and we'll see people from church at the restaurant. They'll sit down at the table and grab a menu and order some super deluxe nachos with extra cheese, some chicken-fried steak, a soft drink, and for dessert, cheesecake with a bottomless cup of coffee. And what amazes me is that, as the food is served, they'll bow their heads and pray something like this: "Dear Lord, bless this food to the nourishment of our bodies."

Now, don't get me wrong; I think we should thank God for the food and ask him to bless it. But how can we ask God to bless unhealthy food like this to the nourishment of our bodies? Here's a suggestion: Pray *before* you order from the menu. Say, "God, help us to honor you as we order," and then order with the phrase "honor God with your body" in the frontal lobe of your mind.

A couple of years ago I preached a message on nutrition. Right after that message, I became public enemy number one to all the junk-food junkies in the area. A clandestine movement began: "Donuts Anonymous." Twinkie support groups were popping up everywhere. We found that our dinner invitations started to disappear. No one invited Lisa and me to dinner because they thought we only drank carrot juice and ate grilled swordfish.

I am not saying that you cannot enjoy your favorite steak and baked potato or even those super deluxe nachos and chicken-fried steak now and then. I like that stuff as much as the next person. But I eat those foods only on rare occasions.

Why? I want to present my body as an opportunity to worship God. And I know that if I treat my body like he designed it, my body will respond to all the challenges of my busy workweek. I have seen in my own life that taking care of my body is another great way to take care of the increasing demands on my already busy schedule. I'm confident that I wouldn't be where I am today if God hadn't shown me these truths about my physical body. I've seen how taking care of my body has spiritual and pragmatic implications. There's no way I could be the husband, father, pastor, author, speaker, and leader I am without a commitment to the body God has given me.

In the Old Testament sacrificial system, the priests and people would sacrifice the cleanest and the very best animals. The same is true for us. We have the opportunity to give God our very best by presenting our bodies as living sacrifices. When we do that, we can be used as a tool in the hands of God. But if I'm dumping trash into my system and neglecting my exercise program, I won't be honoring God, and I certainly won't be able to handle the high stress of my busy schedule.

Worship Through Exercise

The second important aspect of physical worship is exercise. Our bodies are truly a work of art. The complexity of the body is still beyond the understanding of even the brightest minds. But these works of art were not meant to hang in an art gallery or sit in an office chair. Our bodies are meant to be used, to be worked. Much like the Porsche 911 GT2, we can only truly enjoy the engineering marvel we have been given by getting on the autobahn. We do better when we are revving up our RPMs and burning up the fuel in our systems.

Go back to that beautiful Porsche. If we had a Porsche, would we keep it in the garage, locked up? I know I'd only lock it up during vacation or a severe storm. You've got to drive a fine automobile like that because the engine is made to rumble, it's made to really fly. Our bodies are made to go, they're made to rumble. I'm talking about regular exercise.

The FDA has advised that adults need thirty minutes of moderate exercise most days each week. It should be a lifestyle decision to get out there almost every day to walk, run, or go to the gym. Those who are overweight need a minimum of sixty minutes in their regular exercise regimen to start losing weight. I would not be wasting your time talking about this stuff if it were just for vanity. Using our bodies for worship is a biblical principle that we are missing in our overindulgent culture. We are getting the wrong messages from GQ, Cosmopolitan, and Glamour. Our bodies are not objects to be exploited. Our bodies are temples, literally housing for God himself. And these "temples" are made for worship.

Now, most of us feel that our schedules are so full that we need all the rest we can get. Believe me, I'm right there with you. We think we simply can't justify adding exercise to tire us out further when we can barely keep pace as it is. When it comes to exercise, a lot of us believe that it steals time away from our schedules. However, the reverse is actually true. When we exercise, we have more energy—more energy to do other things we need to do.

Let's make a commitment to honor God with the way we eat and the way we exercise. After all, we have been given something a lot better than a Porsche 911 GT2. The body that God has given to you and me is an engineering marvel that we should use to the best of our ability as an act of worship for our Creator. And when we do honor God, he'll add extra octane to our system that will take us to greater heights in everything we do. Remember, even small tweaks in your routine can take you to giant peaks.

STOP AND THINK

FOLLOW THE SIGNS: God is deeply concerned about the condition of your body. Our bodies are unique masterpieces that are made in the image of God. And we can honor our Creator with our bodies through a commitment to nutrition and exercise. An added benefit to taking care of our bodies is the extra energy and stress management we'll gain to combat the rigors of our busy schedules.

CHECK THE MAP: "Do you not know that your body is a temple of the Holy Spirit, who is in you, whom you have received from God? You are not your own; you were bought at a price. Therefore honor God with your body" (1 Corinthians 6:19–20).

"Therefore, I urge you, brothers, in view of God's mercy, to offer your bodies as living sacrifices, holy and pleasing to God—this is your spiritual act of worship" (Romans 12:1).

TAKE THE NEXT STEP: Look at the government's food pyramid (http://mypyramid.gov/) and consider its recommendation to do thirty minutes of moderate exercise most days of the week. How are you doing? What have you eaten in the past twenty-four hours? Have you engaged in at least thirty minutes of physical activity? If you are not there yet, set some realistic goals that will help you get closer to this ideal. And starting today, begin to achieve those goals toward a healthier you.

PART 5

WHAT ARE YOU WORKING FOR?

Happiness is not in the mere possession of money;
it lies in the joy of achievement, in the thrill of creative effort.
—FRANKLIN D. ROOSEVELT

Take rest; a field that has rested gives a bountiful crop.
—OVID (43 B.C.–A.D. 17)

18

MUTUAL FUN

*Success is not the key to happiness. Happiness is the key
to success. If you love what you are doing, you will be successful.*
—ALBERT SCHWEITZER

The adrenaline was pumping and our hearts were pounding as we feverishly paddled down the Snake River. Our guide, Dave, barked out orders to us as we negotiated the rapids. "Paddle left. Paddle right," he would say. We had a white-knuckled grip on our paddles as we tried to stay afloat in the angry water. We couldn't believe the intensity of this alleged "leisure" activity. After we made it through each section, Dave would turn to us and say, "Great job! Now, relax. Isn't this fun, guys?" As we relaxed our aching arms, we tried to soak up the beauty of our surroundings, but not for long.

Almost immediately another section came up. The wilder the rapid, the more he tried to encourage us. "Hey, we are dialed in now. We are paddling great. We are going big," he would tell us. Though we got bounced around quite a bit, we conquered yet another section. When our favorite command (to relax) was heard, I turned around to look at Dave for a moment or two. It wasn't hard to tell that he lived for this. He could do this all day long and not get tired. There was no way he would ever be bored. There was no doubt that Dave was experiencing vocational fulfillment. But just to make sure, I asked him. "Dave, how do you like your work?"

He answered, "I absolutely love it."

Dave is one of the best guides around. He is married to Sandy, a nurse who is successful in her own right, and they also have two kids. He loves his job, and he loves his wife and kids. After years of dedicated service to the rafting company, his supervisor took note and promoted Dave. Now he is the lead guide of the company, and business is booming. People from California and all over the Southwest are flooding to this river. Dave is repeatedly told that he has brought these visitors more fun than they've had in years. He gets fired up when he hears things like that. The more people come, the more Dave wants to be part of the action.

Meanwhile, back at the local hospital, Sandy is doing well in her own job. Her fellow nurses love her attitude, and the doctors seem to really value her opinions. Even though she performs the same tasks day after day, she truly loves what she does. She knows that people are placing their lives in her hands. Her work requires accuracy and discipline, two things she has in spades. Last month, Sandy won Employee of the Month for the second time this year. It gives her great satisfaction to know that her hard work is appreciated.

Dave and Sandy have a lot of things going for them. They are healthy, young, and talented, and share a great family. They also experience true satisfaction in the workplace. This is a phenomenon that is becoming increasingly rare these days.

How about you? Are you fulfilled in your work? You might be surprised to read what the Bible has to say about this thing called "work."

THE GIFT OF WORK

To look at what God says about it, we have to go back to Genesis. We've been going back there a lot, haven't we? There's a good reason for that. Genesis is the book of beginnings. It chronicles the beginning of everything we know today. And in that pattern, we can figure out a lot about what God intended for his creation.

Many of us have the wrong idea when it comes to work. A lot of us think that work was given to us as a punishment for the rebellion of Adam and Eve against God. We think that God made us to enjoy leisure and stress-free living, and the first couple messed it all up when they ate that forbidden piece of fruit. But it all comes down to timing. Did God create work for mankind before or after their rebellion?

If you go back to the creation account in Genesis 1–3, you'll find that work was part of God's original plan. Before they rebelled against God's authority, Adam and Eve were given the gift of work (Genesis 2:15). God gave them the blessing of finding fulfillment through their work. They were given the gift and freedom to create, a quality that they shared with God. They were given the freedom to be productive in their own way.

After they sinned, God did not take away this gift of work, but he did throw a wrench into his initial plan. His original plan was for them to enjoy everything he created for them in a utopian setting. But, as a result of their sin, work became more difficult. Now Eve would have terrible labor pains in the work of delivering children. Adam would have to endure the back-breaking chore of growing his own food in less fertile ground that was susceptible to weeds and insects. This was part of the curse (Genesis 3:16–19). But the gift of work remained the same. Creativity and fulfillment in their work was still very much a part of their existence after their sin.

God could have made work some benign, boring activity, void of any productivity or fulfillment. But he didn't. He gave us work as a *gift*. God wants us to find fun and fulfillment in our various fields of labor. Based on the creation story, we can see that our work is good. When we work hard and produce something, it pleases God. When we use our God-given inge-nuity to create something unique, we demonstrate that we are made in the image of God. It makes God's heart beat faster to see the people that he made with his own hands being fulfilled in their work—and having fun while doing it. Is this a radical idea to you? Did you know you should have fun with your work? If it is a gift from God, why wouldn't it be fun?

I suspect that a lot of you are not experiencing job satisfac-tion. You are not experiencing the great rewards of work. I want to touch on a few aspects of finding fulfillment at work. Instead of giving you a long list, I want to limit myself to just a few suggestions that I feel are the most important. This is not an exhaustive list, but it's a good start. If you want to have fun and reap the benefits and rewards of work, put these suggestions into practice. I'm not promising that every day is going to be a bed of roses, but these suggestions will bring you closer to ex-periencing work that is satisfying and fulfilling.

Develop a Passion-Based Profession

The first aspect of finding fulfillment at work is that we have got to develop a passion-based profession. Our creator tells us that we should enjoy hard work (1 Corinthians 12:4, 6). We are also told that we are all uniquely geared and gifted. You have talents that I don't have, and I have talents that you don't have. And these talents express and expose themselves at a surprisingly young age.

Moms and dads who understand this principle give their children the room to experiment with their God-given talents. In other words, they provide their kids with structure and freedom (within a context of discipline) so that their kids have the opportunity to express their talents and allow them to develop it. Children with parents who support them like this will figure out early what their passions are. And one day, they can further develop these gifts as they enjoy a passion-based profession. I truly believe that God wants our profession to be a natural expression of how he wired us.

One night, when the circus came to town, I took my family to the Ringling Brothers and Barnum & Bailey Circus. It was a sight to see. There is so much action going on at the same time! One act that mesmerized me was a family of trapeze artists. Each family member—even the kids—had a unique flair on the trapeze and used their talents to create one great show. What was really amazing was how they encouraged each other's high-flying abilities. Plus, it was clear they were really enjoying themselves as they worked. Watching those kids swing from the trapeze with smiles on their faces made me believe that that family was living out what the writer of Proverbs expressed long ago: "Train a child in the

way he should go, and when he is old he will not turn from it"
(Proverbs 22:6).

As parents, we are supposed to give our children room to
allow them to maneuver and to show their high-flying abilities. We need to help children discover the way they should go
in life. But we cannot force our children into a passion or, ultimately, a profession. We have to try to help them identify their
creative bent, encourage them as they try to exercise their gifts,
and give them countless opportunities to fail and to succeed.
Kids need help identifying their gifts, but most of all, they need
our love and support so they can dare to do great things with
their gifts.

If you talk to anybody who is experiencing job fulfillment,
I can guarantee you that he or she is using the same gifts that
were expressed early in life. There is no question about it. God
just hammered me with this point a year ago.

Bruce, a friend I grew up with, came into town for business. I had not seen Bruce for twenty-five years, but he came to
one of our church services. After the service, he walked up to
me and said, "Ed, do you remember me?" Even though he was
sporting a goatee, I still recognized him from my childhood.
We embraced and relived some of our old times together. He
said, "I haven't hung out with you for twenty-five years. But,
you know, you are pretty much doing the same thing you did
as a kid. You are telling stories. The only difference is that now
you are doing it in front of thousands of people."

I thought that was kind of funny, but the more I thought
about what he said, the more I realized how right he was. God
used that brief conversation to once again confirm my calling
as a pastor. I can't tell you how incredible it is to be in a profession where I am utilizing my gifts on a consistent basis. The

energy that I get from being at work is incredible. And I wouldn't want it any other way.

Now some of you are saying, "I am not in a passion-based profession. In fact, I don't know what my gifts are. Skill set? What is that? Surely, I'm not that gifted. I don't have any special abilities like you, Ed." Yes, you do! You are absolutely gifted by God. Do you want to know how to discover what you are good at?

Let me offer two suggestions that have helped me, and many others, develop a passion-based profession. First, I want you to look back over your life at the successes—the things that you have done really, really well. Then try to isolate the gifts that were used to produce those achievements. Maybe it was the gift of organization, as you coordinated a charity drive in your community. Maybe it was the gift of administration, the gift of leadership, the gift of service, the gift of music, or the gift of poetry. I don't know what it is, but think about those gifts. Then you may be able to say, "Ah-ha, now I see where my passion might lie."

When we trace our greatest successes, we will also find our greatest fulfillment. Our gifts and passions not only make us successful but also fulfill us, because we are exercising our God-given strengths and passions.

The second suggestion to help you discover a passion-based profession is this: Talk to a trusted friend about your life. Talk to someone who knows you and loves you and ask, "Tell me what I am good at. What are my strengths, what are my weaknesses? Help me figure them out." Other people tend to have a more objective view of your life, and are often better at identifying these strengths and weaknesses. They will offer you clues to what your gifts and passions are.

"Life Is More About Climbing the Lifeguard Stand than the Corporate Ladder"
ERIC'S STORY

When he graduated cum laude with an accounting degree, Eric was certain he was headed down the right road. His father and his grandfather were both accountants, and they had everything he thought he wanted. To him, they were successful. Accounting would be the road to his success.

Eric was hired by a prominent accounting firm in Texas immediately after graduating and was given a starting salary that would be the envy of almost everyone. Things seemed to be headed the right way.

But there was no passion, no drive, no fulfillment in his work. In fact, the thought of going to work drained him. It wasn't that he minded working long hours. In fact, Eric knew all about hard work and long hours. Some of his fondest memories came from the hard work he did during his high school and college days as a swim instructor and lifeguard at the local YMCA. Those days were filled with a sense of joy and accomplishment. Helping people gain confidence in the water energized him and gave him a sense of direction and purpose.

Six months after beginning a potentially "successful" career in the field of accounting, Eric quit. He walked out of that office complex, walked into the nearest YMCA, and was hired as a lifeguard for the following spring and summer seasons.

Eric is now the director of a YMCA. For him, life is more about climbing the lifeguard stand than the corporate ladder. And if you were to ask him if he thinks he is successful, Eric would tell you emphatically, "Yes!"

I want to say a word here to those who manage people. When was the last time you sat down with those people under your authority, under your chain of command, and asked them to write their ultimate job description? Ask them about their passions, their greatest accomplishments, and their desires for the future. As you challenge them with this assignment, they will begin to write and verbalize some powerful things. Within this ultimate job description, it won't be hard to energize their passions, and you can be the one to help them develop a passion-based profession. If you are able to identify their passion and match it to their position, you will have workers who are more fulfilled and workers who are having a greater degree of fun in your workplace. The greatest benefit to you, however, is higher productivity and a more satisfied team with which to work alongside.

Cultivate Community-Based Relationships

As I was talking to a good friend of mine about his work, the subject of job fulfillment came up. I asked him about his childhood and, sure enough, it correlated to what he is doing now. He said something, though, that made an important point. "You know, I have really great friends at work. I have rewarding relationships with a lot of people. What I do is obviously important, but the relationships are a huge part of my job."

That is the second aspect of finding fulfillment at work. If you want your job to be fun and fulfilling, whether you are a mother working at home with a couple of preschoolers, a construction worker, or an executive of a Fortune 500 company, you have got to have the "relationship thing" happening. You could have a passion-based profession that allows you to utilize your God-given talents, but if your workplace is contaminated by toxic relationships—a problem with the boss or a problem with a co-worker—you're not going to find fulfillment. Yes, gifts are important. Yes, following your passion is important. But it is equally important that you enjoy satisfying, gratifying relationships within the context of your work.

Can you imagine doing something 40 hours a week, 2,000 hours a year, and 90,000 hours over a lifetime with people whom you dislike? I've heard people say, "I have worked with that egomaniacal, tyrannical, self-promoting so-and-so for fifteen years, and I have hated every day I was there." Or, "I've worked in that environment for eight years, and every time she walked by my office space, I just cringed." Life is too short to go through a career like that. God wants us to cultivate relationships at work. He has put each of us in our particular sphere to influence, impact, and inspire others for his purposes and his reputation. We can't do that if we can't stand the people around us.

I like what the management expert Peter Drucker says about conflict in the workplace. He says, "When you have a couple of objects close together and they are rubbing up against each other, there's always going to be conflict. So plan on it." Take a quick panoramic view of the people you work with. Do you have any frosty feelings? Are you harboring any hurt? I challenge you to go back and reread chapter 12, "Relational Revolution," and follow the wisdom found in the Bible to experience a revolution in resolving conflict at work.

Also, pray that God will help you cultivate healthy relationships at work. Make your relationships a prayer priority. Pray for that person who you think is an egomaniacal tyrant. Pray for that person who makes you cringe when she walks by your work space. Pray for an opportunity to help these people out. Pray for strength so you can speak encouraging words to them. I believe that God really wants all of us to be proactive when it comes to conflict resolution. You have a part to play to make it better and not worse. Prayer is huge. When you begin to pray for these so-called jerks, God will begin to soften your heart and will do some wonderful and mighty things in and through you.

Pursue Worship-Based Work

Not only should fulfilling work involve your passion and include great relationships, it should also be a worship-based endeavor. God tells us in the Bible that everything we do should be an act of worship (Colossians 3:23–24).

I hear a lot of people coming out of church saying, "Wow, wasn't the worship great today? I really felt the presence of God as I was worshipping." That's all well and good, but worship is not meant to be compartmentalized into some sixty- or seventy-minute time slot on Sunday. Worship should infiltrate every aspect of our lives, especially our work. If God gave us the gift and command to work, we should work as an expression of worship to our Creator. Therefore, when you work, no matter what profession you choose (whether it's changing diapers, filling out reports, selling insurance policies, coaching junior varsity football, or grading papers), it is God himself that you're serving. If that doesn't change your attitude about work, I don't know what will.

When you begin to understand what true worship is, then every activity you engage in at home, at church, or at the marketplace becomes an expression of your gratitude and love to an almighty God. I firmly believe that followers of Christ should be the people who are cranking out CDs, seminars, and books on excellence. Ultimately, we are not working for a human boss, or a specific dollar amount; we are working for our Creator, who endowed us with our gifts and passions. We are working for God. So whatever I do, whatever you do, we should do it to the glory and honor and praise of God.

Have you ever recognized your work as worship-based? It will change the course of your career. It will change how you feel about that difficult person at work. It will change your drive and motivation. It will help energize you with more endurance and discipline.

Are you experiencing fulfillment at work? Find and develop a passion-based profession. Look out for work relationships that you can cultivate over the long haul. Finally, pursue worship-based work. Work can and should be fun. It should be mutually fulfilling. God will be there smiling as you express your gifts. And you will have the time of your life as you use creativity and discipline to develop your God-given gifts and see how far they will take you.

STOP AND THINK

FOLLOW THE SIGNS: Work was not created for our misery; it was created for our fulfillment. And when we trace the past and talk to trusted friends, we can identify the calling for which God created us to flourish. Ultimately, work is an opportunity for us to worship our Creator.

CHECK THE MAP: "Whatever you do, work at it with all your heart, as working for the Lord, not for men, since you know that you will receive an inheritance from the Lord as a reward. It is the Lord Christ you are serving" (Colossians 3:23–24).

TAKE THE NEXT STEP: If you haven't already discovered your career calling, look back at your passions and your achievements and talk to some trusted friends for insight. If you are where you're supposed to be, commit yourself to work diligently as an expression of worship to your Creator.

19

MOTION SICKNESS

Man must shape his tools lest they shape him.

—ARTHUR MILLER

I absolutely love to fish. If it's got gills and fins, I'll go after it. One of my favorite ways to fish is off the stern of a boat in the middle of the ocean. A few years ago I had the opportunity to take a group of college students on a once-in-a-lifetime trip to the Cayman Islands, where I could do some fishing.

One of the sponsors on the trip was a good friend of mine named Lee. Lee is a take-charge kind of a guy who was given the task of making sure everyone signed up for any extra-curricular activities they wanted to do while we were on the islands—biking, scuba diving, parasailing, snorkeling, or, of course, deep-sea fishing.

As the students signed up for the different activities, Lee—who had never been deep-sea fishing in his life—made it his personal responsibility to warn everyone about the dangers of motion sickness while deep-sea fishing. He warned us that when the boat started tossing and turning, the captain wasn't going to turn around. Student after student shrugged off Lee's warning and signed up for the open-water adventure.

The morning of the big fishing trip finally arrived. Everyone gathered their gear and loaded it onto the boat, and we headed out for the day. As we began to hit wave after wave on the open seas, I noticed that Lee wasn't looking so good. The exhaust from the twin diesel engines combined with the odor of fish bait and the rocking of the ship was about all Lee's stomach could take. And with every passing swell, his face turned a darker shade of green. Lee, forgetting his own words to the students, shamelessly begged the captain to turn the ship around. But his request was ignored and we continued to head farther and farther out to sea. Finally, the inevitable happened. Lee made a mad dash to the side of the ship and . . . let it all go.

Motion sickness: It's often associated with the erratic movement of a boat, a car, an airplane, or an amusement park ride that knocks one's equilibrium out of whack, resulting in severe nausea.

Many people right now are being tossed and turned by the erratic movement of a different kind. A lot of us are negotiating wave after wave of workaholism.

Maybe you find your vocational equilibrium out of sync and off balance. Maybe you feel like you are unsuccessfully negotiating the currents as the undertow of our corporate culture slowly drags you out to sea. Maybe you feel the effects of motion sickness, and it's only a matter of time before you have to make a mad dash to the edge, lean your head over the side, and let it all go. Maybe you are desperately crying out to stop the boat, turn back, and head for shore. Yet, the boat never turns around.

Instead, you continue working each day at a breakneck speed, your life careening dangerously out of control. You may have started out chasing the American dream to find happiness, but that dream has quickly become a workaholic nightmare.

Workaholism is a real and present danger today. Just ask the heartbroken spouse who is constantly put on the back burner because of her husband's business ventures. Ask the child who rarely sees his mother during the daylight hours. Or ask the student who stands alone at the curb cradling a soccer ball under her arm until Mom or Dad arrives twenty minutes late—again.

Motion sickness is real. And it can damage, devastate, and ultimately destroy your life and the lives of those around you.

Work itself is not a bad thing. In fact, work is a very good thing. After all, God created work; it was his idea. And God created us with a capacity, a yearning, for work.

In the previous chapter, I said that God could have created work as some benign and boring activity, void of any productivity, but he didn't. He made work enjoyable and constructive so that we could have an avenue to utilize our gifts, talents, aptitudes, and abilities to mirror his image. And if we do it right, work can be gratifying, satisfying, and energizing.

But too many of us overload ourselves, taking on too much and finding ourselves stressed out and beaten down by the juggling act. We let work become all-consuming and all-important, causing our other priorities to take a backseat. And what is supposed to be fun and fulfilling instead makes us miserable.

WORKAHOLISM:
AN AGE-OLD PROBLEM

Workaholism isn't something new to our world. It's been around for thousands of years. We can even find examples of it in the Bible.

The Jewish patriarch, Moses—the man responsible for freeing the entire nation of Israel from Egyptian bondage—found himself pounded by the waves of work. Like most workaholics, Moses thought he was indispensable. And he was convinced that his self-worth came from the amount of work he accomplished. He thought that there was no way anyone else could do what he was doing, so he tried to handle all of the Israelite business by himself.

Imagine the president of the United States trying to run the country without delegating anything. No cabinet, no legal counsel, no legislative branch, no administrative assistants, no law enforcement . . . nothing. Just one man running the entire show.

That's exactly what Moses tried to do.

He would counsel someone and then console someone else. He tried to give economic advice to someone and then encourage someone else. He tried to settle legal disputes and then iron out marital issues. He wanted to control the nation's finances as well as the community's farming needs.

But Moses was spread thin and quickly wearing down. The various demands he faced—pulling him first in one direction, then in another—were just too much. I can just picture Moses running for the side of the boat, ready to let it all go.

Finally, someone stepped in and recognized that Moses's

workaholic behavior was not only tearing him up inside but also limiting the burgeoning nation of Israel. Jethro, Moses's father-in-law, told Moses that he couldn't do it all by himself. He instructed his son-in-law to delegate tasks to others. He wisely recognized that if Moses let others handle minor issues, he could continue to do the important work that God commanded him to do.

We see the same struggle with workaholism in the New Testament. One day, Jesus made a statement to a group of Jewish people that snapped their heads and dropped their jaws. "For what will it profit a man if he gains the whole world and forfeits his soul?" (Matthew 16:26, NASB).

That one question forced people to doubt everything they had ever been taught about working hard for a living. *Is it a good thing to spend three or four decades striving and straining to gain the world at the expense of losing your soul for eternity?*

As far as these first-century Jewish people were concerned, they weren't risking their souls. They were just chasing the dream and trying to keep up with the Joneses. For them, their profession and their spiritual condition were distinctly separate. But Jesus came along and told them the two are inseparably intertwined. You cannot strive so hard for worldly gain without running the risk of losing your soul.

Jesus' question cuts to the quick for all people in all cultures. It hits us between the eyes as it did for his Jewish audience in the first century. Many highly intelligent and competent men and women today are risking that same exchange—their souls for worldly profit. It's the end result of workaholism. So often we sacrifice everything on the altar of corporate worship. And we gamble our own eternity for the temporary thrills and chills of earthly satisfaction.

The *Heart* of the Matter

Workaholism is an easy addiction to recognize. It's not difficult to identify the people who struggle with it. So rather than focusing on the telltale signs of a workaholic, I want to focus on the underlying cause of workaholism.

We tend to label workaholics as type A personalities, or as people who love to be on top of their game. And because they are so competitive and love their jobs, we reason that workaholics are happiest when they are working. So, do some people become workaholics because working makes them happy? Sure, that's a plausible reason for workaholism. But I don't believe that is the most common cause for this widespread cultural malady. After more than two decades in ministry and watching family after family fall prey to the negative effects of overwork and overcommitment, I have found the most significant driving force behind workaholism to be insecurity.

Workaholics, for a variety of reasons, are insecure about themselves. And that insecurity leads them to believe they can find happiness and self-esteem through their work. The more they work, the better they feel about themselves. But those feelings of security, those feelings of happiness, ebb and flow with the reactions of the people with whom and for whom they work. And when contentment and joy are ultimately based on happy feelings that ebb and flow, true joy is elusive.

Many workaholics also seem to have a warped sense of love. Many of them grew up in homes where love was conditional. The amount of love they received at home was always dependent on the level of their performance—on the field, in the classroom, at the recital, or on the stage. And yet, no matter how well they performed or how hard they worked, they always heard they could have done a little bit better.

So now, as adults, these workaholics are desperately trying to hear the words of confirmation and affirmation they never heard as children. And these workaholics push harder and harder at work to hear those words from the people around them.

And sadly, workaholics pass this warped mentality on to their families. Workaholics are usually very successful and can provide their families with a lot of stuff, a mass of material possessions. And they often use these expensive possessions as an expression of their love. But so often, the children don't understand why Mommy or Daddy isn't around, and the husband or wife is crying out for the affection, attention, and presence of their absentee spouse, only to be "bought off" with trinkets purchased at the expense of family time.

I've seen firsthand the devastation and destruction workaholism has on kids. I've seen the rebellion, hurt, and anger that build up in the heart of a child because of the absence of a parent who works too much. A few years back, I was privileged enough to go on a beach retreat with our student ministry to South Padre Island, Texas. We had a group of about seven hundred high school students, and I remember sitting on the beach one night as the sun was setting. I was talking to a teenage boy who was absolutely heartbroken. When I asked him what was bothering him, he began to cry almost uncontrollably, explaining that his parents didn't love him. He told me that they were never around, and they let him get away with anything and everything.

I knew this kid's parents. I knew they loved him. But they were workaholics. And from the surface, it seemed like they loved their careers more than their children. Did they love their children? Of course. But because they parented with a freewheeling style that shunned discipline and expressed love through material possessions, their true feelings of affection were hidden. This boy's parents had a warped sense of love, and although they showered him with all the latest gadgets and toys, all he wanted was their undivided time and attention. The families of workaholics are screaming for the attention that the workaholic mom or dad continues to withhold.

A LITTLE R&B CAN MAKE IT BETTER

So what's the cure for this sickness called workaholism? What can you do to prevent your family, your career, your life, from being torn apart by motion sickness? How can you stop the elusive pursuit of corporate happiness and discover real joy in your work life?

God has given us some amazing advice that will encourage you, challenge you, and help you get your vocational equilibrium back in sync, back in balance, and in concert with his desire for your life. It just takes some R&B.

Refocus

R stands for *refocus*.

If you are around the fishing or boating communities much, you've undoubtedly heard the term *old salt*. An old salt is someone who has done a lot of fishing or work on boats and has been on the water for most of his life. Rarely does an old salt experience motion sickness, but he knows exactly how to overcome it.

If you talk to an old salt, he'll tell you that motion sickness is simply a problem of focus. When you bob up and down on the water, your focus is constantly shifting, and this affects the inner ear and messes up your equilibrium. So the best advice that an old salt has for anyone who is experiencing motion sickness is to refocus. Focus on something that is stationary, something that is fixed regardless of where your boat takes you. Find the horizon line. Or, if it's within eyesight, fixate on the land. If you focus on that stationary object, then everything else will come back into balance.

The same is true for workaholics. They have a focus problem. They are focused on their careers, on their performance. They are focused on hearing that they matter from this group or that group. They are focused on rewards and promotions.

But those things are always moving. They ebb and flow as the trends and profit margins shift. So to cure the sickness, they must first focus on the one thing that never changes—God's love.

Because workaholics typically grew up in homes where love was conditional, they often believe God's love works the same way. Yet God tells us over and over again that we don't have to earn his love. He loves us unconditionally. He tells us that we have been redeemed, that we are known by name, that we are his, and that we are precious to him. Just let all that sink in for a minute. Read through it again. Absorb it. Own it.

That's why he loves us. It's not because of anything we can do or anything we have accomplished.

Let me put it this way. *We are not loved by God because we are valuable; we are valuable because we are loved by God.*

You have been redeemed. God knows you by name. He even knows the exact number of hairs on your head (Matthew 10:30). And he loves you so much that he sent his only Son to die on a cross for your sins.

And when you begin to focus your life on the certainty of God's love for you, suddenly things begin to fall into perspective, and your motion sickness will subside.

The Bible gives us a great picture of what happens to the person who starts to refocus on God's unchanging love rather than the approval of man. "He is like a tree planted by streams of water, which yields its fruit in season and whose leaf does not wither. Whatever he does prospers" (Psalm 1:3).

That is God's amazing promise to you. If you want to be firmly rooted, if you want your life to be more than just an endless string of hours at the office, if you want your family and your friends to rely on you and know that you will be there for them, then it all starts with refocusing your life on God's love.

Break

B stands for *break*.

It is so easy to get overinvolved in your work, especially when you are passionate about what you do. I know because I've been there. But too many hours at the office, too many nights in the conference room, and too much time at the drawing board will cause more harm than good. You have got to take a break.

In your mind, limit the hours you are going to work *before* you get to the office. And settle in advance when you are going to take a break. Don't wait until you are in the middle of a melt-

"Jobs and Careers Come and Go"
SCOTT'S STORY

Scott knew all about hard work—and stress. When his father passed away in the summer of 1986, Scott moved from San Diego to Chicago to assume control of his late father's business. He became the managing editor of a local weekly newspaper. But his duties didn't end there. He was also the head salesman, reporter, photojournalist, prepress layout artist, and maintenance guy. The workload was so demanding that it was not uncommon for Scott to sleep at the office so he could save time driving home every night. Eventually Scott hired a staff to run the paper, and he moved to San Francisco to start a new career, although he continued as the bookkeeper for the newspaper.

Scott's lifestyle didn't slow down on the West Coast. He found a position with a youth soccer league and volunteered extra hours to organize international soccer matches between the U.S. national team and other countries. He would work a full day at his paid job and then work until 10 or 11 P.M., and often the weekends. During this time, he also got engaged and volunteered at a local church.

It wasn't long before his ambition and crazy schedule got the better of him. He began having chest pains and discovered that his cholesterol level had exceeded 210. His doctors warned him to change his lifestyle or prepare for more serious consequences. Fortunately for Scott, his fiancée, Diane, was by his side. She was often with him during those long, extra hours promoting the international matches. Her love and support were the driving forces behind Scott's desire to find balance in his life.

He has come to understand that while jobs and careers come and go, those significant relationships in life last forever.

---

down before you take a break. Do it regularly and strategically in order to maintain your edge at the office as well as at home.

Get away daily—even if it's just for a few minutes. Get outside, take a walk, get away from the office, and use that time to detach from work. Each week, choose a day when you do nothing that has to do with work. I don't suggest that you just sit on the couch and eat potato chips all day, but take a full day to relax. Do something that reenergizes you and gets you back in line with God, your family, your spouse. God tells us very explicitly to reserve one full day a week for him (Exodus 20:8–11). That's the day that you can refocus on him and gear up for the week ahead.

Also, take strategic breaks monthly and yearly. Get away for a weekend. If you're married, make that a weekend for just you and your spouse. In chapter 22 I'll talk more about vacations and how they can be either a benefit or a burden. You'll see how strategic vacations and breaks taken the right way can actually help your productivity during the rest of the year.

So often I hear people say they'd love to take a break, but they just can't afford it. I would argue that if you don't take regular breaks, you're going to get strung out and weaken your work performance, and you could eventually lose your job. So, when you look at it from that perspective, you can't afford *not* to take a break.

THE IDEAL

If anyone has ever faced the temptation to become a workaholic, it was Jesus Christ. Think about it. He had only thirty-six months to get his message of love and forgiveness out to the entire world—and this was before the existence of high-speed Internet and the BlackBerry. If anyone was ever justified in overworking or putting in a few too many hours on the job, Jesus Christ was that man. But Jesus knew what his real focus should be—God, his heavenly Father. And he recognized the necessity of taking time off. He realized that time off would reenergize him and give him an edge for when he returned to his work. Jesus knew that if he didn't focus on God, and if he didn't take breaks regularly, his schedule would break him.

Jesus lived in perfect balance between his work life (his public ministry) and his private, personal life. He was always in sync with his work, his values, and his purpose. Every time Christ did some intensive ministry work, he would follow up by taking a break. Sometimes he would take long walks by himself. He might build a fire and make breakfast. Or he would go fishing with his friends. Whatever it was, after working hard and feeling the emotional, physical, and spiritual strain, he would break away to reenergize and recharge. And because he did, Jesus avoided the dangerous possibility of overworking.

What a tremendous example for us in today's fast-paced,

move-it-or-lose-it,   the-early-bird-gets-the-worm   society! Christ put into effect some wonderful practices that are still relevant today. And to gain our footing back, to cure the cause of workaholism, we must follow his lead.

So how about it? Are you being tossed and turned by those erratic movements that cause motion sickness? Isn't it time you refocused, took a break, and got your professional and personal lives back in balance?

STOP AND THINK

FOLLOW THE SIGNS: Work has a tendency to hijack our priorities. We need to practice what Jesus modeled for us by focusing on God's principles and breaking away from our busy schedules to recalibrate our busy lives.

CHECK THE MAP: "What good will it be for a man if he gains the whole world, yet forfeits his soul? Or what can a man give in exchange for his soul?" (Matthew 16:26).

TAKE THE NEXT STEP: Track your hours at work last week. What conclusions can you draw from this exercise? Were you productive during your workday? Did you work too much or too little? How might your family respond if they were asked about your work habits?

20

STRESS AUDIT

Better to idle well than to work badly.

—Spanish proverb

I have to get something off of my chest: I am stressed out! Maybe you can relate.

As any parent can testify, life with kids can be more than a little hectic. With four children, I feel like I'm constantly under the gun. Between church involvement, work responsibilities, the everyday chores of life, and taking the kids to school and a variety of extracurricular activities, it's hard to find any time to relax. And finding time for Lisa and me to be alone takes all kinds of advanced planning. But we recognize the importance of our marriage and the need for time alone, so we are very intentional about scheduling a weekly date night into the three-ring circus that is our life.

Our oldest daughter is in college—stress. Our son is starting high school in a year—stress. And our eleven-year-old twin daughters are not only into basketball right now but also starting to get interested in boys—double stress!

And there's always yard work. And taking care of the dogs. And paying the bills. And maintaining the vehicles. And . . . and . . . and.

About now you're probably thinking, *Ed, relax! Stop stressing so much. It just sounds like you lead a busy life. Join the crowd. Everyone's busy. Everyone's stressed.*

But isn't that what we do? We take a panoramic photo of our lives, and the magnitude of everything around us seems so overwhelming. So we stress out.

We bury ourselves in a heaping mountain of stress, mostly because of the choices we make, and when we finally take some time to come up for air, we wonder, *How could I possibly relax? With everything going on and all I've got to worry about, I don't even have the time or energy to sit down for a peaceful meal at home with my family, much less to take a long enough break to figure out why I'm so stressed out!*

THREE AREAS OF STRESS

You know that life is stressful. I know that life is stressful. That's no new revelation. But if you consider all the anxiety and all the pressure and all the stress that we face, it boils down to three major areas. If we're going to bring some sanity back to our lives, we need to take a serious look at each of these three areas.

Relational stress is the first area. Whether you are single or married, adolescent or elderly, relational stress can take its toll. The stress of being married; raising children; and dealing with family, friends, neighbors, or co-workers is huge.

Another big pressure point in life is *financial* stress. Financial stress is so pervasive that it is the number one cause of divorce in our country. People are stressed out about their spending habits, saving habits, and investing habits. Mortgages, car payments, and credit card bills pile up until we can't seem to find our way to the top.

What about *occupational* stress? Who hasn't felt stress at the workplace? Maybe you deal with an unpleasant co-worker. Maybe it's a demanding and unreasonable boss. Or maybe you're in the middle of changing careers and you don't know which way to turn. You may even be at the top of your game, professionally speaking, but you don't know how to keep up with all the demands on your time.

So life is stressful.

At this point, I could take a very obvious and predictable path. I could break down the three stressors—relational stress, financial stress, and occupational stress. I could lay out some nice neat points that would help you deal with each one. I could then illustrate each one with some personal life experiences or humorous stories, and then direct you to some official-looking graphs and charts that would illustrate how to process stress.

But you didn't pick up this book just to get a few quips or bullet point ideas, or to look at some visually appealing graphs. That wouldn't help you *actually* deal with stress in your life today, now, in this moment. That would not help you get to the real heart of the matter. You need some hard, practical solutions to the difficult issues of life. We all do. And to find those solutions, I can think of no better place for us to turn than the Bible.

The Bible tells us that an anxious heart weighs us down (Proverbs 12:25). I think we can all relate to that. When we're stressed, it's almost as if there's a weight tied to our necks, dragging us deeper and deeper into the dark abyss. So what do we do about it? How do we untie that weight and set ourselves free from our stressful burden?

HANDLING STRESS

The apostle Paul knew all about stress. He penned a letter to a group of Christians who were dealing with some pressures of their own—they were freaking out from stress. And when Paul wrote the letter to the Philippians, he was literally chained to a Roman guard—he was a prisoner. Talk about stress! But Paul had a handle on it and provided some very relevant advice for us today.

Paul says, first of all, "Do not be anxious about anything" (Philippians 4:6).

How often have you dealt with something stressful just to have someone say to you, "Hey, just get a grip. Just deal with it"? We all know it's not that easy. Life is more complicated than that. So Paul dives deeper and gives us some insight on *how* to get a handle on our stress. Paul talks about some conditions that we must meet if we're going to deal with and process this stuff called stress.

Pray Right

Look at the rest of Philippians 4:6, "Do not be anxious about anything, but in everything, by prayer and petition, with thanksgiving, present your requests to God."

Processing stress starts with a conversation. Paul tells us that when stress strikes, we need to strike up a conversation with God.

A lot of us pretend that we know how to talk with God. We go to him when there's a situation we can't handle on our own. We go to him when we want something. We go to him and demand that he fix our problems. Or we turn prayer into a negotiation and make deals with him.

But to deal with stress, we've got to first learn to talk with God. We've got to pray right. How do we do that? Are we just supposed to rush to God with our to-do list and say, "God, do this. Do that. Oh, and by the way, thanks, God."

No. That's not the kind of prayer Paul is talking about.

The word *prayer* means devotion; it means adoration; it means worship. When we pray, we must express our love to God for who he is, what he has done, what he is doing, and what he is going to do. And it's not a one-way conversation. We don't talk *at* God. We talk *with* God. We share our fears, our joys, our desires, and our feelings with God.

Prayer is not something we do to tell God what to do or to inform him of what's going on in our lives. He already knows that stuff. We share all our feelings with God so that he can help us deal with them. We pray so that we can have a relationship with God that is deep and meaningful and real. It's a time when we take our eyes off ourselves and turn them to God. And it's a time when God can speak to us and help us get a handle on the situation.

When I pray, I'm giving up control to God. I'm handing the situation to him and telling him, "God, I can't handle this on my own. I need your help."

Right after prayer, Paul mentions the word *petition*. Basically, petition means asking God for things. It's part of prayer. Some of us are afraid to ask God for things. Or we don't think he'll answer. We may have our to-do list for him, but we don't ever get around to *asking* him for things. But that's exactly what he wants from us. He is our God, but he is also called our Father (James 1:17). And all good fathers want to give good things to their children.

Several years ago I was talking to a man whose life was a mess. He was facing stress and worry and anxiousness. And as we talked, he said, "Ed, I know I should pray about this problem, but it seems so insignificant compared to the other major problems I'm sure God's dealing with."

My friend had it all wrong. I pointed him back to this concept in the Bible: that we're to pray not just about some things, not just about little things, not just about big things, but about *everything*. God is our heavenly Father and is keenly interested in whatever we bring to him because he intimately loves each of us.

When my children come to me, I'm genuinely interested and aware of anything they say. It doesn't matter if they want to show me a microscopic scrape on their knee, a ladybug in their hand, or the world's largest ball of twine they've just created. I'm going to pay attention to whatever they bring my way.

God is the same way. Whatever we bring to him, he's going to give us his undivided attention. Paul doesn't say, "In some things, with prayer and petition." He says, "In *everything*." So go to God with everything—even your stress. That's the first step in processing that stress in your life.

We should also have a mind-set of thanksgiving when we pray. We should come to God with an attitude of gratitude. When we come to God and thank him for all he has given us and done for us, it does something to the heart of God. It makes his heart beat fast. Does he need our thanks? No. He's totally sufficient without any of us. Even still, Jesus told a story about ten lepers who were healed (Luke 19:11–19). Of the ten, only one returned to say "thank you." Jesus was disappointed and surprised that nine of these men treated him more like a genie than their God. God, as any good father, loves to hear "thank you."

Does God need our thanks? No. Does he like getting it? Absolutely. Let me share a story about my son, EJ, to explain what I mean.

One of my favorite ways to destress is to go fishing with EJ. There's one fishing trip in particular that stands out in my mind. EJ was about eight at the time. After a long day of fishing we were worn out, but we had to get a bite to eat before we called it quits. So before we settled in to camp for the night, I found a Dairy Queen—the unofficial fast-food restaurant of Texas. After downing a couple of Hunger-Busters and chocolate malts, EJ and I headed back to our campsite. On the short ride back, we spotted a couple of deer, a wild hog, and a few copperhead snakes. EJ loved it!

He looked out the window up at the Texas sky and said, "Dad, it just doesn't get any better than this." Then he said, "I love you. Thank you for bringing me on this fishing trip." I actually started tearing up. Trying to protect my manly façade, I tried to pretend that my tears came from a rogue piece of dust that flew in my eyes. I knew EJ was appreciative, even without him saying so. But it meant so much more to hear him say it.

God is the same way. He wants to hear you say it, too. He wants to hear your gratitude, to hear your thanksgiving, to hear your appreciation. It's just another part of praying right.

So when stress strikes, start a conversation with God. We're to pray, we're to petition, and we're to thank him. When we do that, we're promised the chance to experience the peace of God. That means that the storms of life won't overwhelm us. We'll still deal with stress, but God will help us process it his way, replacing stress with peace.

That's something money can't buy. It's the tranquility of our soul. It's knowing that our destiny is defined. And that's the beautiful result of prayer. When we're anxious or stressed, and turn to God in prayer, the result is peace that transcends all understanding—a peace that will guard our hearts and our minds.

That is huge, because our hearts are where our feelings happen and our minds are where our thoughts are processed. And if the peace of God flows from these two places, life isn't going to seem so difficult. Yes, you'll face difficult circumstances. Yes, you still have to live in this sin-stained world. But with the peace of God guarding your heart and mind, you will be able to handle things with a peace and a power that you didn't have before.

A member of our church used to play in the NFL as an offensive lineman. He's three-hundred-plus pounds of solid muscle. One day he took me aside and showed me the techniques he used to block the linebackers who were bent on attacking the quarterback. Now I'm not that small. I'm about 6'2", 180 pounds, with reflexes like a cat! But he lined up across from me and did a couple of moves that about broke me in half. After just a few seconds, I realized I was no match for him.

Well, the peace of God makes that NFL offensive lineman look like a barrier made of tissue paper. God's peace will guard our hearts and minds against things like anxiousness and stress, and nothing will be able to break through his protection.

"I Gained a More Balanced and Peaceful Perspective"
MEREDITH'S STORY

"Everything was stressing me out. I was in the middle of a major transition in my life and didn't know which way to go. Though I wanted to follow God's plan for my life, I didn't know what that was. Would I get more involved in my church or pursue a dream of singing and acting on Broadway? Would I pursue a singing career in Nashville or get more education?

"I remember sitting in my car one afternoon. I was a mess! I was rushing to an important appointment but was caught in a traffic jam. My emotions were so frazzled that I became hysterical right there in my car. I felt like the world was closing in on me and I couldn't breathe. Just before I totally lost it, I glanced up at the visor on my car and saw a 3×5 card that my friend had recently written out for me. The card read:

> Rejoice in the Lord always. I will say it again: Rejoice! Let your gentleness be evident to all. The Lord is near. Do not be anxious about anything, but in everything, by prayer and petition, with thanksgiving, present your requests to God. And the peace of God, which transcends all understanding, will guard your hearts and your minds in Christ Jesus.

"Those words prompted me to talk to God. I told him about my problems and my confusion, and all the stress that I was feeling. I also thanked God for the great opportunities that he had already given me in my young life, and for the big dreams he placed within me.

"As I recounted all the ways in which God had blessed me, I became very aware of his power, helping me realize that I didn't need to worry so much. It's really funny; when you are recounting God's goodness, it's really hard to feel hopeless!

"That afternoon, God met with me in my car on a crowded highway. God lifted a huge burden off of me and provided me with the foundation to make the best decision that would honor him. To this very day, those verses from Philippians 4 are a constant source of wisdom and comfort."

That's the confidence we have when stress strikes and we strike up a conversation with God. It begins with praying right.

Think Right

Paul dives deeper in his letter to the Philippians with some more instruction on handling stress. "Finally, brothers, whatever is true, whatever is noble, whatever is right, whatever is pure, whatever is lovely, whatever is admirable—if anything is excellent or praiseworthy—think about such things" (Philippians 4:8).

Paul is saying that we need to focus on things that are based on God's absolute truth, not the relative truth the world so often recites. We need to focus on the things in life that are virtuous, just, proper, pure, winsome, and worthy of talking about, and the things that motivate us to do good. Stress is mostly a mental thing. Whatever you focus your mind on is what is going to be reflected in your emotions and actions. So to overcome stress, you have to think right.

Sometimes you're going to be assaulted by ungodly thoughts. That's an unfortunate part of our depravity as human beings. Have you ever been sitting in a meeting or on an airplane or at dinner and had an impure thought just jump into your mind seemingly from nowhere? All of us have been there. It's what you do with those thoughts that ultimately determines your destiny.

What the Bible says is to "take captive every thought to make it obedient to Christ" (2 Corinthians 10:5). How do you do that? By acknowledging the power that you have available to you through the person of the Holy Spirit.

The moment you step over the line in faith and establish a personal relationship with Jesus Christ, he places the person of the Holy Spirit inside of your life. And the Holy Spirit is your guide and director to capture those thoughts. He's constantly whispering truth to you and telling you to think on things that build you up, to think on things that reflect the glory and the nature of God. The Holy Spirit encourages you to think right.

And once we begin to think right, the things that stress us out won't hold the power they once did. We will be able to overcome the stress by focusing our attention and our thoughts on things that are pure and good and excellent. And once we capture our thoughts and make them our own, we can move to the third step of overcoming stress.

Live Right

Praying right leads to thinking right. And thinking right leads to living right. In his letter, Paul makes himself an example. He tells the Philippians to do what he does. He says to them, "Whatever you have learned or received or heard from me, or seen in me—put it into practice. And the God of peace will be with you" (Philippians 4:9).

That's a pretty bold statement. "Whatever you have . . . seen in me—put it into practice." Paul was able to say that because he lived out what he had learned through right praying and right thinking. He had a relationship with God that allowed him to discover the things that God wanted him to learn. He was able to look at life not through the stressed-out lens of his mind but through the clear lens of the God of peace. And that allowed him to live a life that others could emulate.

Can you say that about your life? Or are you running through life in such a stressed-out frenzy that it's hard for people to keep up? Are you running so fast that you are trying to outrun God? Throughout the rest of this section, you're going to find out just how to live a life that isn't tangled up with stress and worry. You're going to discover how to ramp up your leisure and leverage it for a better, more meaningful life. So let's continue as we discover what living right is all about!

STOP AND THINK

FOLLOW THE SIGNS: Stress is a natural by-product of a busy culture. God tells us that prayer is the remedy that will change our minds, which will then transform our lives.

CHECK THE MAP: "Do not be anxious about anything, but in everything, by prayer and petition, with thanksgiving, present your requests to God" (Philippians 4:6).

TAKE THE NEXT STEP: On a scale of 1 to 5, with 5 being the highest, how would you rate:

1. Your relational stress?
2. Your financial stress?
3. Your work stress?

21

LEISURE SUITS

By the seventh day God had finished the work he had been doing;
so on the seventh day he rested from all his work.

—Genesis 2:2

I want you to travel back in time with me for just a minute, back to the time of tie-dyed shirts, bell-bottom jeans, and disco clubs. Think back to the decade of muscle cars and *Star Wars*; Evel Knievel's stunts, and Elvis's final tour. I'm talking about the 1970s.

The 1970s was also the decade that brought us the leisure suit—one of the world's worst-ever fashion faux pas. The leisure suit—that outfit forever immortalized by John Travolta as he discoed his way across the dance floor to the pulsating rhythm of the Bee Gees.

Chances are you know someone who owned a leisure suit. Maybe it was even you. Okay, I'll admit it. Yes, I had my very own leisure suit. It was a lime green one, in fact. And when I put it on, flipped up the elephant-ear-sized collar, sported the gold chains with the unbuttoned shirt, and strutted down the street in my platform shoes, I actually felt like John Travolta's character, Tony Manero.

Looking back, I can see that I was really more like the poster child of *uncool*. Let's face it. Leisure suits weren't as great as we thought they were in the seventies. I can't think of one person who looks back at that period and honestly says, "Man, I wish I could look like *that* again!"

But I have some fashion news that may come as a shock to you. Leisure suits are still in style. In fact, they were in style long before *Saturday Night Fever* or the funky beats of the Bee Gees hit the scene. And they'll be in style long after those things make a comeback (after all, everything comes back in fashion eventually). In fact, leisure suits have been around for the last five, six, even seven thousand years.

And by the end of this chapter, you will be sized, measured, and tailor-fit for your very own leisure suit. But don't rush out to the nearest thrift store, because I'm not talking about the kind of leisure suit that went out of style with the Farrah Fawcett hairdo. I'm talking about a leisure suit designed specifically for you by God to help you get the most out of this one and only life.

God tells us over and over—from the first book of the Bible all the way through the end—that we need to wear and model leisure. He tells us that leisure suits us better than any tailormade, three-piece, silk suit money can buy.

But before we really get into this, let me ask you a question. Is leisure a foreign concept to you? Have you fallen into the trap of overworking or overscheduling your life to the point of exhaustion? Are you just treading water, desperately wondering if you'll ever make it back to shore? Do you even feel guilty when you relax?

Most of us do. I know I feel guilty when I take some time off because I spend that "relaxation time" *knowing* that there are plenty of other things that I could be doing to pass the time—chores, work, errands, etc.

Twenty years ago you could ask people how they were doing and they'd say, "I'm doing great." Or at the very least they'd say, "Fine." Today, the answer to that question is almost instinctively and uniformly, "I'm busy!"

God, though, tells us that leisure is essential to getting the most out of life; it's a must if we want to discover true joy and fulfillment. It's not optional; it's foundational.

The word *leisure* comes from a Latin phrase that means "to be permitted." That's just what you and I need to do. We need to permit ourselves to take some leisure. It's time to give ourselves permission to relax. All too often, though, we are afraid to take any time off because we have this belief that we are indispensable. But as Charles de Gaulle once said, "The graveyards are full of indispensable men."

GOD COMMANDS LEISURE

God knew when he created us that we would have this tendency to work and work and work without taking regular time off. But because he loves you and me and because he wants what is best for us, he has given us the gift of leisure.

If you are a parent, you understand the desire to give your best to your children. But sometimes your children need guidance and direction. After all, if it were up to them, the rules would be different. If it were up to my kids, they'd stay up and play all night long. They'd run around outside, play on the computer, and chase each other around with the soccer ball in the house. And they'd have a blast; at least until the alarm went off for school the next morning. As a parent, I know better. I know that kids need sleep to learn. And I also know that tired and crabby kids aren't exactly a treat to have around the house! So what do we as parents do? We give them specific instructions in order for them to get the most out of life.

That is exactly what God has done for us. He loves us so much that not only has he given us this gift of leisure, but he has also *commanded* us to use it.

> *Remember the Sabbath day by keeping it holy. Six days you shall labor and do all your work, but the seventh day is a Sabbath to the Lord your God. On it you shall not do any work, neither you, nor your son or daughter, nor your manservant or maidservant, nor your animals, nor the alien within your gates. For in six days the Lord made the heavens and the earth, the sea, and all that is in them, but he rested on the seventh day. Therefore the Lord blessed the Sabbath day and made it holy (Exodus 20:8–11).*

The word *Sabbath* means that we are to stop, to cease, to knock off the work. After we read this fourth commandment, we should step back in wonder and say, "What an amazing God we have. He's given us fifty-two minivacations a year!"

God says that one day a week we are to stop working so we can spend focused time worshipping. While everything you do, say, touch, and feel should be an act of worship to God, he makes it very clear that we are to reserve one special day a week for him.

Labor is a gift from God. We've seen that already. But we have taken this gift from God and distorted it. We have taken work and morphed it into workaholism.

But God says if you're really going to discover what this life is all about, you've got to jump off the treadmill once a week and take a break.

God tells us something that the production analysts of corporate America are calling a new discovery: *we should rest at least once a week*. That's something that God said thousands of years ago, and it's been in the Bible for us to see the entire time.

I want you to think about your life right now. Do you have a time each week that you stop working? Do you ever just break away?

A good friend of mine attended Cornell University for his undergrad work. He told me that when he enrolled, he made a commitment to himself and to God to obey the fourth commandment at all costs. My friend made the commitment not to study or work on Sunday—ever. He dedicated that one day each week to worshipping God. So every Sunday he attended church, prayed, read his Bible, and meditated on what God was teaching him. And as hard as it may be for many to understand the effectiveness of that kind of schedule, my friend graduated number one in his class—at a renowned university that graduates thousands of people every year; students who study seven days a week, many of them more than twelve hours a day!

To many people, my friend's commitment may seem like laziness, an excuse to do nothing. But setting aside that day for worship and rest is critical. It helps us get the most out of life in ways we can't even imagine or understand. That one day a week is time God has given us to connect with the people in our lives, recharge our own batteries, and worship him. How? By doing some simple yet powerful things. When it comes to that day of leisure, try:

- Taking a relaxing walk to the park with your family.
- Inviting your neighbors over for dinner.
- Turning off the television and reading the Bible for an hour.
- Getting outdoors and enjoying the amazing beauty of nature.

But no matter what you do to enjoy that day, thank God for it. He tells us to commit one full day a week to prayer, worship, rest, and the enjoyment of God's creation—only one day. Are you doing that? Or are you on the go 7 days a week, 365 days a year?

God even set an example for us to follow when it comes to leisure.

Have you always done everything you were told to do? Of course not! We don't really like to do something without knowing if it works. We want to follow an example set before us. We think, *If I can see something in action, then it must work.* And it's only then that we step up and do it ourselves.

God knew that we would have that tendency. He knew we would have the propensity to ignore certain commandments and only follow others by example. That's why he took leisure to the next level.

The Bible says that God worked for six straight days to create the universe and everything in it. What did he do on the seventh day? He rested. He took the time off to enjoy what he had done (Exodus 20:11).

I want to make something very clear at this point. God did not need to rest. He didn't get to the end of his workweek and say, "Whew! I'm exhausted. I think I'll just take it easy for a day."

God is all-powerful, and all-powerful beings don't need rest! The inexhaustible one never gets exhausted. So he didn't need to take the time off. But we are not all-powerful, inexhaustible beings. Sorry to burst your bubble.

God deliberately rested as an example for you and me as a way to say, "Follow my lead." He knew that *we* would need the rest, so he showed us how to do it.

THE WHY

I am a self-proclaimed "why guy." I can't just read or hear something and accept it at face value. Maybe you are the same and you're wondering, *Why has God commanded leisure? Sure, he's modeled it, but why? What's the rationale behind it?*

There are three reasons God has given us leisure, and they all center around the fact that he loves us and wants what is best for our lives. He wants us to truly experience an abundant life on this planet, not just exist. He wants us to thrive, not just survive.

The Physical Reason

After we work for six days, our physical bodies just simply require rest. We need a break physically to maintain optimal performance. According to the American Heart Association, there is evidence of a relationship between the risk of cardiovascular disease and stress. Not only that, but stress also causes a kaleido-scopic range of ailments ranging from sleeplessness to ulcers. So how do you begin to fight the battle? It's very simple. Take some time off.

When Jesus was on earth, he recognized how crucial leisure was to his work. Time and time again during his life, Jesus took a break after working (Mark 6:31–32). During his teach-ing ministry, Jesus said that he came to this earth to give rest to those who were weary and burdened (Matthew 11:28). He recognized the importance of retreating and recovering physi-cally from work. So if Jesus, the only Son of God, recognized the importance of leisure, we should follow suit.

The Spiritual Reason

There is also a spiritual reason for leisure. So many people are walking around spiritually malnourished because they don't take any time to get the spiritual food that they need. They are drained and strained because they don't connect with God on a regular basis.

Again, I look to Jesus as a model. The Bible records Jesus' activities and says that on the Sabbath he went into the syna-gogue, "as was his custom" (Luke 4:16). That means that he did it regularly. Jesus understood the importance of connecting with God—together with others in a house of worship—on a weekly basis. In order to get the most out of life, we've got to do the same thing. We have to connect to a local church and reenergize ourselves spiritually.

If you are not involved in church because you're afraid that you're not good enough, think again. The church isn't full of perfect people. If everyone were perfect, there would be no need for the church. The church is a place that we come each week to reconnect, to focus on God, and to learn how he wants us to live so that we can get the most out of life.

After I preach, I always hear the same story. Someone will inevitably come up to me and say, "Pastor, when I woke up this morning, I wasn't going to show up at church. I almost slept in. But when I got here, I was reenergized. I was stressed and strained when I walked in. But I'm glad I came. I am ready for the week ahead."

If you don't worship God weekly, if you don't take that time off regularly, you will be discontented, because you will be breaking an elementary commandment of the Lord— remember the Sabbath. It is a pattern that is set forth for us throughout the Bible and evidenced in Jesus' own life.

The Emotional Reason

There's also an emotional reason for leisure. Think about your emotions at the end of an average week. If you're like me, you are fried. Now think about taking that feeling and having to work another twelve or fourteen hours during the "weekend." If you go through four or five weeks without taking a day to refuel your tanks, to recalibrate, to refocus, to rejuvenate, what's going to happen? Slowly but surely, your emotional battery will drain.

When our emotions are depleted, we want a quick fix. That's why a lot of people get involved in pornography, illicit affairs, overeating, and overspending. They're emotionally drained, and they're looking for something to plug the hole.

That's when the evil one uses his most tempting methods:

when we're emotionally spent. When did Satan tempt Jesus? Before Jesus went out into the desert for forty days and forty nights? No. It was right at the end of the forty days. Satan came to Jesus and tempted him because at that point Jesus was tired, hungry, and emotionally drained. He also tempts us when we are at our weakest, especially emotionally.

We need to take some time to recharge or we'll be vulnerable to the evil one, who is always looking to destroy us and take us further away from God.

PUTTING IT INTO PRACTICE

A good idea is only an idea until it's put into practice. God's model of leisure looks great on paper. But until we put it into practice, we'll be missing out on God's ultimate plan for our lives. And we discover God's best by imitating him.

When my son was two years old, he mimicked everything I did. As I would go through my morning routine, I had a "mini me" who would follow me around. When I got out of the shower, EJ would be there, ready to copy my every move. I'd put on jeans and a T-shirt; he'd want the same jeans and T-shirt. I'd put mousse in my hair; EJ would ask for mousse in his hair. He would even ask for a cup of coffee (until he actually took his first bitter sip).

One time, as I was brushing my teeth, EJ was standing behind me in the bathroom brushing his teeth. When I leaned over to spit in the sink, EJ spit too—right onto the bathroom floor!

That's what we need to do. We need to mimic God's movements. We need to follow his model. But it's not some kind of once-in-a-lifetime imitation. We're to model God's design for leisure throughout our entire lives. In short, we're to take those fifty-two minivacations during the year.

God's routine, his rhythm for life, is six and one. We're to work for six days and take one day off. That's what the Sabbath is. It's taking one day off from work and dedicating it to God.

But here's what so many of us do. We finally get a day off and we think, "Now I can catch up on all the chores and errands I've put off for weeks. Now I finally have a chance to run around and get everything done that is still undone—yard work, shopping, cleaning, etc." If you're doing all that, you're still working. That's not a day off.

And then we get to the end of our "day off" and we think, "Man, I need a day to recover from my day off!" That's not God's plan. He doesn't want us to take a day off from work just to work harder at home. And yet, so often, we use that day off as an excuse to get more done. I'm not saying you can't do any chores around the house or go to the store if you need to. But we must find that balance.

Make your time off count. Know that rest is part of God's plan for our lives and that it's important for many of the reasons we've already discussed. Let me encourage you to take your day off to recalibrate your priorities and thank God for the good things he's done for you in the past week.

Don't Overdo It

Just as we have taken the gift of work and distorted it into workaholism, many people have a tendency to take the gift of leisure and morph it into leisure-holism. They put on the leisure suit and wear it twenty-four/seven.

I know people who are so involved with leisure and taking time off, the only reason they work is to pick up a paycheck that will fund their leisure. These people swing to the opposite end of the spectrum and completely miss what God says about work and leisure. They miss the fact that God created work as an act of worship. They also fail to see that leisure is an act of worship as well (although we must be careful not to worship leisure).

We should leverage our leisure to help us accomplish the work God has given us throughout the week. I know that the balance can be difficult, especially in today's fast-paced world. Are we taking too much time off or not enough? Are we doing the right things when we take a day off? The easiest and most sure way to find that balance is to model your life after the one who created it.

STOP AND THINK

FOLLOW THE SIGNS: God invented work as a way to experience fulfillment and to exercise worship. But God not only worked but created leisure and modeled it for us regularly.

CHECK THE MAP: "Come to me, all you who are weary and burdened, and I will give you rest" (Matthew 11:28).

"Six days are set aside for work, but on the Sabbath day you must rest, even during the seasons of plowing and harvest" (Exodus 34:21, NLT).

TAKE THE NEXT STEP: Spend at least thirty minutes today doing something fun—preferably something different from your normal routine. Don't apologize for the activity; just enjoy it. Go for a walk outside and feel the brisk air fill your lungs. Or watch a favorite TV show and cling to your sweetheart. Spend some time baking your favorite cookies. While you are enjoying your activity of choice, enjoy God's presence. Know that leisure is his gift for you to enjoy as a reward for the work you've already accomplished.

22

THE VACATION PARADOX

Every now and then go away and have a little relaxation.
To remain constantly at work will diminish your judgment. Go
some distance away, because work will be in perspective and
a lack of harmony is more readily seen.

—LEONARDO DA VINCI

Most people realize the need for time off. We recognize the necessity of detaching from our work. And we inherently understand the notion that there is much more to a fulfilling life than simply crunching numbers at the office or developing the perfect portfolio for a client. But how often do we follow our inclinations to take meaningful time off? I'm not referring to taking a day off here or there. I'm talking about an extended vacation that gives you at least a week away from carpools, copy machines, and cranky bosses.

In America today, taking a vacation may be less common than you think. The American worker is already overworked in relation to most other countries. The average American gets fourteen vacation days, while the average German gets twenty-seven days and the French employee gains a whopping thirty-nine days. Of American workers, 16 percent will not use any vacation time whatsoever. A surprising 32 percent plan to take five days or less, and 10 percent of American workers will only take a long weekend away from the office. A recent survey by expedia.com has suggested that Americans will forfeit over 574 million vacation days in 2006.[1]

If we recognize the need to take time off, what keeps us from actually doing it? What is it about taking time away from work that we find so difficult?

For many of us, it may be an unquenchable need to be needed. We are unwilling to take time away from the office because we are afraid that things might actually be okay without us there for a while. Well, the truth is, everything will be fine without you. And if you take time away, not only will the office be okay; you'll be okay, too. You will actually be able to satisfy your need to be needed when you are away from the office. Let me explain.

THE GREAT AMERICAN VACATION

I would venture to say that most of our lifelong memories are formed away from the office. Think back on your life. Many of your own childhood memories are probably centered on a vacation or two. Maybe you have fond memories of piling into the

---

[1]Liz Marlantes, "The Great American Vacation: Vanishing into Thin Air," ABC News Study, August 23, 2006.

family station wagon and making the trek out to the Grand Canyon. Or perhaps your family loaded up the car with the camping gear and headed off to a national forest for some intimate time with nature. Maybe your family boarded an airplane and flew out to visit the nation's monuments. Or perhaps your parents took off for a week and left you behind with your grandparents. However you remember those times, they were all centered on getting some time away on some type of vacation.

The great American vacation is something about which movies are made and jokes are told. Memories are formed and friendships are forged during those times. It's supposed to be a time of rest and relaxation—a time to reconnect with loved ones and disconnect from the hustle and bustle of life. And yet, in today's fast-paced, high-speed world, even our vacations can become another missed opportunity to get away from the stress and strain of everyday life.

When we do decide to finally take some time off, we trade the turbulence and turmoil of daily life for commotion, confusion, and chaos of a different kind. And when we get to the end of our "vacation," we desperately want another vacation to recover.

Family vacation guides, travel agents, trip advisory websites, and itineraries tell us what to do, where to do it, and the order in which everything should go so we can squeeze every last ounce of fun out of our time. But is all that scheduling and planning and fretting over getting the most out of our vacations really allowing us the opportunity to get the most out of our vacations?

The Overstimulation Vacation

A good friend of mine and his wife recently returned from a two-week vacation to Europe. During their vacation, they visited five cities in three countries over the course of just fourteen days. When he returned home, my friend said the trip was great. They saw so much and did so many things. But my friend admitted that he and his wife spent their vacation running from place to place (sometimes literally), and they felt that they had to experience so much in such a short amount of time that their vacation was overstimulating and not relaxing. Rather than taking it easy, they experienced information overload. My friend told me that everywhere they went—every museum, art gallery, or theater—they bought a book to bring home so they could study up on everything they saw. They didn't even have enough time to learn about what they were seeing while they were there. What my friend and his wife experienced was one of the all-too-familiar vacation vandals that invade our time off.

The Desperation Vacation

Another vacation vandal is the desperation vacation. We grow up learning that hard work is the path to success. "You can sleep when you die," we hear. And so, many people push the limit of their occupational capabilities. They work and work and work—not realizing their dire need for some real time away. They convince themselves that they are invincible—at least when it comes to their work.

But inevitably, everyone that heads down that path reaches the edge. And when we find ourselves at the very brink of collapse, we frantically run to our supervisors and plead with them, "I'm fried! I'm totally burned out! I need some time off, please! I can't go another day."

The problem with vacationing that way is that we get to our vacation spot with little or nothing left in our emotional and physical tanks. We are so desperate for time off that we can't even enjoy the time off once we take it. At that point it's going to take more than a one- or two-week vacation. It's going to take three solid months of lying on a beach somewhere and two more years of lying on a psychologist's couch to get over our desperation and exhaustion!

Now I know that there are times when it is impossible to get away for some extended time on the beach or in the mountains. I know how difficult it is to find that kind of time in my own life. There are certain seasons of life when we are unable to take extended time off. That's specifically why those fifty-two mini-vacations I mentioned in the previous chapter play such a huge role in our lives. So if you have to, pencil in those days off. And make sure you take the time off each week to detach from the previous week and recharge for the coming days. At the same time, however, those minivacations aren't enough to sustain you for months or years on end. Don't allow yourself to reach the point of desperation before you take an extended vacation. Plan ahead and get away before the desperation sets in.

The Regimentation Vacation

Another trap we fall into when it comes to taking time off is the regimentation vacation. This vacation seems more like boot camp than it does a vacation. It's an agenda-driven time that

stresses everyone out, including the most organized and me-
thodical of people.

A regimentation vacation goes something like this:

7:30 A.M.	Wake-up call is at 7:30 sharp!
8:10	Breakfast in the hotel lobby
9:00	Depart for the beach
9:45	Sunbathe, but only for thirty-five minutes
10:20	Rent Jet Skis and ride for sixty-five minutes
11:25	Meet for lunch
12:30 P.M.	Head back to the hotel for a nap
2:00	Leave the hotel and head for the mall
3:30	Meet for a movie
5:45	Dinner reservations

With the regimentation vacation, there is always somewhere to go, but no room for flexibility and true down time.
"We have to be there and do that *now!*" Does that sound relaxing to you? Of course, I'm not suggesting it's bad to schedule
your vacation—you can run into trouble if you don't. But
we've taken the vacation and used it as yet another excuse to
cram more into our already busy schedules. Make sure you're
flexible, and leave room for some actual relaxation.

The Perfection Vacation

Then there is the perfection vacation. That's when we think
everything's got to be absolutely perfect. We have to find the
perfect vacation spot, and everything has to run without any

glitches in order for us to enjoy our time. The problem with the perfection vacation is that it doesn't exist. It's simply not reality.

My family and I have had some incredible opportunities to travel to some amazing locations. But if you were to ask our children about their fondest memories, they aren't found in the most exotic places. Their fondest memories aren't even when everything ran smoothly.

One of the most memorable getaways in my children's minds (and I have to admit, in my mind, too) was a weekend trip we made to Houston, Texas—just a four-hour drive from our house in Dallas. The highlight happened in our very own driveway.

Before our trip, I had to put the luggage on a luggage rack on top of our truck so everyone could fit in one vehicle. The trip it-self went fine—no major problems. But as we returned home, I had forgotten that the luggage was on top of the truck. I pulled up to our house, opened the garage door, and proceeded to drive the truck into its designated spot in the garage. I'll give you one guess what happened next.

Crash! The luggage rack clipped the top of the garage, and shingles and lumber came crashing down on top of us! Thank-fully, no one was hurt. But would anyone file that under the "perfect vacation" moment?

The mistakes and mishaps during our vacations are often the most memorable moments. The time the taxi runs out of gas or the rental car dies on the side of the road; the time the tent comes crashing down in the middle of a rainy night or you miss your train to one city and have a blast in another—those are the times that you will remember long after the vacation ends. Those are the times that you will laugh about and share with your family years down the road.

So often we have such an idealistic image of the perfect vacation that we miss the real purpose of a vacation. The place, the activities, and the agenda are not what make a vacation a vacation. It is the relational bonding, the interconnectedness, and the growth that mark great vacations. And yet, so often, we fall into the vacation paradox.

The vacation paradox is the idea that vacations are just something else we're to mark off from our to-do list. But that's not what vacations are designed for. They are designed to be times of meaning and purpose. So when we take vacations, we should be strategic and intentional.

THE TWOFOLD PURPOSE OF VACATIONS

At the beginning of this chapter, I mentioned our unquenchable need to be needed. We're afraid to take time off because we want to be needed at work. But I also mentioned the idea that our need to be needed would be met most outside of the office. There are two areas in which we are truly needed, much more than at the office. And these two areas should be the firm foundation that supports the purpose and direction of our vacations.

Connecting with Your Spouse

The most important earthly relationship we will ever form is the relationship with our spouse. So when it comes to our being needed, there is nowhere greater than within our own marriage. So the first purpose for taking time off is to reconnect with your spouse.

Lisa and I try to get away together—alone—at least twice a

year. Sometimes it's just for a night or two. Other times it's for a week or so. The point isn't how much time we take. The point is that we use that time to reconnect with one another— away from the hectic pace of our lives.

Some people say they'd love to take some time off with their spouse but simply can't afford it. But you don't have to go anywhere exotic or impressive. You can take a vacation at your home. Watch a movie, go out to eat, come home and have a romantic evening together. Spend some time talking about your goals and interests. Or go to a hotel in your hometown for a night or two.

However and wherever you do it, take time to reconnect— emotionally, spiritually, psychologically, and, yes, physically with your spouse. The benefits to your marriage—even if you get away for just a night or two—will amaze you.

Connecting with Your Family and Friends

Even if you are not married, there should still be purpose and meaning in your vacations. Building relationships with your family and friends exceeds the priority of keeping status quo around the office.

Now, with family vacations, you have to be especially careful about not letting yourself fall into the trap of trying to plan a perfect vacation. If your family is anything like mine, you should expect the unexpected and be prepared for anything on your family vacations. And don't expect too much R&R—unless the Rs stand for runny noses and rashes. Someone gets sick or wanders into a patch of poison ivy. Four kids want to do four different things, and there's whining, tantrums, and tears. And car trips are the worst! There are backseat fights, count-

"I Can Remember Almost Every Vacation"
TED'S STORY

"Vacation was my favorite time of the year. It meant that we got to leave home and go see fun, new places we'd never been before. It was so much fun! We'd pack up our bags, lock up the house, and load up the minivan.

"Mom and Dad were with us every day and every night. We wouldn't have to wait until they got home from work to play with us; we even got to eat lunch together with them! My three brothers and I were out of school, so we'd get to do everything together as a family.

"I remember leaving the snowy North for the beaches of Florida. It took us over two days to get there—but it was worth it. We'd cheer the first time we got somewhere that didn't have snow on the ground, which meant we could leave our winter coats in the car. We celebrated Christmas in Fort Lauderdale one year, and then about five years later, we went back down for our March break.

"Sometimes we would go on vacation closer to home. We'd get to stay in a hotel together and go on fast rides at an amusement park, or visit family that we hadn't seen for a long time. No matter what we did, or where we went, we always had fun together.

"Now, years later, I'm a father-to-be. I don't remember a lot of things from my childhood, but I can remember almost every vacation that our family ever took. I now know why our family is closer than most families.

You just can't replace time that is spent together, no matter what you decide to do.

"When you spend over twenty hours in a smelly minivan together, something magical happens. Sharing memories of when the van broke down or that first day on the beach go a long way to bonding you together as a family.

"I can only hope to create great memories like these for my wife and children as we prepare to start a new generation. One thing's for sure: our vacation time will be a big priority on our family calendar."

less bathroom stops, and the inevitable case of car sickness.

I should clarify something at this point. A vacation with your family is not really a vacation at all. No one can convince me that when I go out of town with my four kids and my wife I will be able to relax. It's just not going to happen. Those times shouldn't be classified as "vacations." They should, instead, be classified as family outings.

There's little time to really relax when you are with your entire family. But the real purpose of the family outing isn't relaxation. It's about getting away from the daily routine and doing something different together. It's about forming memories that bond you together. It's about strengthening your family—even when things don't go perfectly. When you look back at those times, just as I mentioned earlier, you will be able to laugh and share in those memories years down the road. It's those times that should bring the family closer together and strengthen your family ties.

ENJOY THE GIFT

When we remember the twofold purpose for our vacations and use them strategically, we will begin to remember what life is really about—that it's not all about working and earning and saving and spending. A fulfilling life is really about the connections, the relationships, and the enjoyment of life.

When I was four years old, the one thing I wanted most for Christmas was a Tiger Joe action figure. I vividly remember pleading with my parents to please give me a Tiger Joe. It must have worked, because when I woke up Christmas morning and tore through the presents, I found a box the exact size and shape of a Tiger Joe box. When I ripped off the paper and saw Tiger Joe looking up at me, I went ballistic. There was no containing my excitement. I remember jumping up and down and then running around shouting over and over, "Tiger Joe! Tiger Joe!"

And the whole time, my parents were smiling from ear to ear. They almost couldn't contain their excitement and joy over my excitement. They were so happy that their little Ed had his Tiger Joe.

Just the way my parents found joy in my joy, God smiles and applauds when we discover this gift called leisure. And when we use that gift strategically and effectively to fulfill our lives, it brings joy to his heart. God wants us to enjoy the gifts he gives us because he wants us to get the most out of life. And leisure is one of those gifts.

The Bible tells us that God has given us everything for us to enjoy (1 Timothy 6:17). Life isn't meant to be spent with frowns on our faces as we endure a humdrum life. We're to take time off and enjoy what God has given us. Yet, so many of us have this belief that we are supposed to hold on with a white-knuckled grip in order to survive through the drudgery of life. But that's not what God has in mind. He wants us to discover the truth of leisure and use it to fulfill our lives and build purpose and meaning into our lives. And when we do that, we will experience the ultimate joy he has promised.

STOP AND THINK

FOLLOW THE SIGNS: Don't neglect your vacation time. Work has an important place in your life, but it does not define you. Plan some time to unplug from work, connect with your spouse and family, and enjoy the gift of extended leisure time.

CHECK THE MAP: "The apostles gathered around Jesus and reported to Him all they had done and taught. Then, because so many people were coming and going that they did not even have a chance to eat, He said to them, 'Come with me by yourselves to a quiet place and get some rest'" (Mark 6:30–31).

TAKE THE NEXT STEP: Review your vacations for the last three years. Where did you go? How long did you spend away? Who did you go with? Now evaluate each of them. Which of these vacations energized you, and which of them brought you back more fatigued?

23

LAUGH OUT LOUD

A day without laughter is a day wasted.

—CHARLIE CHAPLIN

I'll never forget my first public task in the ministry. As a precocious twenty-one-year-old pastor, I went to work at my father's church in Houston, Texas. At the time, that church was the largest church in America. One morning, my boss (not my father) came to my office and asked me to give the morning prayer at the eleven o'clock Sunday service. (For those of you who don't know, the eleven o'clock service is like the bottom of the ninth inning in baseball.)

The morning prayer in the Baptist church acts like the highlight reel for the entire service. It's the final chance to reach anyone who may have dozed off during the music or missed the main point of the message. It's the time that everyone in the church perks up and pays extra attention. In short, this was my big chance to make a big impression.

Not having spoken from the main stage before, I worked hard to make sure I did this prayer justice. I even outlined what

I was going to pray so I wouldn't miss anything. And I thought, since everyone would have their heads bowed and their eyes closed, I could even read some of it as a last resort.

The day finally arrived. I sat through the service, rehearsing the prayer in my head the entire time. Then the moment came for the morning prayer. I got "the nod" and made my way up to the pulpit, very reverently set down my Bible, and announced in my best preacher's voice, "Let us pray."

Then I gripped the sides of the oversized pulpit and began to pray. Everything was going smoothly. My hard work was paying off. About halfway through the prayer, I was on cruise control. I thought to myself, "This is incredible. Ed, this is the best prayer ever!"

At the end of my prayer, I was supposed to lead the entire congregation in the Lord's Prayer. I had prayed the Lord's Prayer so many times in my life that I couldn't mess it up if I tried. I knew I was home free once I got to this point in the prayer.

As I made the transition to the Lord's Prayer, I used the best pastor's voice I could muster as I said, "And we voice this prayer in the name that is above every name—Jesus Christ; the one who taught his disciples to pray, saying . . ."

Somewhere after this, I crashed and burned. Not only did the wheels fall off, but the transmission dropped out, the oil pan cracked, and the airbags deployed.

Anticipating some stage fright, I had written out the Lord's Prayer word for word in my notes just in case I needed a little help. I read, "Our Father . . ."

And the entire church said, "Our Father . . ."

I read, "Who art in heaven . . ."

Everybody repeated, "Who art in heaven . . ."

And then I went completely blank.

I couldn't read.

I couldn't talk.

I couldn't see.

I totally choked.

After a few minutes of standing behind the pulpit like a deer caught in the headlights, I mumbled some unintelligible words and brought the misery to an end with "Amen."

The congregation began to snicker. The snickering turned to giggling; the giggling to all-out laughter. So much for my fifteen minutes of fame!

Understandably shaken, I hung my head, slowly walked down the steps, and slunk into the front pew next to—of all people—my mother. Against the background of raucous laughter, my mother turned to me and, in her soft, southern twang, said the only uplifting thing she could have said, "Ed, your voice sounded real good."

WHY I LAUGH

We love to laugh, don't we? Whether it's hearing a good joke, catching a comedy on TV, or watching the pastor choke on the Sunday morning prayer, laughter is intrinsically woven into who we are. As we get ready to conclude this section on work and leisure, I think we need to include a chapter on outrageous, contagious laughter.

Laughter is a critical and life-sustaining component in a culture that is obsessed with work and inundated with negativity. Leisure, including laughter, is a gift from God that has to be managed God's way if we are going to mimic our Creator and experience the kind of lasting joy that he has promised to each one of his followers.

God is a joyous God. And the life he wants for us is filled with fun and laughter. In fact, if laughter isn't a big part of your experience, something is wrong. Life can be hard. Have you noticed that? Imagine how much harder it would be if we weren't able to have a good laugh once in a while.

It Makes Me Feel Good

One of the greatest benefits of laughter is that it makes me feel good. At first that statement may sound shallow and superficial, as if a fulfilling life is all about feelings. But even though feelings are not everything, it's still okay to feel good and laugh. In fact, it's not only okay; it's essential.

The newest research reports that when we laugh, our T cells increase and our endorphin levels rise—our entire muscular system relaxes. In other words, our health improves through laughter.

But the newest research—as is so often the case—is simply reinforcing old data. God has told us for thousands of years that laughter is good medicine (Proverbs 17:22). Laughter is God's way of helping us get the most out of life. And it can definitely keep us from taking ourselves too seriously.

When I was younger, I was reluctant to go into the ministry. One of the main things that held me back was the fact that so many pastors, clergymen, and lay leaders seem so serious and boring and monotone. I like to joke and cut up and goof around, so I didn't want any part of a profession that didn't seem to be any fun at all.

But as I began to look at what God wanted for my life, I realized that laughter is a big part of the profession I have been called into. I discovered that God wants me to laugh—even at work. In fact, I'd argue that laughter and work go hand in hand. I love going to work most days, and a lot of that is because my team and I have a lot of fun together in the trenches of leadership. Ministry, like life, is tough. One of the best releases from that tension is laughter.

Several years ago something happened at our church that I don't think has happened in many churches. During one of our Easter morning services, a woman showed up in a pink rabbit costume—ears and all. The funniest part of it isn't the fact that she showed up in a bunny costume. The funniest part is what she said.

One of our ushers approached her and politely asked her to remove the two-foot-high ears because they were distracting the people behind her (as if the costume wasn't enough of a distraction). She looked at the usher and said, completely straight-faced, "I can't take the ears off. My hair is a mess, and if I take off the ears, I'll look funny."

Why do I laugh? It just flat out makes me feel good.

It Tells Me Who My Friends Are

Laughter also tells me who my friends are. When you look for friends, you should look for people who make you laugh, because life's too short to be serious all the time. If you are trying to live a life of outrageous, contagious joy, you should look for friends who share your love of Jesus Christ. Another important quality is a good sense of humor.

This is true in the dating world as well. So often singles look for the wrong things when it comes to finding "the one."

Men and women both concentrate too much on looks in their search for a life partner. Don't make looks the most important aspect of the person you're dating. The first thing, as I mentioned, should be a relationship with Jesus Christ. Second, you should look for someone you can laugh with and with whom you have a great time.

We don't put a high enough priority on laughter when it comes to our friends or to those people we date and ultimately marry. That's sad because laughter is a great indicator of good chemistry. It's a key to building each other up and encouraging one another. Laughter is especially important when you are having a heated argument. It's amazing how a funny face or quick joke can defuse a tense situation. Laughter is vital to establishing healthy, vibrant relationships.

The most difficult thing I do as a pastor is speak for God in public. The stress can be exhausting. But I'm not alone. In fact, public speaking is the second greatest fear for most people—just behind death. After nearly two decades in the ministry, I wish I could say it has gotten easier. I wish I could say I never get nervous before speaking. But I can't.

Week in and week out, I face the same fear. When Wednesday morning rolls around, I feel this enormous weight on my shoulders beginning to build. But I can't cower to the fear. I can't call in sick on the weekend. I've got to show up with my "A" game, because I have a responsibility to speak a word from God. How do I deal with the stress? One word—friends.

I have a lot of friends that I can call on just to get a laugh. There have been many times that I've called a friend of mine at 6:30 or 7:00 in the morning—just to start off the day with some laughter.

When my friends laugh with me, they are affirming me.

They're building my self-esteem and fueling me with the octane I need to face the tough and stressful times. If I didn't have
friends whom I could laugh with, the stress could easily overwhelm me. Laughing with my friends, though, lets me know
who has my back and whom I can rely on.

It Gives Me a Proper Perspective on Life

Laughter also gives me a proper perspective on life. It keeps me
from taking myself too seriously. But what this really means is
that I think too much of myself, that I'm probably suffering
from an inflated ego. Laughter helps me lighten up, helps me
laugh at myself, and knocks the hot air right out of me.

A few years back, my son, EJ, got on this kick of listening to
every one of my messages. Each Sunday, EJ would ask me if I
brought that weekend's tape home. After a few weeks, I started to
really build myself up. I thought I must really be making an impact on his life! He was really interested in hearing what I have to
say each and every weekend! And I started to think that my
teaching was helping my son mature and grow spiritually in leaps
and bounds.

Finally, I asked him about it. I wanted to see how much
this chip off the old block was really learning from his father.
When I asked him if he would like to talk about what he was
learning from the messages, he looked at me with a puzzled
expression and said, "Dad, I play those tapes each night because they help me fall asleep."

Talk about a blow to my ego! But once I got over the initial
shock, I had a real good laugh over it. That moment, along with
many others in my life, reminded me not to overestimate my
own importance and not to take myself too seriously. If I think

too much of myself, I'm not thinking enough of God, and I'm limiting my opportunity to discover the truth of what he wants to teach me.

An inflated ego is like looking at a masterpiece painting from one inch away. When you step back, the details become more apparent and you see the genius of the work. It's the same way in our lives. When we back away from our own perspective, God will show us the amazing things he has in store for our lives.

It Pleases God

While laughter helps me feel good, shows me who my friends are, and helps me gain a proper perspective on life, I also laugh because it pleases God.

There is nothing better than the laughter of children. Parents can attest to the amazing thrill that comes from watching their children laugh. As a father, nothing pleases me more than knowing my children are joyful and enjoying life.

Our heavenly Father is the same way. And he tells us in the Bible that the true mark of a fulfilling life lived the way he has designed it is outrageous, contagious joy (Galatians 5:22). He also says that his own joy is our strength (Nehemiah 8:10). And when we rely on his joy for our strength, and allow that joy to infiltrate our lives, we cannot help but laugh and enjoy life. After all, laughter is the direct by-product of joy.

If we are living a full and meaningful life, we will be known by our joy and our laughter. But we don't use that joy and laughter for our own selfish reasons. And we don't laugh at other people's expense. We use laughter to bring meaning and purpose to others around us, because one of the greatest keys to discovering a fulfilled life is sharing what we have been given—and that includes the gift of laughter.

But laughter can have its downside. The Bible tells us that Satan is a thief who comes to steal and kill and destroy anything that God is trying to build in our lives (John 10:10). How does that relate to laughter?

Every time we have a gift—like laughter—Satan supplies a counterfeit. Laughter that is disrespectful, dirty, or degrading is not godly laughter. It's not the kind of laughter that we were designed for. It's not the kind of laughter that leads to a meaningful existence.

So many comedians today use laughter in a way that God never intended it to be used. It's easy to make fun of someone who may be different from us. It doesn't take real intelligence to make degrading and racist jokes. That's cheap laughter, laughter that tears people apart.

But it takes real creativity, real innovation, and real originality from God to laugh and enjoy life in a wholesome way.

Many times Lisa and I will be at a restaurant with some friends, and we'll be enjoying ourselves and laughing so hard and loud that people will come up and ask us what we're drinking. It's sparkling water and iced tea! You don't have to drink alcoholic beverages to really laugh. You don't have to make fun of someone to really enjoy life. That kind of laughter is not true laughter. It's not the kind of laughter that God intended us to enjoy. And it's not the kind of laughter that leads to a meaningful existence.

I Have Been Healed

I know that life is not all happy and joyful. Anyone who tells you that life is all positive and uplifting isn't living in the real world. We live in a fallen and fallible world. I know that life is tough. And we're all going to face times in life when the last thing we want to do is laugh. We will face times of sickness, fear, uncertainty, doubt, and death. But the Bible promises that those of us who have committed our lives to Jesus will have their tears turned to songs of joy (Psalm 126:6).

Years ago I visited Jackson Hole, Wyoming, during a tragic time. Acres upon acres of densely wooded forests had burned to the ground. When we got there, the fires were still raging. Helicopters were dumping thousands of gallons of water, and hundreds of men and women were putting their lives on the line in an attempt to put out the fires. Most of the area, though, was devastated by fire.

I've been back to Jackson Hole since that time. And as I looked around at the trees, the grass, the flowers, and the wildlife that had returned to the area, I couldn't help but think of our lives. Many of us have been devastated by circumstances beyond our control. Yet, God is a God of restoration. Through him and his gift of lasting joy and laughter, we can make it through those difficult times.

The Bible tells us that the tears that we shed are like seeds. They hit the ground, and if we are walking with God, he allows those seeds to germinate and grow. And one day, they are going to produce joy. And the by-product of that joy is laughter.

Ultimately, my laughter comes from knowing that I have been healed. It comes down to the security of knowing who I am in God's eyes and the fact that he has healed my wounds.

Laughter is about enjoying the life that he has given us on this earth. And it's about experiencing joy and fulfillment that comes from discovering the amazing way in which God has healed us from our sin.

God loves you and me so much that he sent his Son to die for us. And I have a relationship with him—not because of what I have done but because of what he has done for me. And when I think about that, when I realize that I'm freed up to have the kind of joy and the kind of excitement that come from God, I can't help but laugh out loud in joy and amazement.

STOP AND THINK

FOLLOW THE SIGNS: Laughter is one of life's greatest gifts, and it does so much good in our lives. Don't take it for granted. As E. E. Cummings said, don't let a day go by without at least one laugh.

CHECK THE MAP: "There is a time for everything . . . a time to weep and a time to laugh, a time to mourn and a time to dance" (Ecclesiastes 3:1, 4).

TAKE THE NEXT STEP: Think back to an embarrassing moment in your life, like the one I shared in this chapter. Are you able to laugh about it now? Spend some time today looking at the lighter side of life, thanking God for the gift of laughter.

24

IT'S ALL ABOUT
THE MONEY

He that is of the opinion money will do everything
may well be suspected of doing everything for money.
—BENJAMIN FRANKLIN

People say, sometimes scornfully, "It's all about the money."
Well, in a manner of speaking, it *is* all about the money.
That statement has ramifications from the stock market on Wall
Street to the meat market on Main Street, USA. And it is true
and powerful in God's economy.

As a young pastor, I was struggling with the idea of talking
about money in the church. Then one day, I uncovered some
amazing research. I discovered that there are over five hundred
verses in the Bible that talk about prayer, around five hundred
verses that talk about faith, but more than *two thousand* verses
that cover the subject of money and possessions. And if you look
at the teachings of Jesus, you'll discover that he talked more about
money than he talked about almost anything else. For instance, of

the thirty-eight parables (teaching stories) that Jesus told, sixteen of them center around the topic of money, possessions, and our responsibility with those things.

I also think it's interesting that the word *believe* is used 272 times; *pray* is used 371 times; *love* is used 714 times; but the word *give* is used 2,162 times! That's why we can't ignore the money issue. I learned that since God talks about money so much, Christian people can't be shy about discussing our attitudes and actions when it comes to money.

This chapter is all about money. After all, that's one of the primary reasons you get up and go to work every day, isn't it? If you and I were to sit down for some espresso and talk about life, the subject of money management would surface. We could talk about our budgets, our financial goals, or our financial stress. All of these touch on the issue of financial stewardship.

This chapter is not about gimmicks or stock tips that'll beat the market. I want to talk to you about managing money God's way. I realize that you get advice from a lot of different sources regarding money management—friends, family, financial gurus, television commercials, and magazine articles all bombard us with tips that give us the best way to spend, save, or invest our money. Too many of us, though, have never listened to the right advisor when it comes to financial matters—God.

Money is powerful, powerful stuff. It relates to almost everything we do. Many people are drowning in debt. Others don't seem to have a financial worry in the world. Some people feel guilty about the amount of money they make. And still others worship money—it fuels them, rules them, and dominates them. For many of us, our self-esteem is determined by the size of our bank account or portfolio or condo or ocean liner. In these cases, net worth and self-worth are woven together seamlessly.

We spend a lot of our time trying to earn, save, and spend money; it's a representation of who we are—especially in America. And in a very real sense, it is a piece of who we are. Jesus said that our money and our hearts are inseparably linked (Matthew 6:21). The way we handle our money reveals a lot about our character. And to accomplish what God wants to accomplish in our lives, we must understand what to do with what God has given us. Some people are totally oblivious to the spiritual realities that are interconnected with our financial situation.

Did you know that money is actually a test from God? It reveals everything about us. If you want to find out what makes someone tick, just look at that person's bank account or credit card statement. Remember, "money talks."

If that's true, what is your money saying about your life? Money reveals your priorities, loyalties, and affections. But did you know that the manner in which you manage it dictates how many blessings you will receive, or the amount of blessings you will miss in life? So read ahead to discover the joy of being blessed by God and then—as you are blessed—learn to leverage those blessings to make the world around you a better place.

MANAGEMENT vs. OWNERSHIP

Do you want to have true success in life? Do you want your money to have real significance, now and forever? Then you must understand one pivotal principle about making and spending money: True success is about management, not ownership. We don't own even one thing. We came into this life with nothing, and we'll leave this life with nothing.

People may say, "Well, Ed, you don't understand. I've pulled myself up by the bootstraps. You don't know what I have made of my life. You don't know my background. I'm a fighter."

But I have to ask, "Who gave you your life, your creativity, your drive, and your people skills? Who gave you your intellect? Who enabled you? Who empowered you? Who blessed you?"

The answer is: God! God gave everything to us with the snap of a finger. And if he gave it to us that easily, he can also take it away that easily. (If you don't believe me, check out my boy Job in the book that bears his name in the Bible.)

Jesus illustrated the principle of management beautifully in the parable of the talents, in Matthew 25:14–30. He told the story of a wealthy landowner who was going out of town on a business trip. This rich man entrusted his money to three servants. To the first servant he gave five talents ($4,800), to the second he gave two talents ($1,920), and to the third he gave one talent ($960).

While the rich landowner was away, the first two servants doubled their master's money. The one who had five talents parlayed his into ten talents. The one who had two talents parlayed his into four talents. But the one who had one talent dug a hole in the ground and just sat on the money.

Then the day of accountability arrived. The wealthy landowner came back. He said to the first two, "Men, those of you who have multiplied the talents, good for you! You were faithful over little, now I'll make you faithful over much."

To the one who dug a hole and sat on his talent, the master said, "You wicked, lazy servant! So you knew that I harvest where I have not sown and gather where I have not scattered seed? Well then, you should have put my money on deposit with the bankers, so that when I returned I would have received it back with interest." He then took the talent from him and gave it to the one who had ten talents.

Jesus concluded the parable with this sobering statement: "For everyone who has will be given more, and he will have an abundance. Whoever does not have, even what he has will be taken from him. And throw that worthless servant outside, into the darkness, where there will be weeping and gnashing of teeth."

Jesus' point is clear. We are to use what he has given us to advance his work in his world. As a Christ-follower, I am called to develop my gifts and abilities and parlay them for God to use them. But that's not all.

There's another vitally important aspect to Jesus' story. I am also called to care for and invest the financial resources God has entrusted to me and give them back, *as an act of worship to God*. I am not supposed to take all of that stuff, dig a hole, and sit on it. I'm called to utilize it. And then, as I use my gifts, abilities, and money within the context of the local church (and give back to God what is his), God says: Well done. I have given you the ability to communicate. I have given you the ability to make money. I have given you the ability to work with people. I have given you the ability to organize. You have developed that and returned it as an act of worship. Well done.

There is more wealth in our nation today than ever before. According to *Money* magazine, the average American made $10,171 in 1957, $17,931 in 1980, and $27,237 in 2004 (all in the year 2000 dollars). But that wealth has also made people more selfish than ever before. By and large, we are greedy. As our earnings have increased, our yearnings have increased. And many of us who claim to be Christ-followers are just throwing God some pocket change here and there. We are not worshipping God the way that he calls us to do.

One day, though, he is going to come back and look at each of us face-to-face; and a lot of people who go by the label of "Christ-follower" will hang their heads in shame because their greed and selfishness has kept them from being in the center of God's will. It has kept them out of the zone of God's blessings.

Money is a very personal subject, I know. You may be feeling your blood pressure percolating a little right now. Money cuts to the heart of who we are. Any time I talk about money, it gets a lot of people worked up and immediately puts them on the defensive. But attitudes like that are billboard advertisements of biblical ignorance—of not knowing how important an issue money is in the Bible—or even greed. A lot of us think we own our stuff. We have an ownership mentality instead of a management mentality.

Generous people don't say things like that because they realize, "Hey, I don't have any stuff. God gave me my stuff; he owns it all." Consequently, they are very generous with what God has given them, and they don't mind when I, or anyone else, talks about money management.

When we are God-hearted, we understand the fact that God owns all of the stuff and that we are just managers. And when we understand that reality, our God-heartedness will be evidenced by God-generated generosity to others! To get in on the sweet spot of God's success, we need to move from an ownership mentality to a management mentality. And once that happens, we put ourselves into a position to be blessable. And we can turn around and be a blessing to others! That's what I call living in the zone.

The ownership mentality, on the other hand, is a blessing blocker. It clogs what God wants to do in and through your life. When you think that your stuff is your stuff; when you think that *your* mind, *your* drive, *your* creativity, and *your* ingenuity did it; you are following a guaranteed formula for frustration.

That's not the way God wants you to live. God wants to put his "super" on your "natural." When you get this God-hearted perspective, your resources, abilities, and position in life will change dramatically. You'll realize that God is in charge, that he is the owner and that we are simply called to steward his stuff. And that's when you move from a clog to a conduit of God's unlimited and unmatched blessings.

You can do a lot of great things in life, but if you're holding back from blessing others financially, if you're keeping from God what is already his, if you think that your stuff is your stuff and that you can do whatever you want with it, then you're not living in the zone. You're missing out on the blessings of God.

Do you really want to experience joy in your work? Do you want to live for something other than that weekly or semimonthly paycheck? Then let me challenge you to start giving. Bless others with what God has blessed you with. Be a mirror of God's generosity in your church, in your family, to your friends, and to others in need. Nothing can break the back of greed and materialism faster than a lifestyle of generosity, because when you give, supernatural things will begin to happen in your life.

And, by the way, it's no coincidence that this chapter follows the chapter on laughter. When God said that he "loves a cheerful giver" (2 Corinthians 9:7), that word *cheerful* actually means "hilarious" in the original language. The most joyful people I know—the ones who laugh and enjoy life the most—are those who understand the power of money and enjoy the incredible satisfaction that comes from laugh-out-loud giving.

WHY I GIVE

One day I was lifting some weights in a local gym and ran into a couple of high school guys who attend the church I pastor. After we exchanged the usual chitchat, one of them said, "Do you mind if I ask you a personal question?"

I said, "No, go ahead."

He took me over to the side and said, "Does Fellowship Church force you to tithe? I mean, you're the pastor. Do you have to give because you're a preacher?"

I started laughing. I said, "No, man, I don't *have* to give. It's not like they force me to do it." I then explained to him in a nutshell why I give.

Over the last few months, I've asked myself a lot of questions. And in the course of this reflection, I've also lobbed a few questions to God. I've asked myself, "Why do I live?" and then lobbed that same question God's way. The question from the high school guy has given me another answer to chase down.

So, why do I give? I'm not just talking about myself. I'm talking about what God has told me. And when I tell you about why I give, I'm not coming from a preacher's perspective or a pastor's vibe. I want to share this from the perspective of a man who has followed (though not flawlessly) Jesus Christ for a number of years. After thinking and praying on the question, I came up with seven reasons why I give.

My Creator Says To

The first reason I give is because my Creator instructs me to give. I've already given my life to him, and part of that is trying to follow his principles. When you look at what God has to say about giving, it's not an optional thing. It's not a gray area, or something even worthy of a debate. We've already touched on a lot of biblical examples that describe God's plan for giving.

When Lisa and I married twenty-four years ago, we made several commitments. We obviously committed ourselves to each other. But we also made several commitments to God. One of them included giving a minimum of 10 percent of our earnings to our local church. That hasn't always been an easy commitment to keep, but it has certainly been one of the best. None of our money belongs to us anyway. It's all from God—and for God.

When we were newlyweds, Lisa and I made about $25,000 a year. And, at that time, I had no problem writing my check to bring the tithe into the church—$2,500, that's 10 percent of $25,000. Boom! Drop it in the offering plate. No problem there. Well, now we make more than that. And sometimes I hack, cough, choke, and sputter while writing that check. Do you ever feel like that? It's a lot harder now to write that check. The more you make, the more you'll be tempted to keep God's stuff for yourself.

I know, I'm supposed to be different. I'm a preacher, right? And we all know that preachers are superspiritual, superhuman people. We're members of the God squad. In reality, I'm no different from you. We're all the same. And sometimes I struggle with the giving. I give because my Creator instructs me to give; and selfishly, generosity makes me feel good. I want to be such a generous giver that I give my accountant heart palpitations. But my goal is to please my Creator, not my accountant. The world struggles with God's principles. They don't always "make sense." Remember that "turn the other cheek" teaching? Or that "the servant is the greatest" idea? God's principles are not what the world teaches us.

I believe a key reason for God wanting us all to be generous givers is due to the joy factor. The kind of absolute, unadulterated joy I've been writing about comes when our lives are done God's way. Joy comes when we discover the amazing agenda that our Creator has for our lives. As we've seen in previous chapters, generosity is at the core of God's nature. So every time I give, I'm reflecting his nature and his character.

Have you ever wondered why other people give? I mean, it's not like Christians are the only people who give their stuff away. There are a lot of people who are totally disconnected from God but still give generously. Why do *they* give? I think a major reason is because they are unwittingly reflecting the image of their Creator. They can't deny their nature. Even in our selfishness, man is often compelled to give because it is ingrained into who we are. A lot of people who are away from God don't necessarily give for the right reasons. It may be to see their name on a building. Or perhaps they give to relieve guilt. Or their reason is as banal as a tax break. But one thing that all people have in common is that giving mimics the character of our Maker. And emulating him is the best way to live our lives.

I Like Myself When I Give

The second reason is quite simple: I like myself when I give. There is something inside me, call it a conscience, that compels me to give even when I don't want to.

Yes, sometimes I don't want to give. One of the first words I learned as a kid was this word: *mine*. I still struggle with that same word today. Mine. That money is mine. That car is mine. That house is mine. Mine. Mine. Mine. People are either givers or takers. I know I don't want to be a taker. I just don't want to be numbered among them. So that means I gotta go against my sinful nature to be a giver.

I'd much rather be numbered among the givers, because every time I give, I'm mirroring the majesty of my Maker. God is a giving God. He's a gracious and generous God. And as our heavenly Father, he wants to give us good stuff so he can flow it through us to other people. But sometimes we need less spiritual reasons. Giving will also make you feel good about yourself. You'll smile when you look yourself in the mirror.

What about you? Do you struggle with the word *mine*? Do you get to get? Or do you get to *give*? I've gone through periods in my life where I had a get-to-get outlook. But anyone who is trying to mimic our generous God shouldn't do that. In God's economy, I'm supposed to get to give. When I reflect on his character, I give more naturally. But when I focus on myself, I become a taker. I like myself a whole lot better when I'm giving rather than taking. I just feel better about the person I am. I have a healthier self-esteem when I give, and you're probably the same way.

"It's the Easiest Way I Know of to See God Working in Our Lives"
SARAH'S STORY

"I grew up watching my parents put money in a plate at church, but I never really understood what it was about. Then, just before I got married, my fiancé and I went home to visit his family. While we were there, his grandfather pulled the two of us aside and said, 'If you will tithe when you get married, God will bless your marriage. If you are faithful in bringing the 10 percent to his house, he will bless you and provide for you beyond anything you can imagine.'

"That advice, along with the example my own parents had set, made a profound impact on the two of us. So when we got married, we began to bring 10 percent of everything we made to the local church. And it has been amazing to see the blessings God has returned to us. He has blessed our marriage, our children, and even our careers.

"I started out, like most people, working for someone else. But over time, I had the opportunity to start my own business. And the more I involved God in my business, the more I gave back to God, the more my business grew. And it hasn't stopped to this day!

"I don't look at tithing as something I have to do. I look at it as something I have the privilege to do. Tithing puts a new spin on life that brings excitement

and the blessing of God. It's the easiest way I know of to
see God working in our lives."

It Keeps Me in the Zone

That brings me to the third reason I give. Giving keeps me in
the zone, in the blessed place. I like living in the blessed place.
Don't you? We throw the words *blessing* and *blessed* around all
the time these days. "Blessings on you, brother." When someone sneezes, we'll say "God bless you." When people are happy,
they'll say, "I'm blessed." What in the world does that mean?
The word *blessing* means to be on the receiving end of the tangible and intangible favor of God. Usually when we talk about
blessings, or being blessed, we're talking about the intangible
stuff, the kind of things that we can't feel or touch or smell or
even pick up. And that's part of it. God does bless us with those
intangibles.

But don't limit your definition to the intangibles. The
word *blessing* also has concreteness to it. It's also about the tangible stuff. In other words, matter matters. God made the world
with matter. He invented it and then formed matter into something tangible for us to see, touch, taste, smell, and hear.

The blessings of God are both intangible and tangible. So if
I'm in the blessed place, I'll be on the receiving end of the tangible and intangible favor of God. That's what the zone is all
about. If I'm in the zone, I'm protected and blessed. I'm in the
safe place—the sweet spot of God's success.

I discovered a long time ago that I'm not rich enough, I'm
not powerful enough, and I'm certainly not smart enough to

secure God's protection and blessing on my life without his influence. I can't do it by myself. I've got to follow him and his
ways to be in his zone. Giving is definitely a paradox. The
Bible says that if we want to receive, we have to give. If we
want to be wealthy, we need to be generous (Proverbs
11:24–25). That's not what financial advisors tell us. And
that's exactly the point. We need to follow God's ways before
man's ways. God formed each one of us and has a life full of
adventure and joy waiting for us. When you understand the
purpose of God's blessings (to bless others), you'll be in the
sweet spot of God's success and be used in incredible ways to
touch the lives of the people around you.

Let me ask you a question. When it comes to the blessings
of God, do you want to be known as a river or a reservoir?
When you're in the zone, you're a river. You are allowing God
to bless others through your intangible and tangible blessings.
It'll be like refreshing water running through you to many people around you. You'll allow the blessings of God to slide off
you so others can receive God's goodness. And when that happens, God will continue to pour his blessings on you. And the
cycle of fresh water will continue. Reservoir people, on the
other hand, hoard God's blessings until they become a slimy,
stinking, pollution-infested body of water. Because of selfishness, God's goodness flows to you and then stops. It doesn't filter to others and eventually clogs up the source so that fresh
water can't come in.

It Breaks the Back of Materialism

Here's the fourth reason I give. It breaks the back of materialism. Do you struggle with materialism? You can be honest with

me. I would guess that most of us struggle to some degree in this area.

I have the opportunity to travel around the country, and people oftentimes say, "Hey, Ed, I hear that Dallas–Fort Worth is really materialistic. You know—Texas: big hair and big cowboy boots, big belt buckles, big Rolls-Royces, big ranches. It's got to be really materialistic." And there's some truth to that, but I also chuckle to myself. I don't think Dallas–Fort Worth has a corner on the materialism market. I don't care if you live on a farm in the Midwest or if you live in a Beverly Hills mansion near Rodeo Drive—everybody struggles with it.

What is materialism, anyway? It's a preoccupation with things. It's being obsessed and possessed with things. "Those are *my* things, and I made those things, and they're *mine*." That's really what it all comes down to.

Let me ask you a question. Have you ever seen a U-Haul trailer behind a hearse? We can't take it with us, can we? So how do you break the back of materialism? Here's how I do it. I'm sure there are other ways, but this is what does it for me. I regularly give stuff away. I'm not talking about mangy stuff, stained stuff, or ugly stuff. I try to give away something that I value. But that doesn't come naturally at all. Naturally I want to protect my turf and my stuff. In my mind I'll say, "It's mine!" Really I'm no different from a toddler with his favorite toy.

I'm a big fisherman, and so my fishing gear is really important to me. My rod and reel are almost like my children. They are most definitely *mine*. That's my natural mentality. But God has shown me how good he really is. He has helped me break this mentality by giving some of my most precious fishing gear away. I love to tie fishing flies, and I'll spend hours and hours tying them, and I'll buy the materials and invent these patterns to catch fish. Often God will whisper to me, "Ed, give away those flies." God doesn't say it audibly to me, but I can just sense it. It's not easy, and I'll usually stage a mini protest, but I always feel good when I do give stuff away. And it helps me have a loose grip on the things of the world.

You know what's hilarious about materialism, though? I was talking to my brother about this a while back. He shared with me how most of us, without even knowing it, define materialism: *Materialism begins where our income ends.*

Let me unpack that for a second. People who drive the same car that you drive—you don't think they're materialistic. But if they are driving a better car than you? Look out! Suddenly they are money-hungry, evil, and materialistic! Isn't that true? We'd never admit it, but that's how our brains work. Aren't we all like that to some degree? Materialism is a slippery thing to get a handle on, because how do you know if someone else is materialistic? How much money does a person have to spend in order to be materialistic? What kind of car, house, or clothes puts people in that category? It's harder to define than you thought, isn't it? And here's where I have messed up in this area. In the past, I have judged people, and I've labeled them materialistic. But over the years, God has shown me that I don't really know if someone is materialistic unless I know all the pieces of their spiritual and financial picture. I'm not God.

A few weeks ago, I flew to another city to meet an owner of an NFL football team. The guy is worth literally billions of dollars. He has the jets and the yachts and all that stuff. But I had never met the guy before. So how can I say that he's materialistic? I really have no idea. What if he's giving half of his money to a local hospital? How do I know if he inherited most of his money and possessions from his family? What if he's bankrolling some great missions program overseas? Only God knows the heart of someone. Be careful not to judge others, especially in the area of materialism. It's not our place.

I relearned this lesson recently as I read about Warren Buffett. For years, the financial genius and chairman of Berkshire Hathaway had been accused of being greedy and selfish, refusing to fork over his money to charity. In July 2006, this "greedy and selfish person" pledged over $40 billion (yes, I said "billion"!) to charitable organizations, "the largest philanthropic gift in history," according to *Fortune* magazine. It proves the point that things aren't always as they seem. Only God can make a judgment about materialism.

God is our jury and judge. Leave it to him and take care of yourself. Be generous with your own money and possessions so you can be an example to others. That's the best way to combat our problem with materialism. So let's quit worrying about other people—comparing ourselves, contrasting ourselves—and instead, let's worry about an audience of one. Regularly give stuff away and break the back of materialism. Material is cool. It's the "ism" that messes us up.

It's a Wild Ride

The fifth reason for giving is that it's a one-of-a-kind adventure. If you want to see God working in your life, really *alive* in your life, read the Bible, pray, get to know God, and then, after that, start giving. All heaven will break loose! That's the quickest and easiest way to see God move in your life. When you start giving, it reveals a selfless heart, and God promises to bless givers.

God has shown me some amazing things through giving. He's gotten a lot of stuff to me and through me by his grace and power. Not through my hard work and effort, but through him. It's been an amazing adventure. Some married people will look for an adventure through an affair. Some will take up extreme sports. Others will look for a red sports car. Let me suggest that you start giving instead. You won't believe what'll happen.

When we started Fellowship Church, we had to scrape up enough money to put a down payment on this lonely tract of land we acquired. We were this fledgling church and didn't have a lot of resources at our disposal. We didn't know how we'd cover the millions for this new tract of land, but we really believed God gave it to us.

Not long after we stepped out on faith and bought the land, some big developers started moving into the area. Several months after acquiring the land, we were able to sell 22 of the 159 acres for the exact price we owed on the entire acreage! It covered everything—right down to the last penny. The value of our property had shot through the roof. We looked like real estate geniuses, but God was the genius. All we did was pray and listen to his voice.

So many people gave sacrificially to acquire the land and then finance the building we use. It was unbelievable what went on. I'm not necessarily talking about large amounts of money. The amount doesn't matter. It's all relative. You know, one of the greatest gifts to our church could have been a $2,000 gift from someone making $20,000. This kind of gift is much more sacrificial than someone making $3 million and then writing a check for $100,000. That's how it works in God's economy.

During our building campaign, Lisa and I were trying to

have another child. We had our firstborn, LeeBeth. We also had our son, EJ. But we still wanted more children. (Yes, we are gluttons for punishment!) The doctor informed us that infertility treatments would be needed and some serious expenses would be incurred.

So we saved and saved, and we had some money set aside in an account earmarked for the infertility treatments. We were praying, and we were talking about building our church facility, and God just spoke to us and said, "Give the infertility money to the church, Ed."

So Lisa and I prayed about it, wrestled with the decision, and then we wrote the check to the church. A year later, without any medication, without any medical procedures, Lisa had twins. That's what I call the blessing of God!

If you're a giver, God is going to bless your life. He doesn't always bless financially—although at times it is financial. I could tell you some stories of how God gave us money when it was really tight and we didn't know where it would come from. But he blesses in more ways than with money. He's blessed my own life in much bigger and broader ways: relationally, occupationally, spiritually—stuff that money can't buy. It's been a wild ride of blessings, sacrifice, and watching God work. And I wouldn't trade the ride for anything.

Several years ago, I bought Lisa a car. It was the first time in my life I was able to pay cash for a car. I was really excited about that. I was excited as I bought the car, took the keys, and then drove it up to the house. She was so excited, too. "It's yours, honey! It's paid for and everything."

Eight months later, I was sitting in my office when a car dealer called and told me someone had donated a brand-new car to me and Lisa.

I said, "We don't need a car. I just paid cash for a new one." I was kind of bragging, you know.

He said, "You don't understand. The car is coming. I'm delivering it in a couple hours. So what kind of car do you want?"

Not wanting to disappoint, I quickly said, "Okay, a black Suburban with tan interior!"

Several hours later, this Suburban pulled up. I was thinking I was going to sell Lisa's car and pocket the money. So I called Lisa.

And she gave me a quick gut check with just one question: "Have you prayed about it?" (Behind the Holy Spirit, Lisa is my second conscience.)

I put the phone down and prayed for God to give a quick and clear direction on what to do with this car. I walked outside of my office with a little spring in my step, and I walked into one of my staff member's office. And you know what he said to me?

"Hey, Ed, there's a needy family at Fellowship Church, and they have some handicapped kids. They need a special van to transport the kids around. Do you know anybody who has any money to buy them a van?"

And I'm telling you, I felt God tap me on the shoulder and say, "You're the man!"

Now, again, I didn't hear it audibly, but I just knew that I was supposed to do this. So I decided to sell Lisa's car and use the money to buy the van for the family in need.

But then I found out that there was a huge mistake on my taxes, and I owed the government pretty much the same amount of money that I made in the sale of Lisa's car. (Ouch! I told you it was a *huge* mistake!) Oh, man, I thought. Talk about a roller-coaster ride. Sheepishly, I called Lisa on the phone.

"Lisa, I'm sorry. I just can't do it. I'm not going to give the money to that family. We need to pay these taxes, and we can't afford it. I do have some money in retirement, but I'm not going to take that out to pay for this tax mistake. They'll penalize us until the cows come home. We can't do it. We've got four kids to think about. It's just not going to happen."

But Lisa and I prayed together for two days, and I knew in my heart that God wanted us to give that money to this family to get the van. So we did it. And I cannot tell you what a God-sized thing that was for me, for Lisa, and for our four children. Even though some of our kids were really small, we prayed and talked about it as a family. It had such an amazing impact on our family. I'm not telling you this to brag on me or my family. I'm telling you this to brag on God and what he can do in and through you when you give.

You see, God knew that I did not need a car. But God gave me that car to test me to see if I was ready to put my money where my mouth was. And God knew that he could use something as simple as a car to break me out of my ownership mentality. And God does that in all of our lives. It's what I call a treasure test. He just tests us to build our faith.

Let me tell you what's happened since that situation. I've had the opportunity to write about a dozen books since then. And these book contracts came at a time when our family really needed the money. So don't believe the lie that God does not bless his children. God's a God who blesses—both intangibly and tangibly. And if you want to see God show up in a big-time way, start giving. I'm telling you, it is awesome. These past few stories are just the tip of the iceberg in terms of the adventure that my family and I have enjoyed as we have allowed God to work his blessings through us to other people.

So My Kids Will Mimic Me

The sixth reason I give is that I want to be an example to my kids. I want to press this stuff into their lives because I've discovered that values are more caught than taught, and oftentimes I wonder if my kids are getting it.

They watch Mom and Dad give, and we give them some money so they can learn how to give when they're in children's church. But do they *really* get it? I know that I learned so much about giving just through watching my mom and dad. I'm so thankful to have grown up in a very generous family. I've seen my parents give away their net worth on two or three different occasions.

I remember one Christmas I asked my dad, "What are we getting for Christmas?"

And he said, "Nothing." He wasn't kidding, either.

But that was the best Christmas we ever had because we made gifts for one another. I look back on that as one of the fondest holiday memories we ever had as a family.

When I was speaking on the East Coast a few months ago, I took Landra, one of my eleven-year-old daughters, with me to an event. My father had just given her a hundred-dollar bill. I know I never got a hundred-dollar bill growing up, but that's another story! It's the grandparents' job to spoil their grandkids, I guess.

So Landra and I were sitting in the front row with some other people. Before I speak I get a little funky. I was a little bit nervous, and this was a big church; and the music was going, and all of a sudden the pastor took the platform. He said, "Are you ready?" And everybody in the church began to cheer. Then he said again, "Are you ready?" And then they started doing a wave. The entire church was doing the wave in unison. I was thinking, "Why are they doing this? I mean, it's a little bit crazy." You know what they were doing? They were preparing to give the offering at the church. That's how excited they were. And I got so caught up and pretty excited myself. As the offering plate was passed to us, I looked over to Landra and saw her put her entire hundred dollars in the plate. I said, "Yea, God, she gets it. She gets it. She's learning to be a river, not a reservoir. God has gotten through to her. Now, already, he's working through her to bless others."

Again, we're blessed so we can be a blessing. That's why God has given each of us gifts. I want to be a blessing. And I want my kids to live in the zone and be a blessing to others.

I Believe in the Church

The seventh and final reason I give is that I love the purpose and vision of the local church. I mean I *love* it. Remember, Jesus told us that he was going to build his church, not his hospital or school or whatever. Those are all great things, but none of them are the main thing. So Jesus has taken away all of the debate, all of the guesswork, for us. He said, "Direct your tithe to your local house of worship. That is where life change will take place." Because there are three things that will last forever: God's Word will last, people will last, and the church will last. So I have the opportunity to invest in eternity when I bring my money to the church. That doesn't mean that we shouldn't give to mission efforts or relief organizations like the Red Cross; it just means that our tithe (our first 10 percent off the top) should go to the church, and then we can pray about getting involved in other causes that will allow us to reflect God's blessings to others.

So how does Jesus build the church? Well, he gives stuff to us so he can pass it through us. That's how he builds it. He blesses the members of the church one person at a time. And he blesses us with different talents and different piles of stuff. Forget how big or small the piles are. All that matters is that you use them to bless others.

I know the story of Fellowship Church is a total God thing. He has done things at Fellowship Church that I wouldn't believe if I didn't have a front-row seat for all the action. And for me just to be a part of it, just to hook up with what God is doing, has been a supernatural ride. It's truly, truly amazing. And I know that he has similar plans for your local house of worship. He wants to use you to be a blessing in your context.

The amazing thing is that God never rests. God is continuing to do some amazing things through the people of our church. There have been some amazing things happening just in the last year that I'm so excited about. That's the kind of excitement that you sign up for when you commit yourself to a local church. You commit to a living, breathing organism that is blessed by the hand of God. And you have a role, and I have a role, to carry the message of Jesus to the masses.

It really is all about the money. For some, money is about greed and power. It becomes a relentless pursuit that leaves a trail of broken lives in its wake. For others, money is dirty and carnal. People in this camp love to quote the Bible verse that says, "Money is the root of all evil" (1 Timothy 6:10). The only problem is that these people are misquoting what God said in *the Bible*.

If you look at the verse more closely, you'll see that the love of money is the root of all evil, not money itself. We can't over-spiritualize money. In God's economy, matter matters. God created physical bodies and gave us resources to construct buildings and the infrastructure for a society to function. Money itself is neutral. The issue that God is most concerned about is our hearts.

To live in the sweet spot of God's success, he wants our hearts to reflect his character and nature. We do that by being generous with the money he's given us, and by being sensitive to the needs of the people around us. As we learn to see and spend money through God's principles, we'll receive blessings that will allow us more opportunities to be a blessing to the needs around us. That is the kind of life I want for me and my family. What about you?

STOP AND THINK

FOLLOW THE SIGNS: There are many reasons and benefits to living life God's way when it comes to your money. You'll experience the thrill of worshipping God in the sweet spot of his success, you'll break the back of materialism, and you'll have the satisfaction of knowing that you are helping to further God's work.

CHECK THE MAP: "Whoever sows sparingly will also reap sparingly, and whoever sows generously will also reap generously. Each man should give what he has decided in his heart to give, not reluctantly or under compulsion, for God loves a cheerful giver. And God is able to make all grace abound to you, so that in all things at all times, having all that you need, you will abound in every good work" (2 Corinthians 9:6–8).

TAKE THE NEXT STEP: If you were to write your own "Top 7 Reasons Why I Give" list, what would it look like?

1. _____

2. _____

3. _____

4. _____

5. _____

6. _____

7. _____

AFTERWORD

IT'S THE REAL THING

I begin this section in the same way I began the first, with a question:

Does God want you to be happy?

Does he?

No, he doesn't.

God wants something much better than happiness. Much deeper and greater. Something much more real and authentic.

What God wants for you is joy.

And you can find the joy you seek when you abandon at last the relentless pursuit of happiness that leaves so many empty and disillusioned. Happiness does not satisfy because it comes and goes as often as the circumstances in your life change.

Joy, on the other hand, is deep and abiding. It is a lasting quality of life that grows and matures as you commit your life to the things that matter most. We've looked at those major areas of priority throughout this book. Have you centered your life on the priorities of relationships, worship, and work? Are you committed to replenishing relationships that bring you closer to God? Have you discovered that your reason for living is to worship the one who created you? Do you enjoy a life of balance between work and leisure, and are you regularly and strategically giving back a portion of what you earn to the local church? In every area of your life, have you learned to regain the lost art of laughter, fun, and life-giving joy?

That kind of joy is waiting for you. Are you ready to experience it? Are you ready for a life of ultimate peace, contentment, and fulfillment? If you are, I want to make sure you don't miss several important truths before you end this book and begin your lifelong journey toward joy.

JOY IS A CHOICE

First of all, joy is a choice. It's the inner delight that comes from choosing to enter into a relationship with Jesus Christ. And it comes from living a life committed to the priorities Christ has given us. It doesn't matter what's happening in life; whether it's sickness or financial pressures or relational issues or emotional ups and downs, we can experience that joy and inner delight God promises for those who love him and are committed to him.

I know that doesn't jibe with the "happiness now" mentality that permeates our culture, but good things take time. And great things take an eternity. If you want happiness, you don't need to look any further than your next paycheck or your next relationship or your next fun fix. But if you want the real thing, it's going to take commitment for the long haul. The

Bible compares life to a race, and it says there is an incomparable reward for those who finish well (Acts 20:24, 2 Timothy 4:7). The culmination of our joy is that reward. It is coming into the presence of Jesus Christ with the confidence that we have remained committed to him. It is entering into eternity knowing we have lived life to the fullest. It is receiving in heaven a greater measure of what we have invested here on earth.

So you have a choice to make every day and with every obstacle and hurdle that comes into your life. The subtitle of this book is "Five Big Questions to Help You Discover One Great Life." That great life doesn't just happen. It takes work and perseverance. That's why the metaphors in the New Testament so often relate to athletic events or battles. We have to push past the barriers and tear down the walls if we want to discover God's best for our lives. I know that this flies in the face of popular thinking. Most of us have been taught that we can have what we want. Right now! Don't wait! Buy now, pay later! That's what we see advertised on billboards and TV ads day in and day out. Get it while the getting's good! You know what I'm talking about, right? Life is there for the taking, so take it.

But it's not that easy. The best things in life really are not free. If you want the best for your life, you have to make a choice to persevere and stay with it for the long haul. You'll feel like quitting many times, but when you make the daily decision to stick with it, you'll find a reward in the end that is unimaginable and unbelievable.

So, when circumstances come down the pike, you can either choose joy or you can choose misery. Joy leads to eternal rewards; misery just leads to more misery. The Bible says,

"Consider it pure joy, my brothers, whenever you face trials of many kinds, because you know that the testing of your faith develops perseverance. Perseverance must finish its work so that you may be mature and complete, not lacking anything" (James 1:2–4). When I choose joy as I encounter various problems, it brings perspective to my problems. It reminds me that there is a purpose to everything that happens. And that even in the worst of times, God can produce something good. The bottom line is, it's our choice to rejoice.

JOY IS A PROCESS

Not only is joy a choice, but joy is a process. It doesn't happen overnight. Like every other good thing in life, it takes time, patience, and commitment. There is no such thing as microwave joy. It's a quality that builds in your life over time as you submit your life to the very embodiment of joy: Jesus Christ.

I know that this is a fairly abstract concept to grasp. What does it mean that Jesus is the embodiment of joy? Basically, I'm talking about a spiritual relationship with someone who cares more about you than you could ever imagine. Every day, Jesus waits for you to come to him with your hopes, dreams, concerns, and desires. He wants a relationship with you and is patient enough to endure the ups and downs of your life. He knows what you're going through.

And make no mistake: Jesus will give you that lasting joy if you are faithful to him. The apostle Paul, in the book of Philippians, talks of "being confident of this, that he who began a good work in you will carry it on to completion" (Philippians 1:6). The word *began* indicates a process. We don't just get to know

Jesus and boom!—"I've got joy. My joy is complete." It doesn't happen that way. It grows and matures over time. That's why the Bible calls joy one of the fruits of the Spirit. If you've ever tried to grow fruit trees, you know that fruit doesn't just appear on a tree. The tree springs forth from a seed and takes years to grow, and then as the tree is fertilized, pruned, and cared for, the juicy fruit emerges during the growing season. It often takes many years for a fruit tree to mature and produce a decent crop. Talk about patience!

The same is true with joy. God wants the prevailing attitude of his people to be one of joy—outrageous, contagious joy—so he's placed the person of the Holy Spirit inside of our lives. And, over time, the Spirit fertilizes, prunes, and cares for our hearts so we can produce the juicy fruit of joy. Over several years you might produce grape-sized pieces of fruit. And then, as you grow, you might produce kiwi-sized pieces of fruit. Then one year, grapefruit-sized pieces of fruit will appear. Finally, a bumper crop! It's a lifelong process of growing fruit produced by the Holy Spirit of God.

As I mentioned earlier, before I entered the ministry, I hesitated about my decision to become a pastor. I was hesitant because most pastors I knew (with the exception of my father, of course) looked like they held down a night job at the local mortuary. I said, "Lord, I don't want anything to do with that!" But I knew that God wanted me to become a pastor, so I took a dive into the ministry with the resolve that I would not allow the profession to rob me of my joy.

Being a pastor is one of the most serious professions in the world because we deal with eternal ramifications, with life in the raw. Every week I'm talking about problems: addiction problems, marital problems, health problems, spiritual problems, and even death. Many times I feel low, and I have to remind myself that joy is a process. It doesn't come and go with the winds of change. It is a constantly growing and developing characteristic that God wants to produce in my life. He wants me to laugh in spite of my circumstances and regardless of how serious life becomes.

Remember the words of Jesus, "I have told you this so that my joy may be in you and that your joy may be complete" (John 15:11–12). What's Jesus saying? He is saying he wants the joy to snap the heads of a joyless society. People ought to come up to you and me and say, "What's different about you? Why are you so positive about life?"

People around us should see Jesus in everything we do and in everything we are about. You can't have joy in your life unless Jesus is in your life. And you can't produce this fruit unless the Holy Spirit is working in your heart. Some people try to manufacture the false fruit of happiness, but it does not last. The fruit withers on the vine almost before we can eat it, and it does not satisfy. Only the real thing will last—outrageous, contagious joy. It's the kind of fruit that satisfies every hunger in our lives. And it's the kind of fruit we just can't help but share with others. As we share it, it changes not only our lives but the lives of everyone around us.

JOY IS A CONFIDENCE

Look again at what the apostle Paul says in Philippians 1:6— "being confident of this . . ." What is he confident of? We saw it earlier: "that he who began a good work in you will carry it on to completion until the day of Christ Jesus."

This word *completion* is an interesting term. When Jesus was dying on the cross for our sins, he uttered seven sayings. One of those sayings was the term *tetelestai*, which comes from the root word *telos*, meaning "It is finished." Jesus paid the price. The work was complete. It's the same term used here in Philippians. You may know someone—a daughter, a son, a friend, a co-worker—who at one time was close to God, following the Lord and producing true fruit. Now, though, this person is straying away from God, drifting off course. Some people erroneously think God has folded his arms and shunned them. He's forgotten about them. That's not true. When God begins a good work, he will *tetelestai* it. He will finish it. He will complete it. He will use anything and everything at his disposal to complete the good work in you and the good work in me. God is not a quitter; he always keeps his promises. And one of those promises is that he will never leave us or forsake us (Hebrews 13:5).

I don't know about you, but that gives me confidence. As his child, I can trust in the fact that God will not give up on me. And that confidence brings a joy beyond understanding. There are many days when I think, "You mean God is going to complete this work in my life? I'm just a self-centered sinner. He's going to make something good out of *my* life?" I'm sure in your moments of true introspection you think the same thing. And the answer is a resounding Yes! When you blow it with your spouse or your kids or your friend, God is still there. When you say hurtful things out of anger, God has not given up on you. When you go back to that destructive habit, God is still working in your life. Do you believe that? Have confidence in God. He will not abandon you. Even when people have strayed away, God is a finisher. If he began the work, he will complete the work.

JOY IS A PERSON

The person of Jesus Christ is central to a life of joy, and without him this book is just a five-point plan to living a better life. Jesus, though, offers something much deeper, much richer, and much more significant to you and me. He offers an eternal transformation of the heart that provides peace and contentment that is beyond our finite understanding. If you really, sincerely, want to find the ultimate life—a life that is full and rich and meaningful—you must embrace the fundamental truth that joy is a person.

Two thousand years ago, God moved through time and space and stepped down from heaven. He became a man named Jesus. And for the last three years of Jesus' life, he confronted us in love and showed us the hope that we have through him—the hope of knowing and reaching God.

The truth is, there is a road that leads to God. The blueprint for God's road is drawn out for us in a single verse of Scripture, John 14:6. I call this passage of the Bible "Highway 146." When asked by his disciples how they could reach God, Jesus spoke these words, *"I am the way and the truth and the life. No one comes to the Father except through me."*

Highway 146 should look very appealing to all of us. As we're driving in the wrong direction through our own efforts, we should be able to recognize the road signs and the detours that have been pointing us to God. We should, but many of us don't.

Instead of following God's highway, many people decide to white-knuckle the steering wheel of their lives, turn off God's navigational GPS system, and go their own way. And then they

spend most of their lives bouncing back and forth from destination to destination.

God offers us a better way to live, the ultimate way. It is a
better way than chasing the short-lived highs, the stockpiles of
stuff, or the skeptical questions. And it's a *free*way because
Christ has already paid the price—it is literally free to you and
me.

The Bible teaches that the path to God has already been
built and is free for anyone who chooses to accept it. That
path has not been constructed because of anything that we
have done, can do, or ever will do ourselves. We can't earn it
and we don't deserve it. It is simply a gift from God. Even
though we are all sinners, Christ died for us. And his death is
what enables us to reach God. *He* paved the way.

Have you discovered the source of true joy? Have you
made a decision for Jesus? Are you ready to admit the obvious
to yourself and to God? Each of us is a sinner and is in desperate need of a savior. That is a fact that each of us must face at
one point in life or another. And you have two options—you
can either choose to ignore that fact or accept it. But if you
want to truly know God and reach his final destination, you
must turn to him and say, "I'm ready to take your highway. I'm
ready to confess the obvious to you, God. I admit that I am a
sinner and have fallen short of your standard of perfection. I
realize I am separate from you and that I am in need of the Savior, Jesus Christ. I'm ready to get on Highway 146."

In order to make the decision to follow Christ, all you have
to do is think about the road signs God has shown you. Think
about the times you have felt his presence. Think about the
people in your life who have pointed you to Highway 146.
Think about the situations in which Jesus has revealed himself

to you. God has been seeking you. Are you ready to accept him?

Don't continue to deny him. Don't choose to dismiss his truth as simply a piece of friendly advice that you can ignore without consequence. You will only have so many chances in life to accept Jesus Christ as your Savior. And you just don't know how many opportunities God is going to give you. Your last chance could be right now. Or you may have a thousand more opportunities. But don't take that risk.

The Bible says, "The Lord . . . is patient toward you, not wishing for any to perish but for all to come to repentance" (2 Peter 3:9, NASB). But it also tells us that life is a vapor, a mist, which is here today and gone tomorrow (James 4:14). Life is too short to put off this decision about your eternal destiny. Don't wait to choose Highway 146. Get on that road today. All it takes is a willing heart and an honest prayer:

God, I admit to you that I have messed up and that I have fallen short of your perfection. I turn from my sins and want to do a U-turn right now. I am willing to let go of the white-knuckle grip I have on the steering wheel of my life and give you control. I want to get on your highway, your freeway. Right now I ask Jesus Christ, who lived a sinless and perfect life, died for my sins, and rose again from the grave, to come into my life and be my Savior. I open up my hands to you, my heart to you, and my life to you. I ask this in Jesus' name, Amen.

When you do give your life to Jesus, you become a Christ-follower. You will begin to see every area of your life from a whole new perspective. You will begin to finally see that joy is not a feeling; it is a person . . . and that person is Jesus Christ.

"The Benefits of Trusting God Are Almost Impossible to Describe"
KEITH'S STORY

"I was one of those kids who was dragged to church growing up. As soon as I turned eighteen, I turned away from the church. I moved away from my parents and started what I call my 'drinking career.'

"Alcohol eventually led to drugs, and it wasn't long before I became a cocaine addict.

"That kind of lifestyle ultimately destroyed my marriage and my relationship with my two children. My wife and kids left, and for the next ten years, I did whatever I could to get as far away from God as possible.

"One Sunday, a friend of mine invited me to a church in the area. I felt like God was planting a seed within me, but I didn't allow it to take root. I wasn't ready for God to be a part of my life. I wanted to live life on my own terms. So instead of turning to God, I tried to fill the void in my life with anything else I could get my hands on.

"One night, though, I got tired of running away from God. Suddenly I wanted him to be very near. So I got on my knees in a dark and lonely house, and I asked God to take over my life.

"I had no clue where that was going to take me. All I could do was ask God to keep me sober one day at a time and try to build on that. I am about to celebrate ten years of sobriety.

> "The benefits of trusting God are almost impossible to describe. He has restored my marriage. He has restored my relationship with my kids. God has totally changed my life. I have really been blessed beyond what I could have ever imagined."

Whatever circumstance you're going through, whatever heartache you're enduring, whatever obstacle you're facing, God is watching and working. You can say with confidence, "I know God's not through with me yet." And because of that, regardless of what comes your way, you can live a life of outrageous, contagious joy.

Don't give up on God, because God has not given up on you!

SCRIPTURE REFERENCES